The Center for Western Studies is a cultural museum and a study and research agency of Augustana College, Sioux Falls, South Dakota, concerned principally with South Dakota and the adjoining states, the Prairie Plains, and with certain aspects of the Great Plains and the Trans-Mississippi West.

The Center serves as a resource for teachers, research scholars, students and the general public, through which studies, research projects and related activities are initiated and conducted, and by which assistance can be provided to interested individuals and groups. Its goal is to provide awareness of the multi-faceted culture of this area, with special emphasis on Dakota (Sioux) Indian Culture.

The Center was founded in the conviction that this region possesses a unique and important heritage which should not be lost or forgotten. Consequently, the Center for Western Studies seeks to provide services to assist researchers in their study of the region, to promote a public consciousness of the importance of preserving cultural and historical resources, to collect published and unpublished materials, art and artifacts, important to the understanding of the region, and to undertake and sponsor projects, to sponsor conferences and provide permanent displays and shows which reflect the art and culture of the West, particularly the Sioux.

The Center maintains an archive and possesses one of the finest collections available of books relating to all aspects of the American West. The Center continually seeks to expand its collections in order to provide maximum assistance to interested scholars, students at all levels, and the general public. The collections include excellent representative Sioux Indian art, bead and quill work, western art consisting of original oils, water colors, bronzes, photographs, and steel engravings.

BOY OFF
THE FARM

A Memoir of a
Southwestern Minnesota
Boyhood

By
Irid Bjerk

To Roberta
 . . . my devoted wife who kept the homefires burning while
my time was spent at the typewriter.

To Mother and Dad
 . . . who made boyhood such a memorable period of my life.

For Ken, Bob and future generations of the Bjerk family
 . . . were it not for them, there would have been little reason
to publish this book.

Published by
THE CENTER FOR WESTERN STUDIES
AN HISTORICAL
RESEARCH AND ARCHIVAL AGENCY
of
Augustana College
Sioux Falls,
South Dakota

ISBN: Number 0-931170-20-6 Hardcover
First Edition 1982
Second Edition 1983
Printed by Crescent Publishing, Inc., Hills, Minnesota
Manufactured in the United States of America

PREFACE

In the words of the eminent American historian, Daniel J. Boorstin, Librarian of Congress, "We cannot know our past or begin to feel at home there unless we read."

Unlike children born during or prior to the first quarter of the twentieth century, today's children most generally move away from their past. Seldom do they remain on the premises where they could keep up the old homestead and pass it on to their children, Boorstin observed.

Thus, it is reasonable to conclude that unless the memories of those premises are preserved through the medium of the printed page, they could be forever lost.

I was one of those who moved from the family homestead of my youth, but was never so far removed from it that I was not aware of its impact upon my life. Likewise, I had a distinct awareness of the role that the times had played in shaping my physical, mental and emotional being.

When it fell my lot to write a personal column for my hometown weekly newspaper, THE ROCK COUNTY STAR—HERALD (Luverne, Minnesota), I immediately felt that I was being afforded the opportunity to reflect from time to time upon the commonplace experiences that were mine during my boyhood and early youth spent on a farm in Southwestern Minnesota. And in doing so, I would be able to provide generations yet unborn with a first-hand account of Mid-American rural life as it was lived by a boy during the 1920's, should there be those sufficiently interested in their roots to want to research their heritage.

These reminiscent essays were published over a period of about ten years during the 1970s under the heading "Boy Off The Farm." The title is a phrase from the old cliche, "You can take the boy off the farm, but you can't take the farm off the boy."

The selections included in this volume are those which in the judgment of the author, give the best insight into "the way it was back then."

If some reminscenses are repeated, it's because the columns in which they appear were written and published in the newspaper several years apart and repitition did not pose a problem.

ACKNOWLEDGEMENTS

I'm sure if I had not received encouragement and help from relatives and friends, this book would never have been printed. To them I wish to express my thanks.

First and foremost, my deep appreciation to my beloved wife whose insistence and persistence kept me from putting off until tomorrow what had to be done today. Had it not been for her, and her conviction that the reminiscent columns I had written were worthy of preservation, it is unlikely that I would have undertaken the task.

Secondly, I will be ever grateful to my cousin, Ione Bjerk Backus, who saved every "Boy Off The Farm" column after clipping them from the newspaper, and preserved them in scrapbooks which she made available to me when I decided to compile them in book form.

Lastly, my sincere appreciation goes to Bruce and Jean Harrison, owners of The Star-Herald for permission to reprint the columns; to my brother, James, my sister, Lorraine, Julia Eitreim, and Frederick Manfred, Sr., who provided photographs, and to the Center for Western Studies for encouragement, suggestions and willingness to become my publisher.

—The Author

FOREWORD

For years I've read Irid Bjerk's Boy Off The Farm columns and always enjoyed them. They were full of marvelous details telling of the old days before the mechanical age set in. There were also in the columns good stories to read, so real they made our country come alive. And now here we have the best of them all caught up in one book.

Frederick Manfred

TABLE OF CONTENTS

FAMILY — HOME — CHURCH

WORKING ON THE FARM

SPRING — THE QUEEN OF SEASONS

CHRISTMAS MEMORIES

THE WAYS OF THE MODEL T FORD

THOSE WERE THE DAYS

THEN CAME ADULTHOOD

The Ole J. Bjerk Family, 1906

Back row: Judith, Malinda, Helma, Andrew, Minnie, Ole, Olga, Lizzie and James. Front row: Edwin, Dina, Malla, Ole J. Bjerk holding Olaf, Lucy, Randi Hoven Bjerk, Melvin, Maria and Ragna. Olaf died at the age of five in 1910. Three children were born after the picture was taken: Jeanette, Edna, and Olaf. Three children had died before the picture was taken.

Family - Home - Church

Straight Were The Rows
Where Dad's Plow Ran

While I never made a count, I'll venture to say that I've mentioned my Dad a hundred times in "Boy Off The Farm"
reminiscences over the years. But in all that time, I've never written an account dealing with him alone so it's about time I do.

Grandpa and Grandma christened him James Olaus Kolman
Bjerk shortly after he was born December 22, 1878 in a sod shanty northwest of Beaver Creek, about three-quarters of a mile
southwest of our farm place.

Grandpa was great on giving his kids two middle names. I never
did know how they happened to choose James for his first name,
since James is not a Norwegian name. (The Norwegian Bible
refers to the Apostle James as Jakob.) Olaus, of course, is
Norwegian, but I've never heard of a Norwegian, or anyone else
for that matter, with the name Kolman.

Dad was child No. 3 and the eldest son in the family that eventually numbered 23 children. (Grandpa was married twice.) He
barely remembered the sod shanty where he was born, only that it
had two windows. He was about three years old when they moved
into the frame house which Grandpa had built across the road on
the quarter section he acquired by planting a 20 acre tree claim. It
was there that Dad spent his boyhood and youth.

He attended school in the same rural school house that I did. I
don't know whether he actually finished the eighth grade. Likely
he didn't as he had to stay home and help with the farm work during the early fall and spring. He had enough elementary education,
however, to be admitted to Lutheran Normal School in Sioux
Falls where he spent at least one winter session. Lutheran Normal later became Augustana College. Years later, when I attended Augustana, I lived in Men's Hall, the same dormitory in
which Dad roomed when he was there, and I had some classes in Old
Main, which was the principal building on the campus in Dad's
day.

I have only a vague memory of Grandpa Bjerk. He died when I
was five. But from what I have heard, he was both a practical
joker and a taskmaster. He'd do anything within reason (but

always honestly) to make a dollar or save a dollar, with the result that businessmen, while anxious to do business with him, kept their guard up so they wouldn't be "taken". At one time he farmed a quarter section several miles north of the home farm. That year, he raised an unusually fine crop of barley, and in a conversation with a banker in Garretson, he made the statement that he had more barley to sell than the banker had gold in his bank to pay for it.

It fell Dad's lot to have to haul the grain in to the Garretson elevator. When he left with the last load, Grandpa instructed him to take the check for the grain to the bank to cash it and to demand the entire amount in gold.

The banker had anticipated that this might happen. When Dad handed him the check, the banker counted out $1,055 in $5 gold pieces, placed them in a money sack, and handed it to Dad. With the cash at his side on the wagon spring seat, Dad drove home, a distance of 13 miles without mishap.

As more children were born, and living room in the house began to become tighter, Dad set out on his own. He worked as a hired hand for a couple of years, then he started farming with his brother, Andrew.

He never told me much about his youth or his young manhood days prior to his meeting the young lady, a neighbor girl named Mary Aaker, who was eventually to become my mother. They dated for a couple of years or so, and then they were married.

A few days later, they were settled in their home in the northwest part of the county where Dad had rented a quarter of a section of land for the coming year. A little over a year later, I was on the way. The day I arrived, December 10, 1914, the snow was fence-post high. Dr. DeVall, of Garretson, came by team and bobsled to help with the delivery. Dad told me years later that he was plenty worried that I wasn't going to live. The umbilical cord was wrapped around my neck and was choking me. But Doc DeVall knew what to do. When he slapped my bottom, and I gave out a healthy yell, Dad was delighted.

When I was old enough to hold my head up and sit on his lap, Dad proudly took me to Myhre's Studio in Luverne so I could pose for my first picture with him. Very few people owned their own cameras at that time, so it was going to the studio or nothing at all.

As soon as I was able to walk and talk, Dad often took me with him when he was working about the yard. He was always quick to point out the beauties of nature. He delighted in showing me the baby pigs, baby calves, baby colts, baby chicks and baby kittens, warning me that mothers of little things were extremely possessive, and that I should never venture into pastures or pig pens alone.

He was an excellent story teller, and I never tired of hearing the same ones over and over again. We never had bedtime stories at our house, always morning stories, but they were told to us in bed. My sister and I slept in upstairs bedrooms that were unheated. When we awoke on cold mornings, we scurried downstairs as fast as we could because it was warmer there. Mother was usually up first to fire up the kitchen range, and while she busied herself in the kitchen, Lorraine and I would clamber into bed with Dad and ask him to tell us a story.

Funny thing, he always told the stories in Norwegian. Now, I realize that that is the way he learned them, no doubt from his father and mother, or his grandmother. Above the bed, I recall, was a framed print of a little child at the edge of a cliff, reaching for a butterfly, and behind the child was an angel. That story, the one of the guardian angel, was one of our favorites. The other one I best remember was the story of the Three Billy Goats Gruff . . . in Norwegian "Bukken Bruse". How we loved it when he almost whispered the "trapp-trapp-trapp" of the smallest goat as it crossed the bridge, and how he growled the same words as he described the hoof beats of the biggest goat. He knew other tales of Norse folklore as well, particularly about trolls and how they loved to grab naughty children.

Dad liked to use the Norwegian language when visiting with other Norwegians. He used it in conversations with Mother when he wanted to discuss something he didn't want others to hear or understand. He had trouble doing that when Lorraine and I were around, however, because with Grandma and Grandpa Aaker living with us, we had learned to understand Norwegian as well as English.

Another place he liked to use Norwegian was in the barn when he spoke to the horses and cows. He'd talk to the animals sometimes as though they were human and could understand what he was saying. Sometimes, he used complimentary terms. But when a cow switched a wet tail in his face or kicked a milk bucket from between his legs as he sat on a milk stool, or when a horse stepped on his foot, he emphasized his unhappiness with the situation by using a few choice Norwegian words which we as children were forbidden to speak.

When he picked corn or when he hauled hay or bundles with horses, he usually addressed the team in Norwegian. I never did know why, but the animals seemed to grasp his orders just a bit better.

Dad liked to fish, although I know of only a couple of times he actually went on an overnight fishing trip. He'd buy a couple of bamboo poles every spring and fit each one with line, hook and cork, and he and I would fish bullheads out of the creek in our pasture. If we were lucky enough to get enough for a meal, he'd dress them out and invariably we'd have them for breakfast. If there was anything he liked better than sour cream on bread for breakfast, it was fresh bullheads, crisp fried in butter, the way mother always prepared them. If there weren't enough for a meal, we'd put them in the water tank by the well until we could catch a few more.

Dad also liked to hunt during his younger days. When I was in elementary school, there were still huge flocks of prairie chickens that would settle in the corn fields or around haystacks. Dad would take down his trusty Model 97 Winchester 12 gauge when he'd see the chickens fly in and would crouch down and even crawl to get close enough to get a shot. He also enjoyed walking out across the farm and through the weed patches to take a cottontail or jackrabbit, which he would dress and mother would fry like chicken. I was like Mother, I never did care much for wild game. But Dad loved it. Years later, after he had moved to town and our youngest son, Bob, became a hunting enthusiast, Bob would go out and bag a cottontail and he and his Grandpa would enjoy a rabbit feed. Now, my big regret is that I didn't like rabbit when I had the opportunity to do the same thing a generation earlier.

Dad loved the soil and the grasses and grains it produced. But he hated with a passion the weeds that competed with his plants for a spot in the sun. The Canada thistle and the cocklebur were his sworn enemies, and he fought them with every weapon at his disposal. Those were the days before herbicides, so he had to depend on the hoe or sharp spade when he set out to battle them. Whenever the cultivator missed one of the weed plants in the corn field, he'd yell "Whoa!" to the horses and get off the seat to pull the weed by hand.

As a result, neighbors liked to buy their seed oats, barley and flax from Dad because they could be sure they contained no noxious weeds. He could guarantee that, knowing that he had personally eradicated any weeds that might have infested the fields. Just to be doubly sure, he sent seed samples to the University of Minnesota which sent back germination and weed seed count in writing.

A good grain crop was his pride and joy. He liked to try new seed varieties as soon as they were available from the University. I think he grew the first smooth-bearded barley in Rock County. It was called Velvet. For years, everybody planted Green Russian oats, but Dad introduced a new early variety, called Gopher, which not only outyielded Green Russian, but could be harvested a couple of weeks earlier.

Every summer at County Fair time, Dad would devote several days to getting his samples ready for exhibition. He had as much fun getting ready as he did in seeing the blue ribbons on the samples after the judges had made their rounds. He'd run the grain through the fanning mill several times, and then would sit down and go through them a handful at a time, removing any light kernels, or other seeds that might catch the judge's eye and keep him from winning a prize.

Even after he retired and moved to town, he exhibited garden vegetables. One year, he was given recognition for having been a continuous exhibitor at the fair for over 50 years.

He almost didn't make it to one fair. We had a Model T Ford that had been converted into a small pickup truck. He had it loaded down with fair entries, which included a number of rather fragile bundles of oats, barley, flax and alfalfa. The wind caught them, and he noticed one of the bundles was about to fall over the edge of the box. He reached back to catch it. In doing so, he turned the steering wheel just enough so that he drove into the ditch, upsetting the pickup on its side and dumping everything out of the box into the ditch. The grain was in bags, so that wasn't hurt. But some of the seeds shelled out of the bundles so they weren't the best. Dad escaped unhurt.

Someone came along and helped tip the pickup back on its wheels. Dad loaded up his treasures and drove to the fair. The accident made a two-column headline in the paper but his fair entries won fewer ribbons than usual.

I think Dad was a voting Republican before the depression, but the bank failure in Beaver Creek, and Herbert Hoover's handling of the presidency led him to be one of Franklin Delano Roosevelt's strongest supporters. He was convinced that Roosevelt and the Democratic party turned the economy around and ended the depression. He remained a staunch Democrat the rest of his life.

He dabbled in politics once himself. He ran for county commissioner and was elected to a four year term. Four years later he lost his bid for re-election by a vote so close that there was a recount. He appeared more dejected then than when he lost every cent he had in the Beaver Creek Bank some 10 years earlier. He thought he'd done a good job on the county board. I don't think he was rejected because of what he had done or not done while he was in office. I think he was a bit over-confident, and his opponent did a more effective job of campaigning.

I've said many times that Dad was born 20 years too soon to get the most out of life financially. He had just gotten a good start in life when the depression hit. When the Beaver Creek Bank was

about to fold, he, being a director, had to dig up every possible
nickel he could in an effort to save it. It closed anyway.

The farm was mortgaged for about half its value or more and
he'd probably have lost it had it not been for the compassion and
generosity of the man in Algona, Iowa who held the mortgage.
For several years, he let Dad pay what interest he could and asked
for nothing on the principal.

Dad was hurt by the drought in the early thirties when he had
virtual crop failures two years in a row. Livestock prices were
depressed, plus the fact that the Great Depression had stifled all
segments of the economy.

I remember it was extremely dry the spring I completed my
first term at Augustana. There was little prospect for even grass
in pastures, so Dad decided to sell a few head of young stock
rather than permit them to become thin for lack of forage. He had
a trucker pick up the cattle the day he came over to get me to take
me home from school to spend the summer. On our way out of
Sioux Falls, we stopped by the stockyards to pick up his check for
the cattle. The cattle hadn't been sold yet, he was told, but as soon
as they were, they would mail him the check. He waited a couple
of days before there was a Steele-Siman envelope in the mailbox.
He opened it when he got in the house, looked at the invoice, then
sat down heavily in a chair beside the dining room table. He handed the paper to Mother. She started to cry. The cattle were sold,
all right, but they didn't bring enough to cover the yardage, the
hay they had eaten, and the commission fees. In fact, the invoice
showed that Dad owed the stockyards firm a few dollars.

From that low point, farming became a bit more profitable as
the years went by. He was even able to pay a bit on the mortgage
every year. The years of World War II were even better from a
farm income standpoint but by that time, Dad was approaching
70 years of age and was no longer able to work the long hard
hours he had been accustomed to during his younger years. But
he managed to pay off the mortgage finally and the farm was
clear. At least he had accomplished that goal.

All during this time, Dad maintained his good humor and op-
timism. It was tough going, sure, but he was confident that the
good Lord would not let him down. And He didn't.

Dad taught us — my sister, brother and myself — a lot of
things, not out of a book but by what he said and the way he lived.
Love, honesty, self-reliance, appreciation, gratitude, respect for
others. While not one to display affection with a lot of hugging
and kissing, he used numerous other ways to show he cared, not
only for the members of his family, but for others less fortunate.
He and Mother had a beautiful relationship. I never heard them in
a heated argument. They worked together and planned together.

He was a strong disciplinarian but it was seldom he used his hand to punish us unless we had done something that merited more than a good scolding.

"Never tell a lie," he told us. "Be honest in everything you say and do, and you'll never regret it. Every time you tell a lie, you're going to have to lie again and again to try to cover up. If you're confronted with having done something wrong, admit it no matter how great or small it is. It might hurt at the time, but you'll always feel better when it's no longer on your conscience." Over the years I've been grateful many times for that good advice.

Dad had no bad habits, unless it was cigar smoking. He liked his cigars, and got more mileage out of one cigar than any other man I know. He'd light one, smoke about half of it, and then put it out by rubbing the lighted end in the bottom of his ash tray. Later on, he'd light up again. When the cigar became so short that the burning end almost touched his lips, he'd stick a toothpick in the stub and keep puffing until there was virtually nothing left.

During his younger days, he chewed snuff. Mother hated the cigars but not as much as she hated snuff. Then one day he came down with appendicitis and had to go to Sioux Falls for an appendectomy. He took his snuff box along, but never touched it. From that time on, he never chewed again.

A "bum leg" hastened his retirement but he was ready to quit anyway and enjoy life by taking it a little easier. Taking it easy meant plowing up the entire back yard of the little house he and Mother bought in Luverne and planting it to potatoes and garden vegetables. There he spent a good share of the summer hoeing, weeding and harvesting the produce. When the leg problem became so painful he couldn't get around without a cane, he took a little stool to the garden and sat down while he hoed and pulled weeds around him.

As I said, he was born 20 years too soon. Social Security regulations were changed after he moved to town so that a person owning a farm and collecting rent could do a little work and be eligible to get into the Social Security program. By paying into the fund several years, it was possible to collect the minimum Social Security after age 65. But he missed the boat, as they say. He sold the farm a couple of years before the regulation went into effect, and he never qualified.

In spite of all the hardships he experienced, I never heard him complain. Oh, he would say "ow" when his leg pained him, and express his disgust at the way the Republicans were handling the government, but that was about it.

After he died, however, I heard about a complaint he made to his doctor. Dad had heart trouble and was 90 when he went to the hospital a couple of different times. The doctor prescribed certain pills and one time he was put in an oxygen tent. When this happened, he expressed his displeasure to the doctor: "Why do you fellows insist on giving us all this stuff to keep us alive when we're in this kind of shape? Don't you suppose us old duffers know when we've had enough, and want to get out of this world and go home?"

His wish to "go home" was granted June 10, 1968. He was laid to rest in the cemetery beside the church which his father helped to organize, where he was baptized, confirmed, and where he had worshiped regularly all of his 90 years. The Reverend E.W. Rossing delivered the funeral sermon, then paid a tribute to Dad by reading a 20 line poem which described Dad in a few words far better than I have in these reminiscenses. Here's the poem by S. Omar Barker:

My father was a farmer,
A strong, good man.
Straight were the rows
Where his sharp plow ran.
Straight were his thoughts
In his unschooled head,
And straight out of Scripture
The life he led.
Gnarled were his fingers
From lifelong toil,
But mellow his heart
That loved the soil.
Close after God
In his soul came labor,
And an equal feeling
For every neighbor.
My Father was a farmer
Who knew the worth
Of the kinship he had
With the planted earth.

What more can I say about Dad? I can pay him no greater tribute than that.

Dad and eldest son

When I was seven
months old, Dad
took me to the
photo studio in
Luverne to pose for
this picture with
him.

Dad loved the county fair

For over 50 years, Dad never missed a county fair.
Even after he quit farming and moved to town, he
won ribbons on his garden produce.

The Ole J. Bjerk Family, 1887

Dad, the boy on the left, was 9 years old when this family photograph was taken. Grandpa (Ole J. Bjerk) is holding his namesake, Ole O., on his lap. Standing in back are Maria and Dena. Next to Grandpa is Andrew. Grandma is holding Minnie. Next to her are Lizzie and Malinda. Grandma died in 1889.

House on Grandpa's farm

After spending the first three years of his life living in a sod shanty, Dad moved into this frame house which Grandpa had built on his tree-claim quarter.

Mother Listened To Lawrence Welk And Billy Graham With Equal Enthusiasm

My mother is Mary. It hasn't always been. She was christened Marit. I know that for certain because I found the record of her christening in the office of the pastor in Sunndalsora, Norway, when I visited there. She Americanized her name after she came to this country.

She was born in Sunndalsora and came to this country at the age of five. She remembers crossing the Atlantic. It was a rough crossing.

Many times when I was still at home I wondered how she ever made it. I never knew anyone who had as "weak" a stomach as my mother.

Mother knew what poverty was from the old country. The only wealth Grandpa and Grandma had when they came to this country was their large family, love for each other, and a strong faith that things would get better and not worse.

Mother inherited a happy-go-lucky outlook from Grandma.

She could be serious, but she liked fun. She liked people, and made it a point to enjoy them.

She went to country school. She developed a beautiful handwriting, a good vocabulary, and an ability to spell. She's an excellent letter writer today, as her grandchildren, with whom she corresponds regularly, will tell you.

Like so many teenage girls during the early 1900's, she worked as a "hired girl". At that time, she was lucky if she received pay in addition to her board and room.

For that, she cooked, waited tables, baby-sat, washed the dishes, did the laundry with a wash board and tub, ironed with flat irons, scrubbed the floor, and baked bread, just to name a few of the duties.

It was early morning until late at night. But if she objected, she didn't show it.

Work in those days — any kind of work — was considered honorable.

And it was absolutely necessary if one was interested in three square meals a day, and some money with which to keep clothes on one's back.

Mother loved music. She could sing. And she could dance.

There were some who then said dancing was sin. Mother wondered about that. But she found dancing was fun, and she had a hard time believing that a schottische, a square dance or a waltz with a man as a partner was so wrong. Besides, it helped her become acqainted with a lot of different people and it provided a pleasant diversion from the drudgery of day to day housework.

Then Dad came along. He enjoyed a good time the same as Mother did.

They made the Saturday night dances in Beaver Creek regularly after they started "going steady".

Their friends knew they were serious about each other, and they kept asking them, "When are you going to get married?"

Their stock answer was, "Next week."

Next week finally came. On Feb. 27, 1913, they bundled up in Dad's buggy and headed for Luverne where they were married by the Rev. L.P. Lund.

Their first home was in Springwater Township, about three miles north of the Palisade Church, and a half mile west.

It was there that I was born.

We moved to Beaver Creek Township a couple of years later. My uncle moved out of the house, and we moved in. We inherited Grandpa and Grandma who didn't move with my uncle.

Things went good for a few years. Dad was buying the farm. My sister was born. And then my brother.

Then came the depression. Dad lost what he'd salted away . . . and then some . . . in the First National Bank of Beaver Creek because he was a director.

The house Mother and Dad had hoped to build some day didn't materialize. But the old house did get a new basement, replacing the dirt walled cellar that served so well for many years. Mother liked that.

Our home, small though it was, became home for others, and Mother never seemed to object.

Bachelor uncles would drop in from time to time and stay a night or maybe a month. Other bachelors, who had no other place to go, would happen to stop in to say hello and Mother and Dad would insist they stay for a meal or two and spend the night.

If Mother cared, she never showed it. "You're supposed to help the less fortunate," she said.

Mother was a strict but loving disciplinarian. She wasn't above administering a sound spanking, if it was necessary. But it was her own attitude toward others, and her acts of love and respect to parents, brothers, sisters and neighbors, that taught us the virtues of obedience and appreciation for our elders.

Mother worked hard during those early years, helping Dad whenever and wherever she could.

As I look back on it now, she did more than she had to because she enjoyed being with him, and missed him when they couldn't be together. She didn't seem to mind going to the barn and helping with the milking one bit because that meant Dad would be back in the house that much sooner.

Some of the neighbor men took their afternoon lunches with them when they went out to the field to work.

Not Dad.

Mother thought nothing of walking a half mile just to deliver Dad's lunch in person. They both enjoyed sitting down together and visiting 15 or 20 minutes while Dad drank his coffee and ate his sandwich and piece of cake.

I remember well the corn picking season when we had the most hired help around. Mother delivered lunch to them, too, and there were times that the weather "wasn't fit for man or beast."

While the men were harnessing their teams before going out to the field, she'd be getting ready to feed them their breakfasts. And what breakfasts she would stack on their plates when they came in.

Mother was generally the first one up in the morning. I can remember lying awake in the upstairs bedroom where I slept, and hearing her quick footsteps as she moved from kitchen to dining room to front room.

She not only helped milk cows, there were times she went out into the field. Particularly during corn picking time. Dad would pick two rows, as she picked the one nearest the wagon.

She was always ready to come out of the house whenever Dad needed someone to drive the team on the horsepower which turned the grain elevator, or when he needed someone to drive the team on the barn hay rope during haying time.

She objected to anyone's doing any work other than chores on Sunday. She'd prepare a delicious Sunday dinner whether we had company or not. But there was no field or yard work done on that day. Sunday was the Lord's Day.

She made sure that everybody made it to church, and everyone was suitably dressed for an hour in God's House. The night before, she'd go over our Sunday school lessons with us to make sure we understood what we were learning and so we wouldn't embarrass ourselves in front of the Sunday School teacher.

When company came for Sunday dinner, and at haying, harvest and corn picking time, Mother "worked her fingers to the bone," as she expressed it, preparing mountains of delicious food.

She was an expert pie and cake baker. Her bread was the envy of other good cooks around the countryside.

Time came, though, when she thought she and Dad had worked hard enough and long enough, so they decided to move to Luverne.

She enjoyed her little house on North Cedar, even after Dad's passing, but when Blue Mound Tower opened, she decided to move in.

She really hated to leave the little house. She felt confined, and she still does, in her one room apartment.

But she doesn't let closeness get her down. She visits with her neighbors, sings with the Blue Mound Tower singers, does her own banking and bill paying. She rides the minibus to church and to senior citizens meetings which she seldom misses unless she doesn't happen to be feeling well.

One day, a little over a year ago, she fell in her apartment and fractured her hip.

We were worried. She was hospitalized in Luverne, then in Sioux Falls, and then she spent a month recuperating in the Palisade Manor at Garretson.

She was finally able to come home. She used a "walker" awhile, but she looked at it as a temporary nuisance. Finally, she told me to return it to Melvin Qualley, from whom she'd borrowed it.

"I want to walk naturally again, and I never will unless I get rid of that thing," she decided.

Today, at 88, she walks as well as ever.

Only complaint I can register about Mother is that she worries too much. "I can't help it," she says.

The sun may be shining but she remembers that the weather man on radio said there was a 20 percent chance of rain. To her, that means that a storm could well be brewing out there somewhere.

She doesn't worry about her own health much, but she worries about mine. And others in the family. Except when we eat at her house. Then she wonders if we're not feeling well if we don't take a third and fourth cookie, when she passes the cookie plate.

But perhaps she's not a great deal different from other mothers. Most of them are solicitous of their children, and do their share of worrying, too.

I admit that I'm glad she cares. I'm glad that she's concerned about me when I leave town for a weekend. I'm glad she's happy as she says she is when I drop in and see her at the apartment.

I'm glad she still sings and reads and writes letters. I like it when she calls up and says, "If you'll stop in, I'll have a loaf of fresh dark bread for you."

I think it's great that she loves poetry and that she listens to Lawrence Welk and Billy Graham with equal enthusiasm.

I'm proud that at 88 she keeps up with the news of the day, both by newspaper and radio. And that if she wants something from the store, she'll go get it herself without calling me. Not that I would mind doing her shopping, but going to the store and to senior citizen potlucks and to church keeps her active, alert . . . and young for her years.

I'm not eligible to nominate her as "Mother of the Year."

It's too late for that now anyway. She earned that honor the second year that Mother's Day was observed in the U.S.

That was the year I was born.

To me, she's been "Mother of the Year" ever since.

Mother and Dad
February 27,
1913

"When are you
going to get mar-
ried?"

"Next week."

Mother
at age 88

Dad
at age 85

Our House May Have Been Lacking In Luxuries, But There Was Love In Abundance

It's going to seem a bit funny not to pay a visit to the old home place this holiday season.

Every year, with the exception of the year that I was born, I've spent Christmas Eve, Christmas Day, New Year's or some time in between in the old house northwest of Beaver Creek.

But this year the eighty with the buildings on it was sold. After having been occupied by members of my family for I don't know how long, there's nothing now to lure me back to the old house, even though I'm a sentimentalist.

My feelings can be summed up in an Old Testament passage I learned in Sunday School:

"To everything there is a season, and a time to every purpose under heaven."

For me, the house has had its season and served its purpose. I am left with a million happy memories.

My Uncle, Ole Aaker, lived there before Dad, Mother and I moved into the house when I was only about three months old. (Because I was born in December and we didn't move there until March, my first Christmas was spent at my birthplace in Springwater Township).

I lived there until 1936, the year I moved to Luverne to take my first job with Nelson Brothers Department Store.

Dad and Mother continued to make it their home until they retired. That's when my sister and brother-in-law, Lorraine and Art Hulbert, moved onto the farm. After renting it for a few years, they bought it, and lived there until September of this year when they, too, retired.

There can be no doubt that it served its purpose, and for me, it served it well.

But it wasn't the house that made it home; it was the people who lived there.

When my uncle moved out, Grandma and Grandpa, who lived with him, stayed with the house and were there when we moved in. They remained with us until they died, Grandma being the last to go, several years after I had left home.

May I tell you about the old house?

It was tiny by today's standards. There was always room for people, but it was lacking in space for things.

No one was ever turned away for lack of a bed or food. But to get another bed into one of the bedrooms, another chair into the living room (make that front room), or another basket of cobs beside the kitchen cook stove, you had to be a miracle worker.

When we first moved there, the house had an attached rear entrance that we always called the shanty. In front of the shanty door was a board walk.

Inside it at one end was an old cook stove. At the other end was a Dexter wood-tub washing machine, laundry tubs and benches. There were hooks on the wall where chore clothes and winter coats were generally hung. Piled in the corner below was a variety of boots, rubbers, and overshoes.

Every Monday, Mother would fire up the shanty cook stove early in the morning. Then she'd fill the copper boiler with water carried in buckets from the cistern at the corner of the house, some 25 to 30 feet away.

By the time the water was boiling, Mother was ready for the weekly wash. That is, if Dad had the little John Deere one-lunger gasoline engine started.

No other piece of equipment on the farm proved more exasperating to him than did that little engine. First of all, it was hard to start. And when it did, he didn't dare leave the house yard, for fear it would stop. For certain, Mother had neither the strength nor the inclination to "twist its tail" as Dad called the cranking process.

Besides heating the water for the laundry, the shanty cook stove also was used at butchering time for rendering lard, and preparing the meat for canning.

A door led from the shanty into the kitchen.

An oil-cloth covered kitchen table, a Monarch range, complete with attached water reservoir and warming oven, a wash stand, a couple of kitchen chairs, a kitchen cabinet and a box for cobs and firewood left a minimum of working space in the kitchen.

The space was even more minimal in winter when we had to bring the cream separator from the milk house into the kitchen to keep it from freezing.

Just off the kitchen was a pantry. Mother sometimes called it the buttery. That's where she kept her baking and cooking needs, pots and pans, flat irons and other household necessities.

On the pantry floor was a hinged door, with a heavy ring attached to it so it could be opened when someone wanted to go down into the cellar.

The cellar was merely an excavation beneath the house, possibly 20 feet square, and seven feet deep. Walls were neither plastered or paneled, just black dirt on all four sides.

At one end was the potato bin. That's where we'd carry the potatoes to store them after we harvested them in the fall.

At the other end was a cupboard with shelves for storing Mother's home-canned goods, jars and jars of meat, vegetables, fruit, pickles and preserves.

On the floor beside it were the big 20 and 30 gallon crocks, used to store lard, salt pork, and pork chops and meatballs which were precooked and packed in lard for future use.

That left just enough room for the cream can, used to store the cream provided by each morning and evening milking, and for a passageway from the cellar stairway to the fruit cupboard.

Amazingly, the cellar was cool in summer and warm in winter except on real cold days.

When temperatures tumbled below zero, Dad would light a kerosene heater, suspended from a floor joist, to keep the canned fruit from freezing.

Just off the kitchen was the dining room.

When Grandpa was living, he had his chair by the window in one corner of the room, and there he would sit, puff his curved stem pipe and read the SKANDINAVEN, the Norwegian language newspaper, when he wasn't outside cutting wood or doing the hog chores.

Other dining room furniture included a round dinner table which usually had at least two extra leaves in it to accommodate the family and, during harvest and corn picking, a hired man. In another corner was the buffet.

Opposite that was Mother's treadle sewing machine. When not in use, the machine itself was folded into the case and a cover dropped down. The top then served as a table or catch all for the newspapers and magazines that came into the house.

On the wall above the sewing maching was the varnished wood telephone with its elongated mouthpiece, the two silver bells near the top, and the black receiver on one side.

The front room was next to the dining room. At one time, there were double doors between the dining room and the front room. These were closed in the early fall before the hard coal heater was brought in, because the best the kitchen range could do was warm the dining room.

The hard coal heater stood in one corner. Against one wall was a library table on which the old Air-O-Bel radio and its horn type speaker were placed when Dad was lucky enough to win them at a drawing at the Booge store one winter.

We had a brown leather davenport with wooden arms. The davenport could be pulled out into a double bed, and it often served that purpose at night, particularly when Dad hired extra hands to get the corn picking done in the late fall, and had to give them one of the upstairs bedrooms.

There were a couple of rockers in the room, and some straight back chairs. A rug covered the floor.

Mother and Dad slept in the bedroom just off the front room. They enjoyed the side benefit of the warmth from the front room heater, a luxury not available to my sister, my brother and myself who slept in bedrooms upstairs.

There were three upstairs bedrooms, one closet and an open area at the head of the stairs that we called the hall. Two of the bedrooms each had a bed, dresser, wardrobe and chair.

Grandma and Grandpa's bedroom had some extras. A little wood or soft coal burning heater stood meekly in one corner. Grandma had a shawl-covered rocker. Then there was a straight back chair, a dresser, bed and a shelf clock. When they were both in good health, Grandpa and Grandma went to their room about 10 o'clock every morning to sing a hymn together, share a few verses of Scripture, and pray for themselves, the family and the world in general.

They had no wardrobe because there wasn't enough room. Their clothes were hung on hooks along one wall, and were protected from dust and lint by a curtain.

The upstairs hall served a variety of needs. The family trunks, used for storage of seasonal clothing and a few family treasures such as the brass candlesticks Grandma brought with her from Norway, were kept there.

Dad would stock up on Ardee or Mother Hubbard flour a couple of times a year, and the dozen or so sacks he bought at a time were stacked along one wall.

The sugar sack also was stored in the hall. When Mother's supply ran low, Dad would go to town and bring home another hundred pound burlap bagful that usually lasted from one canning season to the next. In winter, when it was too cold to dry the laundry on the outside clothesline, Mother would set up a folding clothes drying rack in the hall.

In the early spring, Dad would bring the Little Red Hen incubator in from the granary and set it up in the hall. A kerosene burning lamp heated the water in the copper tubing that provided the heat to hatch the eggs. Mother would check the eggs for fertility by taking them from the incubator tray each night and looking at them through a cardboard cone made for that purpose.

Twenty-one days from the day the eggs were placed in the incubator, we could put our ear to the side of the machine and hear the pip-pip-pip as the chicks pecked their way through the shells. A day later, the red box was full of fuzzy, cuddly, peeping babies and an equal number of factured egg shells.

Over the years, however, the house was changed from time to time and the furniture was updated.

Mother was not a bit enamored with the shanty, so finally it was moved to one side and made into a wash house. An enclosed porch was built as an entry to the kitchen.

One year, she and Dad decided to get rid of the cellar by raising the house from its foundation and putting a full basement under it. That had the effect of eliminating the pantry, because that space was needed for the basement stairway.

I'll never forget going to the farm for Christmas in 1939. That was the first winter for electric lights in the house.

How thrilling it was to sit down for our Christmas Eve supper without the big Aladdin lamp in the middle of the table to obstruct the view of those seated across the table.

Some time after that, the upstairs hall was converted into a bathroom . . . another convenience that really hadn't been missed much up to then, but once installed, we reveled in the luxury of not having to make the trip to the little house out in back.

As I look back at it now, the conveniences and luxuries we lacked were made up by those who lived in the house.

Dad and Mother, sister Lorraine and brother James, Grandpa and Grandma, and even the hired men who spent the winter with us, lived cheerfully, one day at a time, confident that things could only get better.

There was plenty of work to be done by everyone just to keep warm and fed. There was the great out-of-doors to enjoy, and we never lacked for clothing to keep us warm no matter the temperature or windchill.

We had each other and faith in a loving God.

What we lacked in money and things and entertainment was made up by love and laughter and congenial neighbors whose houses were no better or no worse than ours.

So, today I have no longing at all to go back to the old house to spend the holidays.

But I cherish my memories of it, and always will, because it is these memories that make me so appreciative of what I now have.

Our house on the farm

It may have been lacking in luxuries but
there was love in abundance.

Our family during growing up years

Lorraine, Dad, "Boy Off The Farm", Mother
and James, Jr.

In Those Days You Conserved Heat By Banking The House

The other morning, I crawled out of bed, walked to the window, and took a look at the thermometer.

"18 degrees below zero," I exclaimed in disbelief. "And here it is only the first week of December."

The house inside was comfortably warm — 69 degrees, just where I'd set the dial of the thermostat the night before and the humidity gauge showed a comfortable 25 per cent.

All this made me wonder if today's youngsters really appreciate the comforts that today's homes afford with furnaces that can maintain heat at exactly the temperature desired, and where the relative humidity can also be controlled down to a minute percentage point. The great thing about it to me is that all this can be done with only a slight movement of the fingertips.

When "Boy Off the Farm" was a boy on the farm, a person kept warm on an 18-below zero day just trying to keep the inside of the house warm.

If you were ready for winter to come it helped. But if wet weather had delayed corn picking, it was a sure bet that there were a lot of things to do before the house was snugged up tight like it had to be.

The first thing that had to be done, of course, was to bring the hard coal heater in from the granary. We took it apart and carried it out every spring, because our "front room" was so small. Actually bringing it back in wasn't hard work; in fact it was kind of exciting because there was that anticipation of the warm red glow of the coals just before chore time in the late afternoon.

"Banking" the house was usually the next project. If we were delayed in getting started, it often meant that the ground was frozen, and driving the short fence posts into the ground required more than the 16 pound sledge.

The posts were driven in at about 10 foot intervals about two feet from the foundation. Then "hog wire" was stapled to the posts so when the job was finished, there was a neat little fence, about 24 or 30 inches high, all the way around the house.

I'm not sure if it was frugality, stemming from Ben Franklin's "waste not, want not" principle, but invariably, the banking was done with the bedding we had cleaned out of the horse stalls in the barn that morning. It seemed that this material had a quality of moistness about it that caused it to pack and insulate well, and keep the winter winds from whistling through the stone foundation on which the house stood.

The next project was tacking tarpaper over the screen doors. You never bought storm doors in those days, and combination doors were unheard of. The tarpaper was all that was needed to make a screen door into a storm door.

We kept the coal in a little bin in the granary. Dad usually brought a wagon load back with him from Booge, after he had taken a load of oats to the elevator to get enough money to pay the threshing bill. A scuttle of coal would keep the heater going all night if the heater were properly "banked" with ashes to keep it from burning full blast.

As mentioned earlier, I managed to keep warm just trying to keep the house warm, and so did the rest of the family. There was wood to split, the cob box to keep full, the kerosene lamps to be filled and the lamp chimneys to keep clean, coal skuttles to carry in, and ashes to carry out . . . just to name a few of the chores that have now been eliminated because we have dials and buttons and switches and faucets.

Those were the good old days — so they say — and at the moment I'm glad I experienced them. But I like it better the way it is today. It has been said that "you don't miss the water until the well runs dry" and conversely, you don't appreciate the hot water from the faucet for your morning shave until you've had to break the coating of ice on the kitchen water pail before you could fill the tea kettle on the wood-burning range.

The Kitchen Range — A Multi-Purpose Heating Machine

I read a piece in the paper the other day about the business boom that is being enjoyed by the makers and dealers for Franklin stoves.

This year is going to be their biggest in history, and the reason for new interest in the Franklin stove is the energy crisis and nostalgia, says the news report.

There's something quaint about that piece of heating equipment which has been changed very little from the way it was originally designed by its inventor, Benjamin Franklin.

But it's practical, too. As long as trees can be made to grow from the earth, there will always be fuel to feed the flames that produce the heat in a Franklin stove.

We never had a Franklin stove at our house, nor did we have a furnace.

The kitchen range provided the heat necessary until the late fall of the year, then we started the hard coal heater.

While we had to buy fuel for the hard coal heater, we always managed to get by with burning wood and corn cobs in the range. Both gave the little farm house a coziness that is not possible with modern heating plants, and I guess that coziness is what people are looking for now when they buy Franklin stoves.

The kitchen range was a multi-purpose heating unit that's never been duplicated.

It not only cooked the family meals and did the family baking, it heated most of the house. It had a built in water heater on one side, which we called the reservoir. The flat surface heated the flat irons which my mother used to do the family ironing. Warming ovens at the top of the range kept food warm for any hired man who missed supper because he stayed in the corn field a little longer to get his wagon full. They also served as a safe place to dry wet mittens.

The oven door could be opened, and the kids with cold feet could pull up a chair, sit down and soon be toasty warm again.

The kitchen being Mother's domain found her also the official fireman of the kitchen range. There were no dials to turn, buttons to push, or thermostats to set. She controlled the temperature by knowing just how big a piece of firewood, or how many dry corn cobs to add to the fire in the firebox, and also the exact time to add them.

There wasn't a clock timer nor was there a thermometer on the oven door to show what the temperature was inside. Through the years — and no doubt with some trying experiences at the outset

— she had developed a sense that told her when the baking temperature was just right, and when the bread, the cake, or the cookies reached the peak of perfection and should be taken out.

We children didn't think the kitchen range was such a great invention when we had to carry in fuel, carry out the ashes and bring pails of water from the cistern to fill the reservoir. But when the pans of fresh baked loaves of bread or fat, brown molasses cookies came out of the oven, or when a kettle of home made vegetable soup was bubbling atop the range, we felt a lot more kindly to the black "Monarch" (that was the stove's brand name) that took up the greater share of room in the kitchen.

The hard coal heater was a different thing entirely. It had shiny nickel trim, and "stove blacking" was applied to the cast iron parts to make them bright and new looking. New isinglass was put into the little window frames, replacing those that had cracked or been broken out during the summer or previous spring. Then the hard coal was started.

Nothing was more appealing than to come in to the front room in the early evening and sit and look at the glowing coal inside. It not only radiated warmth, but there was something about the fire that could be seen within that gave a person a sense of well being.

Dad was fireman for old "Garland." (That was the brand name of the hard coal heater.) We knew it was soon time to get up when we'd hear him start shaking the ashes down with a nickel plated lever in the early morning, and then pour in a scuttle full of coal on the top of the coals that were left. By the time we came down from the upstairs bedrooms, which were not heated, the front room was already warm.

It's a lot different now. A thermostat keeps temperature constant. There's no wood to chop or carry, and no wagon load of hard coal to unload with a scoop shovel before every heating season. Now, the fuel is piped in and you can't even see it. I admit, I enjoy today's convenience. But I still am enchanted at the sight of a log burning in a fireplace, or seeing a Franklin stove like the Charles Noreliuses have in their kitchen, and the Wally Estensons have in the living room of their lake cottage.

When I can feel the heat, and see the fire that creates it, I again enjoy a sense of well-being that takes me back to the days when I was a farm boy without a care in the world.

Corn Cobs Helped Keep The Home Fires Burning — And They Were Cheap

Disappearing from the farm scene faster than I realized are corn cribs, corn pickers and cob piles.

There are a number of reasons for this, but mainly it's because more and more corn is being harvested with combines and picker-shellers.

This means that when the corn comes in from the field, it's in shelled form, and the cobs are left on the ground to be plowed under. Shelled corn, of course, cannot be stored in a crib so cribs stand empty on the farms where the combines or picker shellers are used.

When I was a boy on the farm, the cobs were almost as valuable as the corn itself.

When there was a corn crop, there was no need to worry about an energy shortage, because once the corn was shelled, the cobs were stacked in a pile and used as fuel for the cook stove, principally, and sometimes in the parlor heating stove when we just wanted to get rid of the chill.

During my early boyhood, kernels were separated from the cobs by what was called the spring corn sheller. The cob that emerged was unbroken.

When the spring sheller was replaced with the faster cylinder sheller, the cobs came out in broken pieces. This made them less desirable, particularly to the housewife, who had learned to control the surface and oven temperature of her kitchen range just by adding the correct number of cobs to the fire in the fire box. She knew precisely how many cobs would be needed to brown the crust of a pie, or finish a roast to the right degree of doneness in a given amount of time.

It was easy to stick the cobs in the firepot when they were full length.

When the broken variety came into general use, they had to be tossed in by the handful, or sometimes, a small shovel was used. Usually, though, it was by the handful from a cob box that stood beside the stove.

The cob box had to be filled daily. When it was real cold, it had to be filled several times a day. This was usually a job for the kids. When we came home from school, we filled the cob box.

Cobs from corn that had been shelled after having been in the crib over summer made a fast fire and a hot one. But cobs burned out quickly, and the supply in the firebox had to be replenished often. And, they made a lot of ashes.

So, the cobs the kids carried in one day were carried out the next morning in the form of ashes to the ash pile.

At our home, the cobs usually supplemented a wood supply which Grandpa provided. He'd worked as a woodsman in Norway, and knew how to cut and split wood better than anyone I've ever known.

He could fall a tree exactly where he wanted it to drop. Once it was down, he'd cut the main trunk into six or eight foot lengths, and they were hauled from the grove to the woodpile area back of the house. There he had a sawhorse he, himself, had made, designed especially for cutting logs into stove lengths with a one-man buck saw.

Once cut into stove lengths, he split the wood into smaller pieces, pieces that would fit handily in the range, and which stacked easily on a well arranged pile out of doors, or in a wood box inside the house.

We used the cobs for kindling, to get the fire started in the morning, and then burned wood for the rest of the day.

When the cob supply was exhausted, we often had to bring in cobs from the hog feeding yard.

The hogs were fed ear corn, and they'd shell the corn from the cobs as they ate it.

These cobs didn't burn as well, and we hated the job of picking them up, one by one into a bushel basket. But energy had to be conserved, then as now, not because coal was scarce but because cobs were cheap, and, by saving money on coal, there was a little extra cash for other purposes.

Today, cobs from shelled corn are seldom burned as fuel. Sometimes they're burned in a big bonfire just to get rid of them. Others are chopped or pulverized and used for bedding. Some farmers just load them into a spreader and haul them out onto the stubble ground where they are buried with the stubble, at plowing time to provide organic matter in the soil.

A lot of oil and gas were conserved in those days. It is hard to realize now that up until about 60 years or so ago, the only petroleum product generally used for fuel, other than gasoline for cars, was kerosene which provided the energy for a good share of the lighting. In that brief span of six decades, we have seen what we thought was an abundant supply of fuel oil, available at a very minimal cost, dwindle to the point of scarcity and the price has, as they say, gone "out of sight."

It makes one wonder how we'll be heating our homes and cooking our meals six decades from now.

Winter Called For Coal, Wood And Ankle Length Underwear

They say we just went through the coldest January in history. Maybe so.

If I had my doubts before, I was firmly convinced when my fuel bill came. And, most everyone else I talked to was as firmly convinced as I was.

I haven't been griping, though. There's not much to gripe about when there is fuel to burn, and you don't have to lay off work or move in with someone else like they have had to do in some places in the country.

Best of all, we haven't had to plow snow like they have in the east, although some of that snow would be mighty nice to have spread evenly over the Upper Midwest farm lands right now.

We've tried to comply with the energy emergency people's requests to cut back on heat. At our house, we added more insulation in the attic, and we've been setting our thermostat at cooler temperatures both during the daytime and night.

I still believe, though, our house is warmer with the thermostat set at 65 than our farm house was when I was a kid at home.

There were spots in the old farm house that were warm, like right around the kitchen stove and the parlor heater, but the heat didn't circulate very well throughout the rooms. And the upstairs, like most houses of that era, had no heat at all in the bedrooms. A glass of water placed on the dresser at night would have a crust of ice on it in the morning.

Some people I know are going back to supplementing their regular heat with wood heaters.

That sounds like a winner. It would most certainly provide a place to get rid of a lot of surplus wood we're going to have because of the dying elm trees.

But I wonder how long the wood burners are going to be enthusiastic about cutting and splitting wood, carrying it into the house and carrying out ashes?

When I first came to Luverne, the first oil burners had just been installed in the furnaces in some of the homes.

That changed the mode of home heating drastically. How the people with coal burners envied those with oil burners.

The first thing the home owners with oil burners did was get rid of the coal bin.

Coal hauling was a booming business in Luverne when I moved here. No doubt there were others, but Joe Toms seemed to have a corner on it. With his trusty team and a single box wagon, he started delivering to the various basements in town in late summer and early fall, and he'd keep it up all winter.

What a back breaking job that was! Shoveling the stuff into the wagon from the coal sheds at the elevator companies and lumber yards. Then scooping the heavy stuff into the coal bins, usually through a small basement window.

By day's end, his face, his hands and his clothing were as black as the fuel he'd been hauling.

Housewives hated coal hauling day. Regardless of the precautions that might be taken, coal dust would find its way up the basement stairs and into the kitchen.

"Make sure Joe wets the stuff down good before he comes," was the housewife's last admonition to her husband when he went to order a load of coal.

Not only did the coal itself cause dust before it was burned, but afterward as well. Sometimes, the furnace would smoke for some reason or other. This meant days of cleaning soot from woodwork and walls.

Coal ended up in three basic forms once it was burned. There was the soot, the ashes and the clinkers.

Clinkers, like ashes, were residue that had to be hauled out, once the ash pan below the firebox was full. The clinkers were brownish-black non-combustible solids that were formed by the intense heat at which the coal burned, resembling some of the modern ceramic art pieces I've seen in recent years.

Everybody had an ash pile in the back yard. If it was a big house, where coal was burned in both the furnace and the kitchen range, the heap looked like a miniature mountain by spring.

This made business for the ash hauler.

At home, we always burned hard coal. There wasn't much ash to hard coal. And it didn't take quite as much in the way of wagon loads as soft coal did either because with a hard coal heater in the "front room" rather than a furnace in the basement, not as much fuel was required.

Without a thermostat, fluctuating temperatures had to be expected. But I can't recall that it was ever miserably cold. Maybe the reason was that we were dressed for the occasion.

Winter came and we all wore long johns — only then we called them union suits.

My favorite kind was the fleece-lined variety, and I never did like the drop-seat kind, but rather the slit seat. Nothing was cozier to put on after a warm Saturday night bath than a clean, fleecy on the inside, union suit which had been warming on the cover of the kitchen range reservoir while I was in the tub.

The thing I hated about long legged underwear was the bulge

it made at the ankle, particularly when I was seven or eight and wore knickers as my Sunday best.

But I guess I didn't hate them nearly as much as the girls did, and all the girls wore them, too.

Besides the longies, boys always wore two overalls, or an overall and a pair of well worn wool dress trousers, and if not two shirts, then one heavy wool or cotton flannel shirt. And heavy sox.

If the temperature in the house had been about 70 degrees, it would have been miserable wearing that many clothes.

But, perhaps that's what we are coming to again.

We could do with a lot less heat both in our homes and our businesses if we dressed in warmer clothing.

And we wouldn't freeze so much when we stepped out of doors on a cold day, either.

This Is The Way We Washed Our Clothes

I doubt if there was ever a Monday morning during the first 20 years of my life that Dad ever ventured out to the field without having to come back to the house one or more times.

In fact, there were very few times that he even bothered to try to do field work on Monday forenoon because that was wash day at home on the farm.

Today as Roberta and I sit and eat a meal, or watch television, while our automatic washer fills itself with the proper mixture of hot and cold water, swishes the clothes through the soapy water, then rinses them, and spins them dry, I marvel at the patience which Mother and Dad had to have to keep our clothes clean.

Wash day meant Mother was up at the crack of dawn to light the fire in the cookstove which was used to heat the water pumped from the cistern and carried bucket by bucket to the copper boiler the night before.

By breakfast time, it was hot, and ready to go into the washer which we always called "the machine".

Our first "machine", or at least the first one that I recall, was a Dexter wooden tub affair, which was powered either by a long wooden lever and human muscle, or by a gasoline engine with a belt running from the engine to the pulley on the "machine".

If I believed in gremlins, elves, or leprechauns, I wouldn't hesitate to swear that the gasoline engine was completely in their control.

And if the John Deere people hadn't gone into the field of wagons, manure spreaders, corn planters and the like, they'd never have been in business to see the advent of the tractor and modern power farm equipment, because their little single cylinder gasoline engine was certainly "Farmer's Trouble Maker No. 1" if our engine was typical of their output.

And yet, maybe it was a mechanical marvel at that.

Ours didn't have a battery, a spark plug, or a carburator, as we think of them today.

And we used a grade of gasoline which, I venture to say, wouldn't bring more than a disgruntled chug or two out of a modern motor.

First, Dad would fill the tiny gasoline tank. Then, he'd turn a little knob below the cast iron case that held the water which cooled the area around the single piston. This knob "turned on" the gasoline, so it would come up to the simple carburetion device.

Then, he'd put his hand over the round hole on the front of the engine, which served to "choke" it, to bring the gas into the firing chamber.

Then, he began turning the crank!

The preliminaries weren't bad, but I can't say that about turning the crank.

That was a man's job, and 52 times a year for more than two decades, Dad proved he was a man!

With his hand over the opening, each time the crank made a revolution, the engine would go, "Frp, che".

If the gremlins were not in their usual playful mood, about three revolutions of "frp, che, frp, che, frp, che" was all that was needed and it would start. Then the sound would change to, "Tuc, tuc, tuc, tuc, tuc, heh, heh, heh . . . tuc, tuc, tuc, tuc, heh, heh, heh, heh, heh!!" and Dad would mop his brow, and stand back and listen to it with a pleased look on his face.

If it appeared that it was going to keep on running, he'd head for the barn or the field, with a prayer on his lips that nothing would happen to interfere with the ultimate completion of the day's wash.

But, if it didn't start, that was another thing.

That meant, he had to start talking to the playful gremlins, who were lousing up the works.

Why he thought that they, or the engine, to whomever it was he was speaking, understood Norwegian better than English, I don't know. He likely figured that it was one way of being expressive without being profane, and while it may not have helped start the engine, it gave vent to his feelings. Had he not been able to do this, I'm convinced his frustrations would have led him to throw the crank into the nearby pig yard, or to pick up a sledge hammer and smash the green monster to bits.

I don't recall that Mother had to use the hand method to wash her clothes very often, because sooner or later, Dad would get the engine to run, and usually, the washing was finished mechanically. Sometimes, though, it was later than sooner, when the day's task was done.

Many was the time that the engine would chug along merrily until Dad was in the midst of doing some chores in the barn, or was already out in the field, and would then stop.

Mother didn't have the strength to start it again, nor the mechanical ability. And besides, if she had to do all the rest of the work connected with washing, she was determined to have nothing to do with the engine.

This frequently resulted in her shrill call, "Papa! Pa-pa!" which brought Dad back to the scene to kneel again beside the engine, take the crank, and resume his one-way conversation in fluent Norse.

If he were out in the field, it was a different matter. It usually meant Mother had to walk out to watch the horses while he came in to put the pride of the John Deere line back into operation.

There were times, however, that the engine absolutely refused to start. If there was a lot of washing that absolutely had to be done that day, Dad, as a last resort, would back the Model T Ford out of the garage over to the wash house. There he would block the wheels so that the car could not move in either direction, then raise one of the rear wheels, attach a spare pulley we had lying around, and put the washing machine drive belt on the pulley. Then he would start the car engine. Throttled down to slow speed, the car's drive wheel would take over the gasoline engine's duties for the day and complete the week's laundry without further delay.

I think we had the Dexter machine and the gasoline engine until after both Lorraine and I were earning our own money, and we bought Mother a washer with a Briggs and Stratton motor on it, which even she could start.

But before that, she would put all her laundry through the wringer, which she turned by hand until finally, Dexter came out with a wringer that operated by power, by just lifting the lever. Even that was a big help.

The end result was a couple of clothes lines strung with sheets, pillowcases, overalls, chambray shirts, long handled underwear, socks and underskirts.

Once they were dry, Mother nimbly unfastened the clothes pins and filled the clothes basket. Later, after all were carried inside, she would "sprinkle" the biggest share of the washing, roll it up, and then came the task of ironing the entire lot with flat irons kept hot atop the cob-fired kitchen range.

I cannot recall ever hearing Mother complain about wash day. But Dad was convinced that some days were meant to try men's souls, and in his case, it was every Monday.

Sometimes we had to wash clothes this way

Throttled down to slow speed, the car's drive
wheel would take over the gasoline engine's duties
for the day and complete the week's laundry
without delay.

Early day Beaver Creek

Joe Dunbar was the candy man in the white brick
store on the corner which for more than a half
century was known simply as Rauk's.

The Candy Man Was A
Good Guy To Know

Ever listen to a song, and then have it so firmly implanted in your mind that you keep hearing it long afterward?

This is what happens to me when I hear "Candy Man" which Sammy Davis, Jr. has made famous with his recording that came out a couple of months ago.

I guess the reason it stays with me is because it keeps reminding me of when candy was my idea of the very best thing that had ever happened to human kind.

Being a boy on the farm, getting to the candy store was maybe a once-a-week thing, on Saturday night in the summer time, or on Tuesday night, which was always band concert night in Beaver Creek. With a nickel allowance to blow all in one place, it required a painstaking period of decision making before giving the instructions to the man behind the counter as to just how you wanted him to mix and match the goodies in the brown paper bag.

My Dad would usually come home with a bag of candy if he went to town for repairs or twine or whatever. But this particular bagful had to be shared by the whole family so there wasn't too much available for me.

That's why, when I could do my own buying with my own money, I was the happiest boy in Beaver Creek township.

What tantalizing delights there were! The colorful jawbreakers that would last all day if you didn't chew them after you'd had them in your mouth an hour or so and softened them up. The all-day suckers. The penny-per-box licorice cigarettes, and the white candy cigarettes which were red on one end to make them look like the real thing. The licorice whips. And the little white wax milk bottles from which you sipped the cherry nectar, after biting off the end.

Well do I remember some of the candy men who made my boyhood days so delightful.

There was Haakon Strand, who with Carl Tveidt operated the store at Booge. Booge isn't there any more. It was directly west of our farm just across the state line in South Dakota. There was a store there, a grain elevator until it burned down, two or three homes, a little building where some car repairing was done and at one time, a little club house. Oh yes, and the Great Northern depot.

But Haakon was the candy man. Haakon didn't say much. He seldom spoke unless he was spoken to, and then his answer was to the point, seldom embellished with any sage bit of philosophy. But he was a good business man, and was there to do business.

Even if it was only a nickel for a bag of candy, he'd have money in the till at the end of the day, and that's what he was there for.

Another candy man I remember is Joe Dunbar. Joe was "vice-president in charge" of a lot of things at Rauk's Store in Beaver Creek, and always had a little better variety of candy to choose from than there was in Booge. Joe wasn't as patient as Haakon while the lad in front of the counter was trying to decide which pieces he wanted.

Joe's favorite sound was also the bell on the cash register. And, he was a little more careful when he weighed the candy than Haakon was. It always seemed I got a better deal at Booge, even if the selection wasn't as large.

Up the street from Rauk's Store in Beaver Creek was another store, bearing the name of Ott and Grout. Alvah Ott about that time had become involved in the radio business, and was busy selling Atwater Kents so it was up to Thad Grout to dispense the candy. Thad, as amiable a businessman as I've ever known, usually put in an extra piece of candy for good measure. I really liked Thad.

Later, Jim Vopat, who with his wife, Anna, operated the White House Cafe after I was in high school came up with the candy delight of that era. It was the frozen Snicker or Milky Way bar. Lucky for me that those were depression years and I never had any money. If I could have eaten as many frozen Snickers as I'd have liked, I'd have been wearing dentures a long time ago.

Then there was another candy man, whose name I either didn't learn, or have since forgotten. I was stranded in town because of a snowstorm, and when this happened, my home away from home was the A.S. Anderson place, just east of Beaver Creek. My buddy, Howard Anderson, and I had talked about how nice it would be if something happened to the candy truck that went past the farm regularly so we could go into it somehow and abscond with a few pieces. ("With that much candy, he'd never miss it.") It so happened that the truck became stalled in a snow drift where the gravel road comes out of Beaver and onto the highway a couple of blocks from the Anderson house. Artie, Howard and I went out with scoop shovels, and in no time, the truck was "unstuck". For our efforts we received a box of candy bars. Can you imagine, a whole box of five-cent bars? 24 of them! Wow!

When "Central" Helped You Reach Out And Touch Someone

"Ma Bell" has come out with a big promotion to give designer style telephones as Christmas gifts.

After seeing the brochure, I asked our local manager one day if the company didn't have some of the old box style with the crank on the side and the two silver bells mounted on the front above the mouthpiece and he said no.

The old ones, like the one we had on the farm "back then" have become collector's items, and are as scarce as hen's teeth, he said. Besides that, they command a fat price if one finds one and an owner who is willing to sell.

Now, if "Ma Bell' had come out with one of the box style phones, I'd be tempted to buy one. I guess it's because I was always fascinated by the resemblance those phones had to a human face.

The shiny bells at the top were the eyes. The elongated mouthpiece resembled a long nose. The little slanted shelf below it, on which the directory was usually kept, reminded me of a long lower lip of a mouth. The receiver side was the good ear side. The crank side, I imagined, got that way because the head had lost most of its ear in some kind of an accident.

Because our farm was so near the South Dakota border, we were always on the "Garretson line". The Garretson exchange served a number of farmers' mutual telephone companies, and Dad was an officer of the Engelson Telephone Company which served 20 or maybe 30 farms in Beaver Creek and Springwater townships. It had been founded, I think, by the Ingelson brothers, John and Alfred, who lived in the area, and that's how it got its name, except they spelled the company name with an "E" instead of an "I".

I guess Dad was the treasurer. I know he'd have to go out twice a year to collect $8.50 from each customer who failed to send in his "phone rent". This amount provided telephone service for a half year.

If we wanted to call McCurdys, Alinks, Christiansens or Sandstedes, we never had to go through the operator. All we had to do was to ring their "ring".

Our ring, I remember, was three longs and a short — ringgggg, ringgggg, ringgggg, ring! Alink's was a short and a long and a short. McCurdy's was two shorts and a long.

When the bells rang, we'd rush to the phone. So did a lot of the neighbors who would hear the same "ring". You could always tell by the sound of lifting receivers, and the noises that came from

the listeners' homes if they weren't careful to hold their hands
over the mouthpiece.

A person-to-person call in those days was community property.
A lot of people got the news of the community just by "listening".

A good share of the people on our line (Line 38) were
"Americans" which was a term my grandmother used when she
referred to non-Norwegians. Often times when my Garretson
relatives called, they'd speak in Norwegian to Mother or Dad, just
so the listeners wouldn't understand what the conversation was
about. The Sandstede families quite often visited in German for
the same reason.

When we wanted to call someone on one of the other lines —
like the Eitreims, the Edmundsons, the Larsons, the Aakers, the
Williamsons or Rademachers — we'd have to place the call
through "Central".

Central in those days was either Minnie or Polly Falk, and they'd
invariably answer not with "operator" or "number please" but
with their own version of "hello" which sounded something like
"harruh". The caller could give the number out of the directory, or
the name of the person he wanted to reach. It didn't make any difference, they knew which socket to plug the cord into, which
switch to press and the right number of shorts and longs to ring
in the proper sequence.

It always seemed that the greater the distance between the
caller and the "party" being called, the louder one would have to
shout into the mouthpiece. Whenever one called anyone long
distance, it was really important to yell.

"Central" provided other services, too. If our clocks stopped, or
each one showed a different time, we'd call her, and say, "Hello,
Central? Can you give me the correct time please?" And she
would.

Now and then she'd ring the "general ring". That was usually an
alarm of some kind. It consisted of seven quick "shorts," followed
by a pause, then seven more quick "shorts". How the telephone
would click as receivers all along the line would go up. She'd then
make an announcement, like the night when Alfred Ingelson's
house burned down and she called for the neighbors to go and
help. Then, once in a while, she'd call to announce a hot special
available at Fresvik's or the Wangsness store in Garretson.

For a time, we were also hooked up to the Beaver Creek exchange, and as far as I know, at no extra charge. Bill Teason was
the owner-manager, and the exchange was in a little building just
east of the Beaver Creek State Bank.

The Teasons had three daughters, Evelyn, Cleo and Hazel, and
each one took her turn at the switchboard. It was fun to go in
there to watch the little gadgets drop and flutter which was the

signal that someone was making a call. The girls, or Bill, or whoever happened to be on duty would ask for the number, and then plug the cord into the socket. They wore headphones, and every now and then would flip a switch to determine if the people were still talking or if the call had been completed.

When we wanted to call the Beaver Creek exchange, we rang one "long". The response there was generally "number please" or "operator".

Just as the old telephones looked like the face of a human being (to me, at least), they also had a personality and a friendliness that is now gone in this era of touch-tone and DDD telephone service.

The operators were always helpful. If you called someone and there was no answer, it wasn't a bit unusual for the operator to come on the line and tell you that "they're not home there today, they're at so-and-so's funeral." If "Central" wasn't too busy just then, she might ask how you were feeling, or if you'd seen anything of your Aunt Lizzie lately.

The old fashioned telephones and central offices didn't provide the kind of service we demand and get now so I'd never want to go back to those days.

But there's nothing I'd like better than to have one of the old box-style wall phones to hang up in the rec room to remind me of the human element that added a special dimension to rural living for this "boy off the farm."

We Fought A Losing Battle With
The Pesky Flies

Judging from the variety of bottles, boxes and spray cans on store shelves that are filled with preparations for eradicating the housefly, it appears that this most common of all insects is as pesky as ever.

The fly has to be the most prolific, the most embattled, and the most survival-prone of all God's flying creatures — at least in our part of the world.

In summer, flies are everywhere. They like it here.

Particularly they like the farm. That's because there's food, water and lots of places to raise families. And can they raise families!

Fly fighting has changed a lot since the days my mother used Tanglefoot fly paper and the egg shaped boxes of fly powder to keep the indoor population at a minimum.

Even then, she had to supplement her weaponry by carrying the old-reliable wire-screen, gingham-trimmed, wood-handled fly swatter in one hand while she was busy doing her many household tasks with the others. She just couldn't stand the sound of a buzzing fly in her house.

I must confess that I contributed to her problem.

When I went out the door, I opened the screen door as wide as it would go and seconds later, it would slam shut with a bang.

I came into the house the same way. A six inch opening would have been enough. The way I opened it, Old Tom, the biggest horse we had on the farm, could have walked through and have had room to spare.

The flies would keep their scouts out and would use their nature-endowed CB system to spread the message, "Here we go again, gang. Here comes that kid who knows how to open screen doors." And each time the door opened, Mother's swatter went back into action.

I think the flies enjoyed Mother's cooking and baking as much as the rest of the family did. When her bread came out of the oven and its delightful fragrance came through the open door, the flies would settle on the screen door in such numbers that it resembled a black net.

When Dad would come in for a meal, he'd wave his straw hat at them to chase them away, and then quickly squeeze through the narrowest opening he could make and still get through. Even then, one or two of the pests would sneak in with him.

I remember one screen door fly deterrent that was used. A discarded green window shade eight or ten inches wide would be slit into narrow strips on one side, and then tacked to the top of the door.

Opening and shutting the door would cause the strips to move, and a breeze would also stir them into movement. This would have a disturbing effect on the flies and many of them sought quieter roosting areas.

One time, Dad came home from an auction sale with a screen fly trap. This round contraption, about 18 or 20 inches high, and maybe 10 or 12 inches in diameter had legs an inch or two high, and the bottom was cone-shaped, with a hole in the center of the cone. It was set outside the screen door where it was most effective.

The flies were duped into the trap by placing a saucer of sour milk or water beneath the opening. Always thirsty, the flies would sip the nectar from the saucer, and then, as is their nature, they'd take off straight up, and into the hole in the trap.

They never seemed to know how to get out that same hole. As the trap filled, the volume of buzzing increased. Somehow, the flies' life expectancy dropped measurably in that trap, and each morning, it had to be emptied of its catch.

The Tanglefoot fly paper inside the house also trapped a lot of the pesky creatures. Attracted again by the idea of food, flies would settle on the sticky stuff that covered the long strip of curly paper suspended from the ceiling or the kerosene lamp bracket, and they were there to stay.

During the peak fly season, particularly in homes where there were a lot of kids running in and out of the house, it didn't take long before the Tanglefoot was black instead of gold in color.

While the flies were mainly a nuisance indoors, they were vicious and blood thirsty out of doors.

Cattle and horses were plagued by their attacks, but hogs never seemed to be bothered.

Flynets were a vital part of the harness set up for work horses. Some of the nets had canvas backs with strings hanging down the side. The canvas kept the flies from settling on the horses' backs, and the movement of the strings kept them off the sides.

The canvas nets, however, were warm, and some farmers used nets entirely made of string or leather thongs — an ancient form of macrame — which weren't quite as hot for the horses.

Even with the nets, the horses switched their tails to keep the flies from their rumps, and when standing still would be lifting their feet and stamping hard on the ground to try to get the stinging creatures off legs.

A person working with a team of horses learned to be wary while unhitching them from a piece of machinery because being hit in the face with a switching tail could be mighty painful.

There was one breed of fly that was particularly distressing to horses. We called it the nose fly. It only sought out the tender nose of the horses, and during the peak season, literally drove them crazy. Someone, however, invented the screen nose basket, which fit over a horse's nose, and kept the flies from settling down to do their dirty work.

I never did find milking a pleasant time in any season, but during the fly season, it was especially disagreeable.

When the cow was out in the pasture, she could swing her head and use her tongue to dislodge the flies from her front quarters, and could use her tail to keep them from settling in too deeply on her hind quarters. Tied with a chain to the manger, or locked into a stanchion in the barn, however, the cow was restrained from moving her head, so her only recourse was to switch her tail, and stamp or kick her feet.

Every year, Dad would buy a couple of gallons of fly spray, and before each milking, we'd have to go over each cow with a hand pumped sprayer, giving her a coating of the insecticide which did indeed kill some of the flies, and deterred others during the hour it took to do the milking.

Even then, it wasn't unusual for the cow to switch her tail into the milker's face, and occasionally with such force as to knock his straw hat off. She was prone to kick, too, to try to get at flies biting her front legs or under her belly.

Another defensive tactic was to grab the busy tip of the cow's tail and hold it firmly against the cow's leg by pressing one's knee against it. The cow would manage to pull it loose and whip her tail around, now and then, but it gave the milker a little more time to duck out of the way to keep from being clobbered.

Some cows were worse than others in this respect. With them, we protected ourselves by wrapping a chain with a pair of shackles around the rear legs. Putting the tip of the cow's tail under one of the shackles added to the effectiveness of the system, and to the comfort of the milker.

If any good ever came from World War II, it was the research done on insect control, and the resulting insecticides that were produced as the result of the research.

Today it is a lot easier to control flies, and I would guess there aren't as many around.

But go to a picnic, or try to snooze in a lawn chair, and one realizes that the battle has not been won. Today's flies have developed greater resistance to chemicals, and have managed to maintain their population levels.

Here is one area where mankind has not disturbed ecology. Fly swatters may be made of plastic rather than wire screen, but they still are a summer necessity. Raid in aerosol cans may have replaced the dusting powder in the yellow egg-shaped boxes, but the flies still gather on screen doors, and deposit black specks on the white trim around front windows.

The Lord must have a reason for permitting the flies to exist despite all man's efforts to eradicate them. Maybe it's His way of letting us know that He's still in charge of His universe.

Fighting flies was a losing battle

Flynets were a vital part of the harness setup . . .
some farmers used nets entirely made of string or
leather tongs.

Every farm had chickens

There was a time when every farm had a flock of
chickens and ours was no different. Here's Grandma Aaker feeding them while Grandpa pumps
water. The building at the right is the shanty
where we kept the washing machine.

There Was A Time When Every Farm Had A Flock Of Chickens

Have you noticed as you drive through the countryside that you seldom see a chicken on a farm yard any more? How long has it been since you had to slow down to let a chicken cross the road ahead of you?

What has happened is that farmers just aren't raising chickens any more. The farm poultry flock of a hundred birds or so may never have been highly profitable, but they furnished eggs, big roasting roosters and plump stewing hens for the table . . . and for a long time, money to buy groceries. They lived on whole oats, shelled corn, and skim milk, all of which the farmer had produced himself, so he had nothing to buy really.

He didn't have to fool much with the eggs, either. Just pick them and put them in the crate. When it was full, whether it took a day or a week to fill it, he took it to the store where he bought his groceries on Saturday or Saturday night. There they were counted and either paid for in cash, or credit was given in trade. I remember well that we never went to town to "shop" when I was on the farm. We went to "trade" and so did all our neighbors.

A friend was telling me the other day how he used to lug egg crates as a boy when he lived at Merrill, Iowa. At this particular store where he worked, it was the custom to take telephone orders from the farmers' wives during the day on Saturday. So, all day long he would carry the slips of paper, on which the orders were taken, around the store, picking up the items ordered and putting them in boxes to await the arrival of the customers.

By evening, he said, the aisle through the center of the long narrow store was lined on both sides with boxes of groceries.

Then, when they were finished with their Saturday night chores, the farmers and their families would come to town. From about 8 until midnight, he'd carry boxes of groceries out to the farmers' cars and carry egg cases in. For this, his sole reward was a big bag of candy, although he suspects that his parents were given credit on their grocery account for the work he did.

How things have changed!

Now people who are in the egg business are in it big. Instead of a hundred hens, they have thousands. The birds spend their entire lifetime in cages, their feet never touching the ground. They have never eaten a kernel of corn, a grain of oats, or a live cricket. Nor have they ever had the enjoyment (at least it always looked like they were having fun) of scratching in the straw around the straw pile for grain or weed seeds.

Not knowing the pleasures that exist beyond the four walls in

the great out of doors, the hens in confinement seem to be happy.
Go into any cage laying house and you can hear a chorus of
satisfied cackles. There they live on a fancy diet of scientifically
formulated rations that is supposed to produce the finest flavored
eggs in the world. The drinking water is clean, pure and generally
fortified with drugs that keep the hens healthy (maybe this is
what makes them sing, too).

The modern egg and broiler "factories" have made it possible
for Americans to enjoy scrambled eggs and country fried chicken
at costs that are unbelievably low in this day and age of inflated
prices. The prices are so low, in fact, that the average farmer can
better afford to buy eggs and chicken at his favorite supermarket,
than he can to raise and feed them himself.

While this is great for the food budget, it takes away a few of
joys that were a part of raising the farm flock. Now there is
nothing to compare with the thrill of seeing a baby chick peck his
way through the shell of an egg; the peeping of chicks beneath the
hover of a brooder; the excitement of finding a cluck hen on a
bunch of "settin" eggs in a manger of the calf-pen side of the barn;
the sense of conquest as you'd sneak out at night in the fall to
catch the chickens that chose to roost in the trees, rather than go
into the chicken coop; the crow of the roosters at sunrise, and the
way they proudly strutted, scratched the ground for food, and
called their harems together to delight in the morsels they had
uncovered.

The old saying is that you never miss the things you never had,
and I suppose the farm youngsters today will never miss the fact
that their parents never had a flock of chickens. As for myself,
I'm glad that I've cuddled baby chicks, picked eggs, been chased
by a cocky rooster, watched a mother hen settle over her brood as
it started to rain, and used a wire chicken hook to unseat a young
cock from his perch on a willow branch on a dark and frosty
autumn evening.

Faith Of Our Fathers Living Still

I've seen the printed program for the three big events that have been planned for the commeration of the 100th anniversary of the founding of Palisade Lutheran Church this coming Sunday.

There'll be a lot of dignitaries taking part, former pastors, and former members of the church. Among them will be Herman Larson.

Herman and I were boys on the farm at the same time, so I am looking forward to seeing him again. It's been a long, long time since we fished bullheads in the creek on our farm and swam naked as jaybirds in its refreshing waters during the summer months.

It's been a long time, too, since we attended Sunday worship with our families in the old church.

And a long time since we "read for the minister".

Most persons of my generation who are of Norwegian descent understand the meaning of the phrase "read for the minister". To those less fortunate ones — the ones not of Norwegian descent, that is — I should explain it. Reading for the minister is the English translation of the Norwegian "lese for presten", the terminology used then for what we today call confirmation instruction. It was a regular Saturday session with the pastor of the church who would instruct us in the basic Biblical teachings for a couple of years.

Prior to Herman's and my time, the instruction was in the Norwegian language. At least, I think Herman did his "reading" in English, because I did.

The "reading" part was serious business. We didn't do much goofing around in the pastor's presence. We were taught at home to not only respect him, but to obey him too, and he made sure we did.

But before he arrived at the church — particularly if he was delayed and all his pupils were there before him, there was plenty of activity.

And Herman, who had an outstanding singing voice then as he has now, did his share to make the goings-on interesting. He received excellent cooperation from Robert Ormseth, and if I remember correctly, George and Iver Eitreim, and Sam Bly.

The pulpit of the church was considered sacred — no one was permitted there but the pastor, but Robert and Herman dared throw caution to the wind. Robert would climb up the stairs (the pulpit was raised about three steps above the floor in the front of the church) and would sing the words of the liturgical chant in Norwegian. Herman and the other boys would respond from the pews below. Occasionally, one or the other would do some preaching, emphasizing words or phrases with exaggerated arm and hand movements.

Then, as soon as they heard the sound of the pastor's Essex drive up in front, they sat down in the pews, doing their best to suppress laughter that had built up during their "fun time".

As I look back at it now, I believe that all of us learned the meaning of respect in those "reading" sessions. While we may have been rascals then, we took with us from those sessions a feeling of reverence for God and His church that has remained with us. I know it has with me.

I have some fond memories of the Palisade Church.

I suppose I have a special feeling for it because my grandfather was one of the founders, and my own father was among those who worked to get the present church built. I was a member there until after I was married. My mother and sister are still members.

There were two churches, a mile apart, at one time. Differences of opinion on some doctrinal matters among some of the members split the congregation. The minority group built the second church and started a new cemetery. A number of years later, when tempers had cooled a bit, both congregations decided to restore their once good relationship and were reunited. Then we had two churches, one called the East (which was the original church and the one we attended) and the other the West Palisade Church. For many years, both churches were used, with services in each on alternate Sundays. There were those, however, who still felt their cause had been just and would not attend church when the services were not held in their "own" building.

The first pastor I can recall is the Reverend T.A. Rodsater, a kindly gentleman who served not only our country church, but the church at Hills.

I remember him in the pulpit. He was an excellent preacher, never having to refer to his notes. Instead he seemed to look up toward the ceiling and to one side as he proclaimed the message of the day. As a boy, I thought he held his head that way because he was in direct communication with the Almighty. Maybe he was.

Pastor Rodsater visited our home on many occasions. Grandma always was happy when he came and Mother always had coffee, fresh bread, or cookies to serve for lunch. I'll never forget his expertise at drinking coffee from a saucer, which at that time was socially permissable and commonplace. He could pour the coffee from his cup with his right hand into the saucer he held in his left and raise it delicately to his lips. How Grandma would beam when he said in Norwegian, "Det var rektig god kaffe."

The Reverend T.A. Mason succeeded Pastor Rodsater. He, too,

was a kind and gentle man. He wasn't the preacher that Pastor Rodsater was, but he was loved by members of his flock, and he loved them. He had served several parishes during his lifetime, but before he died, he told his family he wanted to be buried in the Palisade Cemetery. His wish was granted.

There were certain customs observed at the church which today might be considered "square" or even ridiculous.

When I was about four or five, all the men would sit in the pews on the right side of the church, and women on the left. Husbands and wives separated when they came into the church.

Boys in those days wore knickers as their "Sunday best" pants. One of the incentives for "reading for the minister" was that for confirmation day, your folks would buy you your first long pants suit and Elgin or Hamilton pocket watch.

I can still see the words on the arch above the nave of the old church, "Salige er de som hore Guds ord or bevare det." In English, this means "Blessed are they who hear God's word and keep it."

After confirmation, it was usually a boy's prerogative to sit in the balcony rather than with his parents. This was a sign that he had grown up and all the young fellows would head there when the church bell rang. I can well imagine there were many times that the preacher would have liked to have stopped in the middle of his sermon to give them a stern reprimand, because their behavior wasn't always exemplary.

I remember Andrew Larson was the church janitor.He would always bring a pail of drinking water and a dipper which he set on a chair inside the entry way.

He'd also ring the bell — the first bell about an hour before church started; the second bell when the service was about to begin, and then the three muted gongs proclaiming the end of the service. He also made sure that the single register furnace was kicking out enough heat in the winter and that the windows were open in the summer.

I remember Ed Eitreim. Ed always sat in the same seat, by a certain window, in the old church. Ed had a strong tenor voice that was especially appealing when he harmonized during the three-fold Amen.

And there was Andrew Brekke. Andrew was the last of the area farmers to come to church with team and buggy. There was a barn near the church then and Andrew would unhitch the team, put them in the barn during the service and hitch them up again when the service was over.

Attitudes within the church have changed during the years and for the most part, this is good. When I was a boy, folks who weren't Norwegian were not very welcome in our church. When a

boy or girl married what we termed in those days a "different na-
tionality" it often took years before the non-Norwegians were accepted as equals.

Neighbors might get together on Saturday night for house
dances. Or they might work together in the hayfields or harvest
fields during the week; they might get together on a Sunday
afternoon for a visit, but if one was Norwegian and the other German, Dutch, Irish or "American" they wouldn't be caught wor-
shipping together in church on Sunday.

This has changed now, because there are no Norwegians or
Swedes or Germans any more. All are Americans, who have found
that the differences their parents or grandparents thought existed were mostly imagined.

The other evening, I made a trip to the church to take a picture
of some of the members who are direct descendents of some of the
early pioneers who formed the congregation. Two little boys,
Tommy and Timmy Eitreim, are the fifth generation of two of the
early day families. As I snapped the picture, the words of an old
familiar hymn came to me: "Faith of our Fathers living still . . ."

There are other churches in the county that are 100 years old
and older, I know, where the faith of the founding fathers is living still. This, I think, says that the stability of the people of the
community is the result of that kind of faith.

To me, it is visible proof of the truth of the inscription in the old
Palisade church, "Blessed are they who hear the word of God and
keep it."

The East Palisade Church

Grandpa Bjerk was one of the founders of the congregation. Dad, Mother, my sister, brother and I
were confirmed there.

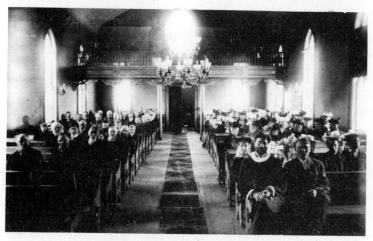

A typical Lutheran Church interior

When I was about four or five, all the men would
sit in the pews on the one side of the church, and
the women on the other. After confirmation it was
usually a boy's prerogative to sit in the balcony
rather than with his parents.

Palisade Lutheran Church, 1939

Dad was on the committee that was responsible
for building the new church. It had the distinction
of being the first rural building in the county to be
electrified by the REA.

Confirmation Day
June 2, 1929

One of the incen-
tives for "reading
for the minister"
was that for confir-
mation day, your
folks would buy
you your first long
pants suit. I was
pretty proud to
have this picture
taken.

We Called It The Young Peoples Society, But Old Folks Wouldn't Miss It On A Bet

Church youth groups seem to have a lot of fun these days. And they have a chance to learn a lot that wasn't taught when I was a boy on the farm.

We never went on roller skating parties. Or swimming at the "Y". Nor did we ever visit a Jewish synagogue or a funeral home. Our youth gatherings were simple family get togethers with a program, lunch and games.

Our gatherings were never called fellowships or leagues. We called our group the Young Peoples Society but there were more "old folks" there, or at least as many, as there were kids.

Our Young Peoples Society met at the Parish School House. Our minister would announce the meetings from the pulpit on a Sunday morning once a month.

"Young Peoples Society meets tonight at the Parish School House. Mrs. Andrew Larson and Mrs. Ole Ormseth will serve the lunch and a good program is planned," he would say.

The Parish School House had been built by our church congregation for use as a "Norwegian School." They called it Norwegian school to differentiate from the public school which the Norwegians called the "English school."

Actually it was built as a school for religious instruction in the summer for the children of the congregation. It had regular school type desks, and a raised platform in front doubled as a stage. It had a basement too, with kitchen facilities, so it served as the meeting place for both the Young Peoples Society and the Ladies Aid. Our country church had no kitchen facilities.

So, one Sunday night a month the families of the congregation would head for the school house for the regular monthly Young Peoples Society meeting. The president of the society served as the master of ceremonies for the program. The pastor was not always there because it meant he would have to drive either from Garretson or Hills where the pastors lived at that time.

For each meeting, a program committee had to arrange entertainment. The president was given the list of "numbers" on the program and he'd announce each one. The president I remember most vividly was Ed Eitreim. Country folks generally were bashful or hesitant to stand before a group of people, but not Eddie. He knew everybody and could inject a bit of fun as the program went along.

Every meeting opened with the singing of a hymn. Then, he would announce, "The first number on the program tonight is . . ."

and he'd give the name of the person who was to sing the solo, speak the piece or play the instrument.

And that's what most of the programs were, generally — vocal solos, instrumental solos, "pieces", and maybe a speech. I wonder now if the expression "speaking a piece" was a colloquialism of our community or if it was used elsewhere as well. It was, in fact, a recitation — a memorized poem, or a humorous or dramatic reading that had been memorized. Or, as we always said, "learned by heart".

Any kid in the congregation who had ability — or whose parents thought his or her child had ability — could usually expect to be asked to be on the program several times a year.

Occasionally, there would be special attractions, such as plays or speakers or musical groups.

The plays were usually skits with a group of youngsters, or on occasion, young people of high school or college age, as the actors. They'd dress up to represent older persons, country bumpkins or city dudes. Bed sheets were suspended from a single wire across the front of the school house and served as stage curtains. Copper hog rings, standard equipment on every farm, were used to fasten the sheets to the wire to make for easy opening and closing of the curtains.

Speakers were sometimes pastors and sometimes dignitaries from town, such as attorneys and school "professors". Every school superintendent in the state was called a professor in those days.

Some of the popular entertainers I recall were Emil Ekberg, the Booge comedian, John Sanders, the Garretson editor and band leader who played a mean cornet, and the Luverne male quartet made up of Einar Lorange, Henry Holmied, Ole T. Olson, and Thorvald Mosby. They'd really make a hit with the "old folks" when they sang such Norwegian selections as "Kan Du Glemme Gamle Norge" and "Ja, Vie Elske Dette Landet". Another good quartet number they sang was "Little Brown Church in the Vale."

They all spoke with a Norwegian accent and sang with one too. When they came to the part about "Come, come, come to the church in the wildwood," they'd pronounce it "komm, komm, komm," the vowel sound being somewhere between a long and short "o", and I'm not too sure they didn't pronounce it "shurch" rather than church. Anyway, they were popular and the school house was jam-packed to the back door when they were invited to sing.

There was one repeat act on every program. That was the reading of the minutes of the previous meeting by the secretary. Usually, the secretary's duties were handled by one of the young women in the congregation. She'd recite the whole story of the previous month's meeting — that it opened with the singing of Hymn No. 1, and that so and so sang a solo and so and so gave a reading. She'd conclude with the words, "lunch was served by . . ." and give the names of the hostesses, and then report the amount of proceeds derived from the sale of the lunch.

Getting everything ready so a Young Peoples Society meeting could be held was no small task, either. During the spring and fall, someone had to make sure that the furnace was started so there would be a little heat. The gasoline lanterns had to be filled and air had to be pumped into the tanks before they were lighted and returned to the wire hooks that dangled from the ceiling.

The hissing of the lanterns as they burned during the programs sometimes made it impossible to hear the younger, more bashful kids as they spoke their pieces.

The hostesses seldom heard or saw the program. They were busy in the basement, preparing sandwiches and cutting cake. The fare seldom changed — cold meat on a bun and two kinds of cake, chocolate (you couldn't call it devil's food at a church function) with white frosting, or white (you could call it Lady Baltimore if you were prone to put on airs) with chocolate frosting.

Electric coffee makers had not even been invented then. The hostess usually brought her own corn cobs or fire wood as fuel for the cook stove and the coffee was boiled in a couple of huge graniteware coffee pots. Beaten eggs added to the ground coffee made the "grounds" settle so the coffee would be clear.

There was no orange drink or Kool-Aid for those who didn't drink coffee. It was either a cup of coffee or a glass of water.

Everyone, it seemed, drank cream in his coffee those days. And it was real country cream, no half and half, or non-dairy creamer such as we get nowadays. A bowl of loaf sugar graced every table for those who liked their coffee sweetened.

Everybody paid 15 cents for the lunch — that is everybody except those who took part in the program. "No, you go free tonight," the treasurer would say to those who had performed.

After the lunch, the parents would sit around for a while and visit. The kids sometimes went out and played games or just stood around talking, the boys punching each other or teasing the girls.

Once in a while, I'd attend Young Peoples Society with a good friend, Howard Anderson. Howard belonged to what was familiarly known around Luverne as "Lund's Church". During the summer months their society would meet at the farm homes of members of the congregation. The program format was the same as ours, with the president as master of ceremonies, and sandwiches and cake for lunch.

The program, however, usually was presented from the big

front porch which most of the farm homes had. The piano was pushed out of the living room onto the porch when there was a solo or an instrumental selection that needed piano accompaniment.

There was another difference, too. Rev. Lund was generally there, and was the speaker of the evening. Of all the clergymen I've ever known, none was more certain of who was destined to spend eternity in heaven, and who would spend it in the nether regions than Pastor Lund, and he never hesitated to inform his listeners of his convictions.

When he carried on too long, it cut down on the after-lunch game time for the kids, which made them a little unhappy. Nevertheless, he always seemed to command their respect.

Were Young Peoples Societies to hold meetings today as they were held then, it is doubtful if even the president would show up. The kids and their folks certainly wouldn't. And who would you ever get to appear on the program?

Then, it took the place of TV. The kids and their parents were together with other kids and their parents at a church function where laughing and a good time were not considered sacrilegious.

Maybe its better for young people to go swimming and to roller skating parties, to observe a Jewish worship service and to be involved in a discussion of death and funerals.

But there's something to be said, too, for the family and neighborhood ties that were made stronger by the Young Peoples Societies.

Autumn Hike Made A Pork Chop Supper A Feast To Remember

It's funny what triggers one's thinking mechanism, isn't it?

Sights, sounds, odors, tastes, feels . . . all the senses have a way of putting a person's brain into motion if one just takes the time to permit them to serve as stimuli.

It happened the other evening. I was walking home from the high school. It was quiet — not a breeze stirring the leaves of my neighbor's poplars. Overhead, I quickly located the Big Dipper and the North Star. There was a faint odor in the air — somewhere, a skunk on his nightly patrol, had been disturbed.

"Fall's here," I mused to myself as I could hear leaves from the birch tree crackle underfoot as I crossed my front yard.

I don't relish fall now like I did when I was a "boy on the farm" but there is still something about it that brings out the boy adventurer in me.

It brings back to me, too, the memories of the long hikes that we farm boys were always taking every autumn. I'm sure a lot of town boys did the same thing, and shared the same experiences and the same love and respect for the out-of-doors that I had then, and still have.

We had a creek running through the pasture on the farm and it seemed the natural direction to take when starting a hike. It had a lot of attractions. It wasn't unusual to scare up a few wild ducks at this season of the year. At least, there would be mudhens. Quite often we'd see the long-legged, long-necked blue herons standing in the water, fishing for minnows or crayfish. Then there were times when a smaller bird that we called a crane, but others called a "shypoke", would rise from the water on its slow moving but powerful big wings and head for another part of the stream.

In late afternoon, it wasn't uncommon at all to see a muskrat head across the pond, forming a "V" in the water as it headed for the bank where there was an underwater entrance to its den. When the bank was reached, the muskrat ducked its head, its rump surfaced, and into the hole it went.

If there had been fall rains, the springs along the creek were sure to be running. I'd get down on my knees just to take a drink of the water as it bubbled out of the ground and then continue my walk. If the fall had been dry, there would be places upstream where the creek was no longer running. There in the mud, it was possible to determine if there were a mink in the area, because his tracks were generally imprinted in the mud.

Crossing the pasture fence into the hay meadow brought other discoveries. The weeds grew tall near the stream there and it wasn't a bit unusual to flush out a couple of cottontails, a pheasant or two, and maybe a hawk which had just swooped down to catch a plump, furry field mouse.

The creek made an S-curve there, then came the big willow which was right to the edge of the stream. The water was a little deeper at this point, but the bottom was solid mud. Usually there were minnows that had been trapped there, when the water level was down above and below it. And the crayfish stuck their heads out of the holes they had made in the bank above the water line. Once they saw you, they shifted into super-reverse and disappeared, back into the hole.

At the quarter section fence line were more willow trees and a big weed patch. There, it was usually possible to find a den of skunks, easily detected by the odor at the den's entrance and the grass and corn husks which had been carried home by Mama Skunk to make her winter home warmer and more comfortable.

Farther along the fence line was a row of box elders about of a quarter of a mile long. The pheasants liked that area. It offered protection, shade and the grass grew tall because it was difficult to mow closely to the trees. Once in a while, a hawk would settle in their branches. So would crows. But neither bird would let a person come close before soaring off into the wild blue yonder.

Back in the pasture was a rock pile and to get there from the box elder trees meant going past the watermelon patch. Usually, only the melons that would never get red ripe remained this late in the season. When summer would hang on until October, there might be a good one or two left. I always checked the melons for ripeness by first tapping my shoe, then tapping the melon. If the sound produced by the taps was the same, then the melon was ripe, and out came my trusty jackknife to "plug" it to make sure.

The rock pile was the accumulation of small rocks uncovered each year during the plowing season. I always checked the rock pile. If there was a faint odor of skunk, I knew that either a skunk or a civet cat had taken up winter quarters there.

Up the hill from the rock pile was a favorite spot for the badgers. Those expert diggers didn't need an excuse to make a hole in the ground with a huge pile of earth in front of it. If it meant getting a striped gopher for a meal, it was worth the effort, it appeared.

Farther down the pasture, near the old sandpit, there were older badger holes. Big brown owls lived in them in the summertime. In the fall, they headed for other climes.

By this time, my circuitous hike was almost ended. I would crawl under the fence beside the box elder where we always left our clothes when we boys went skinny dipping in the creek in the summer time, then I'd walk toward the barn, past the garden and the potato patch.

A yank at one of the big carrots would either produce a husky, orange delicacy for a hungry boy, or a handful of carrot tops. But even a carrot didn't spoil my appetite. As I walked into the house and could smell the big panful of American fries and another frypan filled with pork chops from the big stone crock in the cellar, I swear I was the hungriest kid in Beaver Creek township.

The table was set; the Alladin lamp in the center, and the whole family sat down to eat at the same time.

After a fellow's taken a hike around the farmstead during the late afternoon of autumn, could anything be more delightful?

You Could Learn A Lot
From The Hired Man

When the Minnesota unemployment figures came out the other day, I got to wondering how they ever managed to handle the hired man situation so simply when I was a boy on the farm.

No matter how tough things were, farm workers seemed to have jobs. If they didn't they were bums or tramps who wanted to keep on the move. There always seemed to be a place for a man who was willing to work.

The fact that a man was willing to work, however, didn't mean he was going to get paid. But to a lot of farm hands, this wasn't so all important. If a man had a bed to sleep in — even if it was a refrigerated room with the "bathroom" outside a block or more away — at the end of a snow shoveled path, and a guarantee of three meals a day plus afternoon lunch, he had it made.

The family social structure was a lot different then.

A man who may have been a total stranger the day he was hired, immediately became a member of the family.

He ate at the same table — slept in the same house. A lot of times, because of the lack of room, he shared the bed of one of the boys in the family. He didn't need a great deal of closet space. Usually, all the clothing he owned he carried in one suitcase or was wearing the day he arrived.

Generally, the hired man worked for room and board from the time corn picking was over in November until March 1. Mostly, he did chores — milking, barn cleaning, livestock feeding. Now and then, he'd have to help haul in hay from the stack in the meadow, after the supply in the hay loft was depleted. If there were trees to be cut and firewood sawed, he'd help with that. Otherwise, he took it easy, just sitting around, reading the newspaper or Successful Farming, or listening to the Rosebud Kids, Amos 'n Andy or Oxydol's Own Ma Perkins on the radio.

Once in a while, he might ride along into town or drive his own car if he had one. With some of his summer earnings, he'd stock up on the "makins" — several tins of Velvet or Prince Albert, a sack or two of Bull Durham, three or four packs of Riz La cigarette papers, and a pack of Camels or Luckies for Sunday use.

On Saturday night, if there was a house dance in the neighborhood, he'd accompany the family and before the night was over, he'd be schottisching or waltzing with the neighbor girls as though he'd known them all his life.

Hired men were always single men, it seemed. Many of them were neighborhood farm boys — in their teens or early 20's, who had brothers at home to keep the family farm operating.

Like industry with its apprentices, journeymen and master craftsmen, farming also had three rungs on the success ladder. A man was first a hired hand. After he'd earned and saved enough to buy a team of horses, a few cows and pigs, and some machinery, he'd start looking around for a farm to rent. Once this was accomplished, he'd "batch" it or he'd get his sister to move in with him and do the cooking and cleaning. All this time, he was looking for the "right girl", and eventually he'd get married. Together, he and his wife would work hard, have a family, and earn a reputation for frugality that was good enough to get a loan to buy a farm. Then, he'd be on the lookout for a hired man.

Now and then, however, there'd be floaters who'd show up in town, looking for work. And inevitably, someone would hire them.

You can imagine those first meals when the family was joined by a total stranger. The kids would watch his eating habits and so did Mother. If he didn't take a big helping of one thing or another, he was considered a finicky eater. If he took small helpings of everything, he was just being too polite, and she'd say, "Now you must help yourself. You must make out your supper."

Others were famished every time they sat down to the table. They'd pile their plates with food, and when it was passed a second time, they'd heap it high again. Some would reach across the table to spear a second pork chop or slice of bread.

Some saucered their coffee, then slurped it noisily. Others, when the potatoes and meat had been eaten from their plates, would finish the meal with a slice of bread they'd used to wipe up the last drop of gravy, leaving the plate "clean as a whistle".

Some of the men were the silent type. Some were talkers. The talkers were the story tellers, and were not above embellishing tales of their exploits with bragging and untruths to make them more exciting.

One of those was a fellow I remember only as Henry. Mother always called him "Crazy Henry" because he was always spinning yarns that were obviously untrue, and boasting of all the great things he had done. He had only a couple of teeth. He'd laugh uproariously at his own jokes and stories, and when he did, his face was as funny as a clown's. He was one of the hired men who'd leave the country in the fall and show up again in the spring. He'd bum his way into Beaver Creek and hitch a ride with a neighbor out to our place where he'd spend a couple of days or a week before moving on.

Another fellow who'd come and spend a few days to earn a few dollars doing day labor was Ingebret Klungness. He had come to this country years before from Norway. He never married and he never had a home of his own. He spoke a language that was a mixture of Norwegian and English. He made the rounds of the Garretson-West Beaver community, staying first at one place, then at the next. He never had an invitation. He just showed up. There was nothing to do but ask him to come in and stay. He always did. Mother always seemed glad when he left.

Hired men who had the habit of using foul language never lasted long at our place. Mother could tolerate a few things, but "swearing", as she called it, wasn't one of them. Anyone who used bad words in the house was told about it in no uncertain terms. He was warned to watch his language. If he persisted in his ways, Dad was told about it in no uncertain terms. He, in turn, told the hired man that he had been told, and that in the best interests of all concerned, he'd better pack up his suitcase because he was going back to town.

The perfect hired man, however, was the one with good habits, the one who'd take a weekly bath, who'd shave regularly, who didn't drink, smoke or chew. He was a pleasant sort of fellow to have around. He'd sing when he was milking, keeping time with squirts into the milk bucket.

He'd whistle when he was feeding the horses and the cows. He kept the horses looking clean and neat and he could see things to do on a rainy day.

The mark of a good hired man was his ability to get up in the morning without having to be called.

I remember Mother would call until she was hoarse, trying to get some of the sleepy heads out of bed. Usually, their jobs were terminated when the rush season was oven. They'd never be asked to come back.

The man who could get out of bed at 5:30 without being called or without the use of an alarm clock, was one who'd have his share of the chores done and breakfast eaten by seven in the morning so he could get out to the field.

He'd be home for dinner at 12 and back out in the field at 1.

He'd work the horses steadily, but would rest them when he saw they were getting hot or tired. He'd stay in the field until 6, then he'd unhitch and come home, put the horses in the barn and feed them. He'd milk his share of the cows after supper. Then he'd lie down on the grass under the cottonwood tree and maybe enjoy a cigarette or a few puffs on his pipe before "hitting the hay".

On Saturday, he might knock off a little early so he could go to town that night. On Sunday, he'd be around for chores both morning and night, unless he'd worked out an arrangement to be gone Sunday evening.

Although they were never really aware of it, the hired men were teachers in their own little way. They were the ones from whom the farm boys learned that storks did not bring babies and that the neighbor girl with the protruding front had done more than eat too much watermelon.

They also helped expand the boys' vocabulary with words that could not be used in the home, in front of the teacher, or in mixed company, but were perfectly acceptable in an all-male crowd.

They were the ones who knew and sang the latest songs — songs they learned at the country dances. These — and bawdy barracks ballads that had come down the line of hired men from the days of World War I — were quickly picked up by the farm lads as they worked side by side with the hired hands, both in the barn and in the fields.

They were the ones who could teach advanced whittling with a jack knife, and how to play a harmonica, a fiddle or an accordion.

They'd work for $50 a month from March 1 through threshing. Then, with things easing off, they'd move north with the harvest, making $3 to $4 a day shocking or threshing with board and room furnished but no chores to do.

They'd be back around the first of October for corn picking. During corn picking, they were paid not by the day or month but by the number of bushels they picked. Again, they got board and room and didn't have to do chores.

When the season ended and the hired man left, it was sometimes as though we'd lost a member of the family. It was always more quiet around the house. And there was more work for the kids when the hired man wasn't around to help.

When he left, his employer would give him a check for what he had coming. He'd earned no fringe benefits, no bonus. There were no deductions for income tax, health insurance or social security.

There were those who'd go to town and blow a few bucks of it for moonshine and a good time, but not the fellow who wanted to better himself.

He'd head for the bank, where he'd add to his savings account, or he'd take the cash and put it in a tin box or a sock in a locked trunk if he was one of those who didn't trust banks.

Then he'd go home to spend the winter with his parents or to the home of a brother or sister to stay until spring. If he had no family, there was usually someone who'd take him in to work for room and board.

It used to be at this time of the year that the farmers would start checking to see who might be looking for work come March 1. Gimm and Byrne's and the pool halls were the principal employment agencies in the county and that's where the men looking for jobs would hang out during the daytime.

The era of the single hired hand has passed and with it a way of life. Thanks to the generosity and hospitality farm families offered, no one was ever unemployed. The man maybe didn't have a paying job, but he had a roof over his head, food to eat, something to keep him busy, and he didn't have to pay out a nickel for taxes.

Maybe that's why you still hear someone occasionally refer to that period as the "good old days".

Rx For Coughs And Colds: Camphorated Oil And A Wool Sock

I awoke the other night from a sound sleep — choking and coughing.

Post nasal drip, I mumbled to myself, after I was conscious enough to sit up in bed.

And not a thing in the house to remedy my condition.

I'm usually prepared for winter colds — cough drops, Triaminicin, Vicks Vapo Rub. But I just hadn't gotten around to replenishing the medicine cabinet.

So all I could do was cough, roll over, doze off for a few minutes and cough again.

I wonder now how I ever got through my childhood without the modern day cold medicines that relieve so much misery.

I'm sure there were times I was sicker than some of the guys shown on TV who stay alive only because they take capsules filled with tiny time pills, gulp red or green colored liquids and sniff stuff from a little sprayer that's perhaps more fun to operate than it is effective.

You can bet my mother never dropped an Alka-Seltzer in water and said, "Here, take this." She took a glass of water, added a tablespoon of vinegar, and a teaspoon of baking soda. When it started to fizz, she merely said, "This will do you good."

If we ever had aspirin in the house, believe me, it wasn't available to us kids. I don't think St. Joseph had invented the children's kind yet, and if he had, I doubt if Mother would have taken a chance on our becoming addicts.

We never heard of post nasal drip. We just knew it for what it was, a runny nose in reverse.

If we'd have asked for an antihistamine, chances are Mother would have told us to watch our language and to quit playing with kids who used words like that.

There were no Contac tablets, Coricidin, Congespirin, or Dristan. No Novahistine Elixir or Traminic Expectorant. No Simec, 4-Way or Afrin nasal sprays. No Vicks inhalers.

But there was Mentholatum. We'd get free samples handed out at school. Tiny round, flat containers, the size of a quarter. When the samples were gone, the folks would buy some when they went to town. For a stuffy nose, directions called for placing a bit of the ointment "about the size of a pea" into each nostril at bedtime. If we didn't have Mentholatum, we had the equivalent, Rawleigh's Camphorated Ointment. It worked the same way.

If a cold gained too much headway, then more drastic measures were initiated. Particularly, if it settled in the chest and a cough developed.

The Mentholatum jar was brought out, or the Vick's Vapo Rub. There was also a white camphorated liniment that J.R. Watkins put out, an all-purpose medicine that worked equally well for suppressing colds or rheumatism.

Before the bedtime medication started, Mother would find a piece of wool blanket about 10 or 12 inches square. Or a piece of material cut from a worn out wool or half wool union suit.

While the wool cloth was being heated over the hard coal heater, she'd polish my chest with the Vicks or the liniment.

If the chest congestion was real bad — and that meant being one step away from double pneumonia — there was nothing to do but go all the way and make a mustard plaster. I don't remember that it was more effective than Vicks, but if the blisters it produced on the skin were any indication, the heat most surely reached the source of the trouble.

The same treatment was used for a sore throat. Rub the throat with Vicks or Mentolatum or liniment, and pin a wool sock around it. As I remember it now, there was something cozy about having a wool sock around my neck.

Once in a while, we tried to relieve hoarseness with a gargle. No Listerine or Lavoris then. Table salt dissolved in warm water was the usual remedy and it worked.

Some folks used Piso's cough and cold remedy for relieving hoarseness, soothing throat irritation and easing throat tickle.

Others swore by Hill's Cascara Quinine Bromide which was supposed to "break up a cold in 24 hours and relieve la grippe in three days."

We never went much for those "patent" medicines.

Most frequently used cough remedy in our home was a mixture of honey and pine tar. It lacked the suppressants, decongestants and all the other things the ads say today's remedies have. But it tasted good so Mother had no trouble getting us kids to take it.

Doc Hanson in Valley Springs prescribed a concoction that Druggist O.P. Running made up which was more effective. But it tasted horrible and Mother had to choke it down our throats.

"One teaspoon as needed" and "Shake well before using" were the directions on the front of the bottle. Before the stuff was shaken, however, it looked like creek water with the silt settled at the bottom of the bottle.

One of our favorite cold remedies was hot lemonade. But we seldom ever had lemons in the house when one of us came down with a cold, so we didn't use it often.

More frequently, however, we used Grandma's favorite cold

remedy. Steaming hot milk, on which was floated a pat of butter and a half teaspoon of black pepper.

What the mustard plaster did for the outside of the chest, the hot milk did for the inside.

With all remedies used regularly and properly, we usually were rid of the cold in seven days.

If we did nothing at all and suffered through it without mustard plaster, Pine Tar Cough Medicine and a sock around the neck, it would take all of a week before the only evidence that remained was a sniffly nose.

There was one time, however, when colds represented more than a routine nuisance of winter.

I can't remember it actually, but I do recall Mother and Dad talking years later about the flu epidemic that spread across the country right after the Armistice in 1918.

During a three month period, there were over 412 cases in Luverne alone. Thirteen persons died from the dread disease which began as a type of cold, then quickly developed into a type of flu that settled in the lungs causing pneumonia.

The Red Cross set up an emergency hospital in a big house which then stood at the corner of East Park and Brown Streets. Beds were provided for 18 emergency patients and a Red Cross nurse from Minneapolis was assigned here to manage it.

I'm not sure whether Luverne had more than the two doctors, Dr. Sherman and Dr. Wright, then or not.

I know they didn't have the medicines they do now, because the drugs that are now so effective in flu and pneumonia cases weren't discovered until 35 or 40 years later.

I think of this as I watch the cold and flu remedy commercials on TV and think how lucky our family was that dreadful fall.

As sickening as some of the commercials are, I know that the products advertised may not cure a cold any faster than the remedies of my boyhood, but they do relieve many of the discomforts that accompany a cold.

Since my coughing siege the other night, I have stocked the medicine cabinet with the cold standbys — a jar of Vapo Rub, a box of cough drops and a Vicks inhaler.

Somewhere, I'm going to have to find a wool sock and I'll be all set in case it happens again.

Lydia Pinkham's Vegetable Compound
And Other Staple Remedies

When I read in the paper the other day that the Lydia E.
Pinkham Medicine Co. factory was closing in Lynn, Mass., I
started thinking about some of the great "medical discoveries" of
yesteryear, of which Lydia Pinkham's Vegetable Compound is
one.

Lest any of you are concerned that the compound is no longer
being made, let me assure you that it is. It will just be made in a
different factory, that's all.

Of course, since Lydia Pinkham's Compound was a preparation
for curing "women's troubles" I never used any of it.

But I remember the ads that appeared regularly in The Rock
County Herald when I was a boy on the farm. I always got a kick
out of reading them because generally they contained a personal
letter from a satisfied customer. Sometimes I wonder if these letters didn't eventually lead newspaper editors to publish letters to
the editor because of the readership they commanded.

Just to make sure that my memory was correct, I went to the
Herald files to see if I could find one of the ads. Sure enough, I
found one in the first paper I thumbed through. The headline of
the ad boomed out in bold type:

WOMEN EVERYWHERE
Praise Lydia E. Pinkham's
Vegetable Compound

Then came the testimonial letter, from a lady in Independence,
Ore.:

"I was sick with what four doctors called Nervous Prostration,
was treated by them for several years, would be better for a while
then be back in the old way again.

"I had palpitation of the heart very bad, fainting spells and was
so nervous that a spoon dropping to the floor would nearly kill
me, could not lift the slightest without making me sick; in fact, I
was about as sick and miserable as a person could be. I saw your
medicine advertised and thought I would try it. I am so thankful I
did because it helped me at once. I took about a dozen bottles of
Lydia E. Pinkham's Vegetable Compound. Since then I have used
it whenever I felt sick. Your remedy is the only doctor I employ.
You are at liberty to publish this letter."

Needless to say, the ads were effective. The compound could be
found on the top cupboard shelf in most every household then.
And it's still in use. Look for it the next time you shop at your
favorite drug store and I'll bet you'll see it on the shelf.

I don't recall that there was ever a large amount of Lydia's elixir used at our house, but I do remember some of the other really important medications.

One I remember in particular, because Dad always used to come home with a bottle of it about this time of year. It was J.E. Treat's Honey and Pine Tar Compound for coughs and colds. It not only seemed to work, but it tasted good and that was something one couldn't say about most medicines.

I always thought old Jay personally compounded his cough medicine, as we called it, in his pharmacy. It was years and years later that I learned that a pharmaceutical manufacturer supplied it to him in gallon jugs, together with some free labels with J.E. Treat's name on them and he merely did the bottling and stuck the labels on himself.

Another good tasting medicine we always kept on hand was Syrup of Figs. This was a laxative and one that was kept out of reach of the children for obvious reasons.

For persons who required a medication for a condition just opposite of what Syrup of Figs was used for, there was a compound called Blackberry Balsam. It's still available, the drug stores' equivalent of blackberry brandy. It is made of a half dozen or more roots and herbs, a real combination for anyone who favors organic compounds over drugs.

Then there was wonderful Castoria!! At the least sign of a cold among the children, this sweet medicine was administered. A bottle always stood on a certain shelf. We really didn't mind taking it.

Now something psychological would also help . . . the old platform rocker! Many a time our childish sorrows were whisked away by its rhythm with Dad or Mother holding us in their arms.

We would occasionally have Tanlac in the house. This was a pepper-upper sort of thing, a substitute, maybe, for Geritol. Others, however, preferred the Beef, Iron and Wine Tonic. Teetotalers who would never touch liquor found this to be a blood builder and a nerve quieter.

I remember Grandma talking about Curaco and Peruna, but I don't remember her using them. Alpen Krauter, I understand, was another substance much the same as Curaco. These, too, were health tonics.

There were several kinds of linament, and we always had one or more kinds in the house. Grandma and Grandpa found Sloan's Linament helpful for their rheumatism. (Gee, I haven't heard of anyone with rheumatism for years. Don't people get it any more?) Sloan's had a very strong and distinct odor. When the weather was damp and other conditions were right for bringing on the rheumatic pains, I could always depend on our house to smell of

Sloan's linament when I came in from the fresh air of the outdoors.

A home concocted remedy that many used for relief of chest colds was a mustard plaster. The recipe called for a tablespoon of dry mustard, three tablespoons of flour, and one egg, all mixed together. This was spread between two thin pieces of cloth and applied to the chest and back. After the chest became red, it was removed and was followed with a rub of camphorated oil. Repeated every three hours, it really did the trick.

The "Watkins man" who came around with his suitcase full of medicines and extracts about once a month sold a white linament. This was good for aching muscles, such as one would develop the first few days of corn picking season and also was used for applying to a person's chest when he had a chest cold. You could even mix it with something and drink it for colds, if I remember correctly.

We seldom had a "boughten" antiseptic. Whenever we suffered a cut or a scratch, Grandma in particular made sure we applied kerosene, then bandaged the wound with a white rag tied with store string. But once in a while, when John Connell had a special on Peroxide, Mother would buy it. There was something psychological about peroxide. When applied to a wound, it would bubble up or foam. That showed it was "working" which meant that the healing process was already in progress. After I took high school chemistry and found out what the chemical composition of peroxide was, I'm not so sure that a good washing with clean water wouldn't have been equally effective.

We generally had "sweet oil" on hand. This was an effective earache remedy. I suppose any kind of a vegetable oil, such as we have nowadays, would have done the same thing. But then, if it wasn't "sweet oil", you didn't have the right medicine.

No Tears Over Spilled Whisky

Dad was never what one might call a drinking man.

Not that he didn't like an occasional glass of beer, a taste of wine, or a bit of "schnapps" as he called it.

But never did I see him intoxicated, nor do I ever recall his coming home from town with the smell of liquor on his breath.

This could have been the result of the fact that most of my boyhood days coincided with the days of prohibition — that period between 1918 and 1932 when the 18th Amendment was in effect.

Dad, however, was of the school that believed a little brandy or whisky as medicine was nice to have in the house, particularly for treating winter colds and flu, and for stomachaches.

That was the reason he happened to buy a quart of smuggled-in Canadian whisky when it was offered to him by Emil Harlfinger, a Beaver Creek character who made his living trapping, cutting wood, working as a day laborer, and occasionally, by "bootlegging".

He'd tried to sell Dad "moonshine" whisky on many occasions, but if it wasn't the real thing, Dad didn't want it. One day, however, he made a sale. He'd obtained some Canadian whisky and offered it to Dad for $15 for a quart.

Money was more plentiful than good whisky, so Dad accepted the offer. He brought the bottle home and put it in the basement.

Did I say basement?

One would have to stretch his imagination quite a bit to label the excavation beneath our house as a basement, although it did serve some of the purposes served by what is referred to as a basement today.

As I remember it, it was merely an excavation beneath the house, a place where it was cool in summer and somehow it seemed to be warm and cozy in winter. It didn't extend the full length or breadth of the house, so it was necessary that the house be placed on a foundation, which in the case of our home, happened to be large rocks plastered together with concrete.

The space across the top of the unexcavated area beneath the house to the stone foundation formed a shelf; a convenient place for storing various things and because it was dark in the cellar, that's the place Dad chose to store his costly cold medicine.

How long it had rested unopened in its niche I don't know.

But apparently Dad had neglected to keep his secret a secret, because one day, my Uncle Cornelius came to the house and asked Dad, "Jim, have you got any whisky or brandy?"

"Well, that depends," he replied, knowing my uncle possessed a thirst that required frequent quenching.

"Orval is sick, he's got a cold and Lizzie thought if we had a little whisky or brandy to give him he wouldn't cough so much."

Orval was Cornelius' and his wife, Lizzie's, pride and joy, a baby not yet two years old.

"If it is for medicine you want it," Dad said, "I've got some."

"Mary," he said, addressing Mother, "find me a little medicine bottle or a cough medicine bottle or something that Cornelius can take it home in."

Mother produced the bottle and down into the celler he went.

He broke the label on the unopened quart, unscrewed the cap, and filled the two ounce medicine bottle.

He replaced the cork on the medicine bottle, then screwed the cap in place on the whisky bottle, and returned it to its hiding place when it happened.

The bottom of the bottle hit the sharp edge of a foundation stone.

There was the sound of shattering glass and of liquid gurgling from a container.

In a minute, the dry earth had absorbed 30 ounces of one of the rarest of commodities in Rock County.

Then Dad uttered those Norwegian words I have heard him speak so many times in moments of frustration, "Nay, har du sett", except he used the Oksendal dialect and pronounced "sett" with a "sh" sound, "shett." Translated into America's vernacular, he had exclaimed, "Have you ever seen the beat?"

Uncle Cornelius felt worse than Dad did about the calamity. He wanted him to keep what was in the medicine bottle, but Dad wouldn't hear of it. The sick baby needed it worse than he did. But I think Uncle also felt a pang of sadness as he pondered on how much more enjoyment he would have received out of soaking up the contents of the broken bottle drink by drink than the earth did, swallowing it, as it were, in one gulp.

Forty years later, Dad laughed about the incident and recalled, "Funny thing, we never did need that whisky for medicine. We got along without it and didn't miss it at all."

Great Grandma Norelius

While her husband braved the storm to get help, she gave birth alone to her first daughter during the blizzard of 1881. She lived to be 100 and is shown here with her first great grandchild, Kenneth Bjerk.

Augusta Gilbert

Born in a tiny frame farm house during a blinding snowstorm, "Grandma" Gilbert lived to be 96.

Time To Be Born — A Happening During
The Blizzard of 1881

"Grandma" Gilbert observed her 93rd birthday without much fanfare March 14 at the Mary Jane Brown Home. From her wheel chair, she graciously accepted the wishes for a happy birthday extended her by friends and relatives.

"Grandma" Gilbert is my mother-in-law, a person I have loved and admired all the years I have known her. My regret at the moment is that she is no longer able to comprehend the story I'm about to write. It is one she related to me years ago.

It's the story about the day she was born.

Substract her age (93) from 1974 and you'll get 1881. That was the winter of the big snow and many blizzards. The first storm hit Oct. 15, 1880, and the last severe blizzard of the winter hit the day "Grandma" was born.

"Grandma" was a Norelius. Her parents lived on the farm north and east of Beaver Creek.

I never knew Grandpa Norelius. But people who knew him recall him as a strong and stalwart Swede. Grandma Norelius was a fine-featured, mild-mannered Norwegian with a keen intellect. Her demure stature belied her physical strength and stamina.

They homesteaded in Beaver Creek township. The first of their 10 children, a son whom they named Charles, was born there just 13 months ahead of Augusta, or "Grandma" as I choose to call her.

Beaver Creek was the nearest town, three and a half miles away, Luverne, where the only doctor lived, was six miles away.

"Great-Grandma" Norelius, as I recall, was not a worrier. A devout Christian, she had great faith that the Almighty would supply her needs.

I feel sure, though, that the storms which never seemed to cease that winter did cause her to become concerned about the new baby destined to arrive early in March.

When February arrived, she no doubt had hopes things would get better. But another blizzard came February 3. The Rock County Herald said this started "a sort of serial blizzard in five chapters with cessations long enough only to announce the heading of the next chapter". When it appeared that the weather was finally about to settle, another one struck February 11 continuing through the next day, filling in the cuts that had been made in the drifts on the roads and railroad tracks earlier.

From the first of February to the first of March, only one train had gone through Luverne and Beaver Creek. Dealers' supplies of hard coal were exhausted by the first of February. A week later, what supplies of wood they had on hand were gone.

If "Great Grandma" was worried when she turned her calendar over to March, she had a right to be.

The time for the baby to born was near at hand.

On the morning of the 11th, a heavy snow began falling. The storm continued without letup, through Saturday and into early Sunday, the 13th. Hope was renewed as the weather cleared that day and shovelers could get out once more.

On Monday, "Great Grandma" knew her time had come. The question was, where could her husband go for help?

They decided his best bet was to get "Aunt Jennie" Mickelson, who lived three miles to the west across three sections of prairie land that lay buried beneath several feet of crusted snow. The trip there was shorter than if he were to go to Luverne for a doctor and perhaps more certain, because they knew "Aunt Jennie" could be depended upon to come when she was asked.

Another storm struck at noon on that day. It ended in the evening.

I'm not sure when Grandpa Norelius left or when he came back. But when he returned, "Aunt Jennie" with him, they found "Great Grandma" in bed and with her new baby daughter and a 13-month-old boy.

The baby girl had arrived without anyone's help. After her birth, "Great Grandma" had gotten out of bed, put the baby in a blanket, fed little Charley, added fuel to the fire and had gone back to bed.

Augusta, being the first daughter born in what eventually became a family of 10, was her mother's No. 1 helper from the time she could understand her mother's directions.

Like so many children born to immigrant parents, she learned their mother tongue first. When she started country school, she could speak only Norwegian. She cried the first day she came home from school because the other children ridiculed her inability to speak English.

It was that day that her mother decided that only English would be spoken in the home from hence forth. This was America, she said, and American she and her family would be.

"Great Grandma" sensed the importance of education as well as common sense. Charley, being the oldest, had to stay home and help his father with the farm work, but he did manage to go to high school. Augusta went to high school and then had some teacher training. The third child, Walter, went to business college. The remaining seven attended the University of Minnesota and received degrees.

While Augusta was attending high school, she carried a note

with her every day signed by her mother, so that if there were an emergency at home, she'd have a signed excuse slip to show the teacher. She completed high school in three year's time.

She didn't start teaching right away. She was needed at home to help care for the growing family. One day, when she was about 19, her mother told her she was about to have another baby. Augusta fought back the tears momentarily, then ran down to the orchard and cried.

But she did get her chance to teach — in Hills and in Steen. A summer session at the University led to her getting a teacher certificate. What she hadn't learned in school, she learned at home. She was an expert in home ec. She could do most anything with a needle and thread, sewing machine, knitting needles, and crochet needles. Her bread and cakes, cookies and rolls, beef roasts and fried chicken brought her praise as one of the best cooks in the county.

If she had a fault, it was her insistance on perfection. Everything was always "thus and so" with her. I'll always remember that when she dressed up to go any place, she invariably wore white gloves, as she had been taught that gentle ladies should. Her house was always neat as a pin.

Today, at the Mary Jane Brown Home, she is still the perfect lady. Always polite, always gentle, always gracious, seldom demanding.

She doesn't remember what one tells her from one minute to the next. Her world is a world of her own, a world of strange imagery, like just having returned from a trip to Minneapolis where she had visited her mother, or wondering how she's going to get the horse hitched to the buggy so she can get to her teaching job in Steen on time.

As she sat in her comfortable room in the Mary Jane Brown Home on her birthday, she looked out the window at the lawn and the fields in the distance and could see that the winter snows had disappeared.

What a contrast from the day she was born, when her first weak cry was heard by only her mother and tiny brother!

What a joyous moment — what a great relief it must have been that night for "Great Grandma" when her husband and "Aunt Jennie", cold and snow covered, opened the door to the little farm home and announced, "We're here."

How grateful we are today that they made it.

I'm Really Going To Miss Aunt Minnie

I consider myself fortunate that I have a lot of relatives whom I enjoy. My dad was one of 23 children; my mother one of 10 so it stands to reason that I have a lot of uncles, aunts and cousins.

One of my favorite aunts was my Aunt Minnie, whose funeral I attended last week. She was the last of Dad's full brothers and sisters (Grandfather was married twice). Had she lived until October, she'd have been 89 years old and that's quite a life span.

Aunt Minnie was six years old when her mother died. She was about 15 when she left home to work in Sioux Falls as a house maid. There she met and married G.A. Rystad and they later moved to the little town of Rembrandt, Iowa where Uncle G.A. went into the general store business and Aunt Minnie raised a family of four boys and three girls.

What made Aunt Minnie special to all her nephews and nieces in this part of the country, particularly me, was that she was our only aunt who lived in town. All the rest lived on farms. That made her different in a sense.

And she was pretty. Snappy brown eyes, dark hair, soft voice, and lovely smile. Truly she was a gentle woman.

It was always the event of the summer when Aunt Minnie and our "city cousins" came to visit. "G.A." always drove Dodges. I'll never forget the new touring car he drove one time. It had disc wheels. How I enjoyed getting behind the steering wheel and manipulating the shifting lever. That was something our Model T didn't have and I though it was really class.

Dad always said that of his sisters, Aunt Minnie was the one who had a flair for style. This flair she maintained through the years. She was aware that beauty was something that had to be maintained if it was to be preserved. She always managed to look younger than she really was.

She loved the beauty of the out of doors and of growing things. Even after G.A. died and she lived alone, she had a big garden where she spent many enjoyable hours with her flowers and choice vegetables.

Aunt Minnie never missed a family event in Minnesota that I can ever recall. When there was a reunion, she was there. (First one, usually.) If there was a funeral or a wedding, you could depend on her coming and everyone looked forward to seeing her.

Aunt Minnie lived a good life, a long life, a loving life, and we're going to miss her.

The pastor who conducted her funeral based his sermon on the beauty of a Christian life. No tribute he could have made would have been more fitting.

Her final resting place is a beautifully kept country cemetery
surrounded by lush Iowa farm land. A fitting place for a gentle
lady, born and reared on a pioneer prairie homestead and who in
her own quiet way, made life more beautiful for others.

School - Activities - Recreation

Miss Brindel Was An Extraordinary
Country School Teacher

Of all my teachers, the one I remember most vividly is Ann
Brindel Scott who taught in District 44 when I was in the third,
fourth, fifth and sixth grades.

I remember well when she came, about a month or six weeks
after school started. When school opened, a Miss Johnson was the
teacher. I think she came from the Cities, I'm not sure. But she
had a boy friend someplace and she became extremely lonely.
Finally she decided it wasn't worth it, living away from him, so
she resigned.

How the school board happened to locate Miss Brindel, I don't
know. It runs in my mind that she came from Wabasha. I never
knew there was a town by that name until she showed up.

Miss Brindel was beautiful and vivacious. An excellent
disciplinarian. And a good school janitor. She had a wonderful sense
of humor, but often had to hold back in order to maintain the
kind of composure that is necessary if there is to be order in a one-
room school house.

When she first started teaching in District 44, she boarded with
the Roy Fenstermakers, who furnished her with a buggy and a
driving horse named Prince.

Prince had a lot of spirit. Particularly when he started out of
the Fenstermaker driveway and onto the dirt road that headed
north past Fagan's farm and McCurdy's to the old school house.
He'd start out as if he were running the greatest buggy race in his
life, but by the time he'd cover a mile and three quarter straight-
away, he calmed down enough so Miss Brindel could unhitch him
and tether him to a tree or a fence post without worrying about
having a runaway.

Miss Brindel made a pretty good salary, at least so the school
board and the residents of the district felt. Any single woman
who could get a check for $100 for teaching 20 days a month was
considered as doing very well financially.

The term extra-curricular activity hadn't even been coined
then, although Miss Brindel had her share of such activities and
didn't realize it. One of those activities was custodial service.
(Custodial service is another commonly heard expression around
our education institutions these days which hadn't been coined
then.)

It may have occurred to Miss Brindel that she had signed a
teaching contract, not one for janitorial duties, but she never
complained that I know of. It was just part of the teaching job,
like helping kids to conjugate verbs, to memorize the multiplica-

tion tables, or to make Easter bunnies by drawing a rabbit on a piece of construction paper and covering the drawing with pussy willows to make it look and feel furry.

Doing the janitor work was especially unpleasant during the winter months. It meant getting up an hour earlier to get the school house warmed up by the time the kids started arriving.

There was a coal bin in the entry way to the school house and Miss Brindel would fill the scuttle with chunks of dirty, black soft coal that she would toss in on the embers left over from the day before — if there were any left. Then she'd have to "shake" the ashes down into the ashpan below the fire pot and carry them out and dump them.

Her next task would be to fill the "evaporation tank" at the top of the big black metal jacket which surrounded the pot-bellied heating stove that was situated in one corner of the room. The evaporation tank must have done a good job of providing humidity, because from mid-December to March 1, the frost on the windows was generally so thick that one couldn't see through them.

It didn't take long, particularly after the little room was full of kids, until it was warm and cozy inside. Miss Brindel had a way of knowing just how that stove was to be fed to keep the temperature relatively even throughout the day.

From 9 a.m. to 4 p.m., Miss Brindel spent her full time teaching. We'd always have opening exercises first — the singing of America and new songs we'd learn from time to time, the pledge of allegiance to the flag. Sometimes, she'd read to us or tell us a story in her own words from a book she had read. When she'd tell a story in her own words, it was the most delightful time of the whole school day.

I'll never forget one story that really captured Miss Brindel's imagination. I believe it was published in a magazine — perhaps the Saturday Evening Post or Colliers. Anyway, it was about an Airedale dog. It was a story somewhat on the order of Jack London's "Call of the Wild," with the dog as the hero. It wasn't long afterward that Miss Brindel was the proud owner of an Airedale, whom she called Peter, the same name as that of the dog in the story.

She not only taught from books, but was the physical education instructor and playground supervisor.

One day she brought a pair of skis, which was something that even we Norwegian kids didn't have.

Francis Fagan, one of the "big kids", was the one to try them first. He didn't wait for any instruction, such as how to bend his knees and lean forward. He just started moving his feet, stood straight up, and folded his arms behind his back.

Miss Brindel put her hands over her eyes. She envisioned (1) a pair of broken skis, (2) a boy with broken bones, (3) what will Mrs. Fagan say when she finds out her boy needs a doctor?

A cheer arose from the youngsters as Francis sped down the hill. They had expected him to turn head over heels as the skis hit the corn stalks at the bottom. Miss Brindel lifted her hands slightly, just to take a peek. There was Francis at the bottom of the hill, the proudest kid in school because he'd negotiated the hill without a tumble. He picked up the skis and trekked back up. Recess time was over and Francis had done something none of the rest of us could do.

Francis always wanted to be a cowboy. He liked to ride horses and shoot guns, even though they were toy ones. One day, he brought a real gun to school, a revolver. It wasn't loaded, but Miss Brindel didn't think a school room was any place to be carrying a gun, so she took it away from him. Francis didn't like it, but he gave it up.

Harold Freim must have been in the first grade. When he started school, he couldn't speak English, only Norwegian. Some of us who knew Norwegian would translate for him and help him learn the English words.

Francis, who knew every trick there was, thought it would be fun to heckle Miss Brindel a bit by asking Harold to go inside during recess to ask for the revolver.

Maybe Francis threatened him with a face washing in the snow but, whatever, bashful Harold went in to the teacher and whispered in a mixture of Norwegian and English, "Francis sa I could ha wolverine." Calling the revolver "wolverine" almost caused Miss Brindel to break up with laughter. Harold laughed, too. But the gun remained on the teacher's desk until school was out. Then Francis got it back with strict orders to take it home and leave it home.

Miss Brindel taught at District 44 for 4 years, if I remember correctly. The last year she bought a car. She and a former Beaver Creek teacher, Reeva Merkel, I think, were the first two school teachers in the county to drive cars to school.

Anyway, Miss Brindel wasn't boarding at Fenstermakers anymore, but was living in Beaver Creek.

They didn't have permanent anti-freeze in those days, just alcohol. Miss Brindel and Celos Hettinger at the hardware store put some in her Model T. But he hadn't kept the car running while he was filling it so it didn't mix with the water.

She started out the next morning, without knowing that the bottom of the radiator had frozen. The alcohol started to boil and the car was smoking like a steam engine by the time she was halfway to school. When this happened, she decided it was time to get out.

Suddenly there was an explosion under the hood and the car was engulfed in grey smoke and steam. She didn't know what to expect when the steam cleared away, but at least the car wasn't a pile of rubble. Charley Wallenberg happened to come along. He lifted the hood and found out what had happened. The boiling alcohol had blown one of the radiator hoses off. There was nothing he could do but be a good neighbor and take her to school in his car. He went back and somehow managed to get her car back to town to be repaired.

After that, she left the winterizing chores up to Jim Vopat or the Baustian brothers at the Beaver Creek Garage.

Miss Brindel left District 44 to teach near Jasper. Then, she and her husband moved out to Washington, where she embarked on a successful business career.

She taught a lot of "boys off the farm" like myself and I believe she meant it when she said many years later that she was more proud of the pupils she had taught than she was of any of her own achievements which were many.

A Country School Boy's Uniform Was A Pair Of Bib Overalls And A Blue Chambray Shirt

When school starts, summer is gone for all practical purposes and fall is here once again.

Maybe I get that feeling because I was brought up that way. As anyone who has experienced it will agree, a farm boy (and a farm girl, too, for that matter) was always glad to see school start because it meant that summer's work had ended for all those of school age.

Summertime may have been vacation time, but it was also the time that thrifty farmers and their wives made the most of having the kids around home. There are hundreds of chores to be done on a farm, particularly during the growing season, so no youngster had reason to complain that "there's nothing to do around here". Anyone who uttered those words aloud in front of his elders was certain to be assigned half dozen or more tasks.

So, fall was looked forward to with anticipation. Fall came when school started. The three months of summer work which was referred to as "vacation" was over and we all could take things a little easier.

I just wonder if the kids today are as anxious for school to begin as we were. Maybe everyone didn't feel as I did, but I always looked forward to the opening day and seeing my friends once again because we didn't have much opportunity to get together during the busy summer.

The country school I attended was situated on a tract of ground in the northeast corner of our farm. Our farm buildings were in the southwest corner so we had a mile to walk if we walked the road. If we'd "cut across", that is walk diagonally across the fields and pasture, the distance was a little over a half mile.

Most of the time, we cut across on our way to school in the morning. At night, we quite often walked the road. That gave us a chance to walk with the southbound kids for a half mile before we had to turn to walk west the remaining distance.

I don't suppose I ever started school in the fall without a new pair of blue bib overalls, a new blue chambray shirt, and a fresh haircut.

Bib overalls and blue chambray shirts were the uniform of the day for farm boys in school. Had they worn anything else, they would have been labeled "sissy" by the older boys and shunned by the younger ones.

Mothers always had a choice when they shopped for new overalls of either "high back" or "low back" models. The low back had suspenders with elastic in them and they buttoned to the waist in back. The high back kind was firmly fixed in back, without buttons. A favorite trick of the bigger boys was to unbutton the smaller boy's suspenders which would cause the back of the overalls to drop. This made the girls giggle and blush and resulted in a lot of busy frustration for the boy in overalls. I liked the high back kind for that reason.

Those were the days before non-shrink demins were invented, so the new overalls were always purchased about four sizes larger than the boy really needed. if you were eight years old, you'd be fitted with an "age 12". If you were 12, your size would be 16, and so on.

This meant the first time (or times) you wore the new overalls, you'd have to roll up a five or six inch cuff on the legs and you'd have six inches of room to spare around the waist.

After the overalls had been washed the first time, they'd be quite a bit shorter and less full at the waist. But the extra length and breadth served a useful purpose later on.

When winter came, it was always nice to have the extra length to tuck in at the top of one's overshoes. The extra room at the waist made it possible to wear a second pair of pants beneath the overalls for extra warmth without the discomfort of a tight waist.

By spring, the wearer had usually grown sufficiently so the cuffs had to be turned down the whole way. And the waist was just about right.

Just as a pair of blue overalls was the mark of a country school boy, so was his tin dinner bucket.

Grandpa Aaker, who lived with us, smoked Union Leader tobacco in his pipe and bought it in one-pound containers. Shaped like a basket with a hinged cover, these containers made good "dinner baskets". They had two handles that folded together, making them easy to carry, simple to open and close. There was room for a couple of sandwiches at one end and a piece of cake, cookies, an apple or an orange, or a small glass container of canned fruit at the other.

A lot of the kids, however, carried their lunches in tin pails, which originally had contained corn syrup or molasses, staples on the pantry shelf in a country home. Some had what we chose to call "boughten" dinner pails. These were round, too, but were designed especially for carrying lunches.

I oftentimes chuckle to myself when I listen to the school lunch menu announced over the radio and hear the kids that day are going to have pizza, barbecues on a bun, or fish sticks. Pizzas and barbecues and fish sticks hadn't even been invented when I went to grade school.

But this isn't to say that we didn't have good lunches, even though we had to eat them cold. Mother would make sandwiches with home canned beef or pork, or with "minced ham", and on rare occasions, peanut butter.

But a favorite of mine was mustard. Plain prepared mustard, spread over butter between two slices of bread. Maybe I shouldn't have said plain prepared mustard, because it was a little more than that. Mother would buy horseradish or German style mustard in quart jars from the Watkins man or Rawleigh man and from the very first bite one knew he was munching a real mustard sandwich. A couple of these, with a cold chicken drumstick, a cold pork chop, or a hard boiled egg made a tasty first course. A piece of devils food cake with some home canned peaches, a piece of fresh apple or pumpkin pie, or a juicy crisp apple topped the meal off in fine style.

There were always certain school supplies we had to bring with us the first day. A couple of penny pencils and a jumbo pencil tablet headed the list. Then there were a couple of note books, with brown covers on the outside and ink paper on the inside. (We used these for copying down songs which the teacher would write on the blackboard and of course, for other materials that we wanted to or were required to keep.)

Then there was the bottle of Sanford's blue-black ink with which we filled the ink well on our desks the first day of school. And we started the term with new Spencerian pen points in our pen holders.

Nearly everyone had a soap eraser, an art gum eraser or a double duty rubber eraser, one end of which was for erasing pencil marks, the other for erasing ink. The art gum and the soap erasers were the best for pencil erasing, but the ink erasing end of the double duty eraser was the only effective way to eliminate a mistake that was made with a pen.

On the first day of school, we were issued our books, assigned our lessons, and maybe taught a new song. The second day it was all business, and it remained that way until the end of the term.

Limited in formal training as the teachers were in those days, they nonetheless were excellent instructors in the basic studies of reading, spelling, language, arithmetic, geography and history. How they were able to teach seven or eight grades during the day, do the janitor work at the school, and prepare their lessons for the next day, I will never know.

The rural teachers I had were dedicated to their tasks, and somehow, managed to instill enough knowledge into our thick heads so that we never had to feel inferior when we competed with youngsters who attended "town school".

Today's kids are exposed to a lot more knowledge through the availability of a wider variety of subjects and modern teaching techniques, I know. They're getting science and math in elementary school that we didn't even get in high school.

But when I read some of the things the kids write and punctuate, I wonder. Country style teaching by a young gal with four years of high school and a year of normal training couldn't have been so inferior after all.

District 44 School House

My sister, Lorraine, and her friend, Alice Johnson, are in the foreground. We kept our dinner buckets and overshoes in the entry way except during sub-zero weather. Then we could take them inside.

Winter Transportation

When the weather was really rough, Dad would take us to school or come and get us in the bobsled. With a horsehide robe or a big horse blanket to cover us, it was kind of a fun ride.

Warmth Was Measured By Weight, Not BTUs

"Now you bundle up," Mother would say. "We don't want you catching cold."

If ever heat was conserved, it was during my country school days. Once I was bundled up, there was no way any body heat was going to escape, nor could cold air get to my body unless perhaps it was through my hands and feet. And if I kept moving and stamping my feet, clapping my hands and waving my arms to slap my shoulders, they'd stay warm too.

I wonder, grudgingly, when I see kids on the way to school these days in light weight snowmobile suits, hooded jackets, ski masks, down filled mittens and snowmobile boots, why didn't they think of that 50 years ago.

The prevailing thought then was in order to be warm, it had to be heavy.

Heavy coats, heavy jackets, heavy sweaters, heavy mittens, heavy underwear, heavy stockings, heavy overshoes. If the garment was thick and weighed a lot, it was considered good.

The word heavy, very often, was synonymous with wool.

Wool was the warmest of the fabrics. Down was used only for bedding — pillows and feather ticks.

Of course, there was heavy cotton, wool and cotton blends, but none of the polyester, dacron, nylon, rayon and other man-made materials so common today.

The appearance of the first frost in the fall was the signal for changing from summer underwear to heavy underwear.

Coziest garment in the world, I believe, is a new fleece-lined cotton union suit.

There were lighter weights of winter underwear and heavier ones, but Mother and Dad were of the opinion that fleece lined cotton provided the greatest amount of warmth for the least amount of money.

Stepping out of the galvanized washtub after the Saturday night bath in front of the kitchen range and then stepping into a clean union suit which had been warming on the cover of the stove's reservoir has to be one of the most pleasurable sensations of my childhood.

For the benefit of the very young and uninformed, I should define a union suit. The word union means that the outfit was one piece, a union of the lower half with the top half, the drawers with the shirt.

Some union suits came with short legs and short sleeves, but

they were never worn in winter. The winter variety came with
long legs and long sleeves.

So, when you donned a union suit, your whole body, with the exception of your head, your hands and your feet, were encased in
coziness.

Union suits came also in 25 percent wool, 50 percent wool, and
100 percent wool.

Only person I ever knew who wore 100 percent wool underwear was my Uncle Ole, my dad's brother. He wore 'em winter
and summer, more for their therapeutic quality, I think,
than for warmth. He insisted his rheumatism would immobilize
him if he didn't wear 100 percent wool.

Most people I knew wore wool, or even part wool, only as a last
resort. The wool was scratchy and wearing wool underwear indoors where it was warm could cause the skin to become
unbearably itchy.

You could always tell which of the kids in school wore wool.
They were always moving around in their seats, scratching
themselves here and there, particularly after the big black heater
in the corner of the school room warmed up.

But the heavy underwear was only the beginning in the bundl-
ing up process.

Mother always saw to it that I had a stock of heavy shirts for
winter. When the creek was frozen to the point that it was possible to skate on it without breaking through the ice, then it was
time to switch from the blue or grey chambray shirts which were
standard attire for farm boys during the spring, summer and fall,
to flannel shirts.

Flannel came in different weights, also, depending on the
amount of wool in the cloth.

Mother made my flannel shirts. She'd see a pattern in Farmers
Wife magazine that had a little more style to it than the
"boughten" shirts in H.B. Creeger's Golden Rule store. She'd
order the pattern and then buy the cloth at the Golden Rule.

The shirt I remember as having the most class was a black and
white hounds-tooth check, with extra long collar points. That
shirt not only was warm, but it had style, too. I liked that.

When early December rolled around every country school boy
— in fact, every male in the family — would wear at least two
pairs of pants.

Two pants, generally, meant a pair of wool trousers over which
bib overalls were worn. Or it could mean two pairs of bib overalls.

The wool pants were usually dress trousers that had been
outgrown, or worn out on the knees so that they had to be patch-
ed. Worn beneath the overalls, the patching didn't show, and

neither did the fact that legs came down only half way between the knee and the ankle.

There were two schools of thought on bib overalls.

Some liked the Lee and Oshkosh b' Gosh vest backs because they covered the back better.

Others, however, liked the convenience of the low back models. Low backs had elastic in the suspenders. They didn't bind when you had to stoop and pick up something. The suspenders also buttoned at the bottom, just over the back pockets as well as on bib in front. Boys who had been given permission by the teacher "to leave the room" liked them because they didn't have to take their coats and jackets off if they had low back overalls.

Usually, on cold days we wore two pairs of socks. Grandma knit wool stockings that extended above the knees. When the wool ones were in the wash, a pair of long black stockings worn with a pair of blue or brown Rockford work socks over them were almost as warm.

When the temperature dropped below zero, Mother made sure I wore at least two, if not three, jackets and sweaters. Generally, it was a wool cardigan sweater and a blanket lined denim jacket which everybody called overall jackets.

Active boys like myself usually wore out one jacket a year. Climbing up and down the hayloft ladder, crawling through barbwire fences, and wrestling around in the snow on the school ground was hard on clothing. Every new jacket I got was two sizes larger than I needed. That allowed for wearing a sweater beneath it and two of them if it got really cold.

A lot of kids wore stocking caps, then as now, but I usually had a wool cap with a bill and fur lined earflaps. Sometimes the earflaps didn't cover the tips of my ears and a few times when I came home from school, the tips of my ears were snow white, evidence that they were frostbitten.

"Rub them with snow right away," Dad admonished.

Mother wondered why I hadn't wrapped my knit wool scarf around my neck and face the way she had done it when I left for school that morning. I guess the reason was I didn't like to breathe through it because it always frosted up in front of my mouth and nose.

Now, bundled up as I was from head to toe, I had to put on my four buckle overshoes. No zippers in those days. Overshoes came in the one-buckle, two-buckle and four-buckle size for boys. Dads could get them in five-buckle heights.

With heavy underwear, a flannel shirt, two sweaters, an overall jacket, a pair of wool pants and a pair of overalls on, stooping over to pull on a pair of overshoes, particularly if the shoes one was wearing had rubber heels, was a grunting and puffing struggle.

My friends in school — the Wulf boys, Harry, Arnold and Lawrence — didn't have to go through that. They always had high top leather boots and could get by wearing two-buckle rubbers.

How I would have liked a pair of high tops, the kind you could wear with grey wool socks trimmed with red at the top. But Dad and Mother, for some reason, made it perfectly clear that ordinary shoes worn with four-buckle overshoes were far superior to boots and rubbers and, therefore, with shoes and overshoes I had to be content.

Overshoes on, all I needed then to be fully bundled up were my mittens. Every year, Elmer Alink, who didn't have a Grandma living with him, showed up the first cold winter day wearing a pair of lined leather mittens with an elastic wristband.

But I had a Grandma, who knit mittens as well as stockings and scarves. They were warm by themselves, but were especially so when worn with a pair of boy's size double thumb husking mitts.

You could get them dripping wet when out playing in the snow at recess time, but they dried in a hurry when draped over the jacket around the school house heater. And they didn't get stiff like Elmer's leather mittens did when they were dried after being soaked.

With all that on, the northwest winds had trouble penetrating to the skin, believe me. We were round and firm and fully packed but not agile, because movement in that amount of clothing was anything but easy.

But we were warm, and that's what counted.

We'd head out over the pasture and fields, picking out a route where there were the fewest drifts. If my body would assimilate as many calories today as it did on those days, I'd waste away in no time. It was work to climb over the high drifts. We'd start across a drifted area, perhaps, and half way across, the crust would break and our heavy overshoed feet had to be pulled out of hip deep holes that we'd make with each forward step.

By the time we reached the school house, we'd had our quota of exercise for the day. It felt kind of good to sit down at our desks and do our arithmetic problems.

When the weather was really rough, Dad would take us to school or come and get us in the bobsled. A couple of wagon spring seats on the floor of the bobsled box gave us a place to sit. With a horsehide robe or a big horse blanket to cover our bodies from our feet to our necks, it was kind of a fun ride, particularly if some of the neighbor kids were riding with us. When it was real cold, Dad would light a kerosene lantern to provide heat underneath the blankets or robe.

It wasn't so pleasant for Dad, though, who had to drive Daisy and Bess, the team of bays that generally were given the bobsled duties in winter. Dad, wearing a big fur coat would stand up the whole way. Usually, he tied a knot in the reins (we called them the lines) so he could slip them over his shoulder and not have to hold them with his hands the whole time. Every now and then, he'd swing his arms and slap his hands against his body to stimulate circulation and to give himself some exercise to keep warm. Straw on the floor of the bobsled helped to provide insulation for his feet.

Looking back on it now, I'm fully convinced Mother knew what she was talking about when she told me to bundle up. With all those clothes on, a cold germ couldn't get through no matter how hard it tried.

But it would have been a lot more convenient for me and a lot less trying for her if all I'd had to do was slip on a down-filled snowmobile suit with hooded jacket like kids do now.

That's what comes of being born 50 years too soon.

If You Learned How To Dog Paddle, You Knew How To Swim

I'm not sure how old I was when I learned how to swim. Nine or ten maybe. I was still going to country school, I remember.

I know I liked the water. Even before I learned to swim, I'd go wading in the shallow end of the creek that went through our farm. Then, as I grew older — and more daring — I ventured into the deeper parts.

Some of the older farm kids in our neighborhood came to our pasture to swim and bellyflop in the summertime and they encouraged me to go with them. It developed into a regular thing.

I remember one summer I made a count of how many times I'd been in — something like 93 as I recall. That's better than once a day.

The creek then was about three and a half or four feet deep where we swam.

Farther downstream in what we called the big pond, the water was shallower and the bottom was muddy.

The silt had started to fill in there. It didn't start filling the swimming hole until later. For a number of years, the bottom was sandy there.

A block or so from the spot where we'd get into the water was a small box elder tree. That's where we'd undress and leave our clothes while we were in the water.

I never had a swimming lesson, although my uncle, whom we always called Buster, helped me learn to dog paddle by holding me as I paddled both my hands and feet, then letting his hands drop while I fended for myself for a few strokes before going under.

An old discarded fence post did more than anything to help me learn to swim.

At first, I held the post ahead of me in my hands and paddled my feet as fast as they would go to keep from sinking. The next step was to put the post under my chin and paddle with both hands and feet.

Then, I began to let the post slip under from under my chin while I paddled for dear life to keep my head above water. Eventually I learned how to dog paddle.

As swimming became more and more a part of my summer recreation routine, I found ways to improve the swimming hole. This took some extra manpower, but there was generally a neighbor boy or two on hand to help.

One time we built a pier out into the water of some discarded boards and two-by-fours my dad left lying around. We found an old stone boat which we launched to serve as a raft.

For those who don't know what I mean by stone boat, I should perhaps explain that it was a low-slung sled made of four-by-four runners and covered with planks, running crosswise.

The one we had was about three feet wide and five or six feet long. A stone boat was normally used to haul big field stones from a field after the stones would surface during plowing or cultivating time.

We would use the pier and the raft when we wanted to dive or bellyflop.

When we were diving and bellyflopping, we'd usually hold our noses with one hand while we held the other arm ahead of us or over our heads so the hand would hit the bottom of the shallow pond before our heads did.

A couple of my friends couldn't stand to get water in their ears. They would plug their ears with their thumbs and use their index fingers to close their nostrils.

One of the fun things we often did was to go down to the pond where the bottom was soft and muddy. Where we'd pick up a handful of mud in each hand and then walk up onto the shore and cover our bodies and faces with the gooey stuff. Then we'd run and jump or dive off the pier to wash the stuff off.

One thing we never had to worry about is catching heck when we got home for getting our swimsuits and towels dirty. We never wore swimsuits nor did we use towels.

Usually, by the time we'd sauntered from the creek to the base of the box elder tree, the sun had dried our bare bodies so we could dress without using a towel.

It didn't matter if our feet had collected dirt and dust enroute. We were barefooted most of the time anyway and washing our feet in a white enamel basin was the final order of the day before going to bed.

A half-dozen kids in the little creek was enough to stir up some soil particles, even if there was a hard, sand bottom in the middle of the stream. These particles usually collected on the tiny body hairs and after a couple of hours in the water, we'd come out quite speckled unless we were careful to wash ourselves down before we left the creek.

Generally, this was done while we dangled our feet into the water from the pier and dipped water with our hands to wash our hands, legs and bodies.

Swimming took on new dimensions after a heavy rain.

The otherwise placid stream of about 20 feet in width would swell to a fast moving, muddy current several blocks wide.

While we on occasion tried to swim from one side to the other,

we usually waited until the water returned to normal levels and
cleared. The flood waters were a bit smelly, too, and this
detracted from any desire to try the deep and wider stream.

After public school was out in May, I attended a parochial
school which our church maintained at that time for the benefit
of the children of the parish. The school was located in the ex-
treme northwest corner of Beaver Creek Township, about four
miles from our farm.

When this school was in session, it brought together kids from
several rural public schools in this area and it also brought out a
false bravado in a good many of us.

If any boy challenged another to try something, he hardly dared
not do it for fear he wouldn't be chosen to play on a baseball team.

A mile south of the school house and across the fields was what
was then called the Tokheim Bridge.

Water from Knute Onerheim's spring filled the pond adjacent
to the bridge, also brought the water level under the bridge to a
depth of two or three feet.

Sometimes a few of us "snuck" down to the bridge during the
noon hour for a quick dip.

Diagonally across the field and a bit closer to the school house
was the state line bridge. There was water there only after a good
rain. On occasion, we'd sneak there for a noon day dip, too.

Sometimes I'd spend a day or two with my cousin, Arnie
Gunderson, who lived in what then was Manley, a mile east of
Valley Springs.

He and I would walk the Great Northern track up to the
railroad bridge where we were joined by Duke Okeson and his
brother for a swim in the pond below the bridge.

One time, we decided to make a pond closer to home.

We walked down to the creek in W.W. Bell's pasture, just north
of what is now Sam's Station on old Highway 16, and by digging
up some wet sod along the shore, we managed to build a little dam
across the narrow creek.

The farmer living downstream didn't like the idea because it
stopped the flow into his pasture and he had no water for his
cows.

A night or two after we built it, he opened the dam with a spade
or sand shovel, because the next time we went back, our pond was
gone and the stream was back to its normal five foot width and
one foot depth.

We really didn't care too much anyway. As boys that age
generally do, we had found other exciting things to do like getting
a group together for a game of one-hole cat.

As time went on I had fewer and fewer opportunities to swim.

Sometimes on Sundays, I'd go to Garretson to swim in Split

Rock River with Arnie Ormseth, Galen Meck, Norm Fresvik and Don Williamson.

I never did get a chance to try the Luverne pool which was then a bend in the river at the east end of the Luverne park.

Diving off the rock ledges along the shore of the Split Rock was fun, but dangerous.

The Beaver Creek "pool" had been abandoned before that time.

I think it was maintained by Hettingers or Charlie Harris who dammed up the water in the area at the east part of town, south of the railroad tracks, so they could harvest ice there in the winter.

Thus, I never had a chance to swim there.

In later years, about the only time I ever went for a swim was the week of vacation we took as a family each summer, either to Green Lake near Spicer, Lake Darling near Alexandria, or Big Sand Lake near Park Rapids.

But I never lost my love for the sport and guess that is why I've taken it up again now that I am enjoying more leisure time in retirement.

You Had To Knuckle Down
To Keep Your Glassies

It's marble playing season but where are the marble players?

Business in marbles is anything but brisk nowadays. At least that is what my storekeeper friends tell me.

There's more interest in shooting baskets than there is in shooting marbles. And maybe that's better, I don't know. At least, a person gets a lot more body exercise that way than when he is down on his knees in a marble game.

I never became very adept at marbles. I guess that was mainly due to the fact marbles didn't ever catch on as a spring sport in old School District 44. As I think back now, I can't ever remember seeing the big boys — Harry and Arnold Wulf, Francis Fagan, my uncle "Buster" or Hank and Clarence Top — ever shoot marbles. Maybe, it was because when marble season rolled around, their dads decided they were a lot better off at home doing farm work than going to school and getting an education. So, when the big boys didn't do anything to popularize the sport, us little fellows like Elmer Alink, Harold and Martin Freim, Floyd and Albert Johnson and I spent most of our recess time snaring striped gophers or teasing the girls instead of learning the art of marble shooting. But not so with the more sophisticated kids in town.

They were marble players, believe me. But they should have been good. They didn't have chores to do like we who lived on the farm did.

Oh sure, they may have had to walk down to the town pump a couple of times a day for a bucket or two of water, but there were no cows and horses to feed, no barn cleaning, no milking.

About the time I started high school, Eddie Rauk was considered the marble champ in Beaver Creek. Don Vopat ran a close second and if I remember right, Tommy McDermott, Drake and Bud Drowden, and Eddie LaDue, could hold their own pretty well. Harold and Howard Crawford, Russ Leslie, Werner and Fred Stegemann, Cecil Chesley, Howard Anderson, Otis and Billy Godfrey, and Hank and Clarence Langhout were like the rest of the boys off the farm. They just didn't have the chance to practice and they had no place to play like the alley of the lumber yard building in town.

There, the boys were protected from the chill spring winds. The dirt floor was dry and the marbles rolled perfectly.

The game that was most popular was the one where a big circle was made and the object was to shoot your opponents' marbles outside the circle. First, you'd put your stakes into the ring. If you were playing for glassies and if the players were equally skilled, the marbles would go in on a one to one basis.

If you were lucky enough to own an agate or two, then you'd play for agates, or you'd put in maybe five glassies to one of your opponent's "aggies". If you were on a tight "commies" budget, maybe the only marbles you could afford was a bagful of clays, which were called "commies". Then, you'd probably have to put in 10 commies to each glassy for your opponent.

The game started by tossing a shooter marble toward a straight line, maybe eight or ten feet from the circle. The person coming closest to the line shot first at the marbles in the ring. The next closest one shot second, etc. Each time a marble was knocked out of the ring, the shooter pocketed the marble and was given a chance to shoot again.

Most of the boys had favorite shooters. And they developed a method of holding the marble so that the knuckle of the thumb, not the thumbnail, held the marble against the tip of the forefinger. Ed Rauk and Don Vopat were extremely accurate using this method and could pick off individual marbles from considerable distance. They also developed an unbelievable amount of "fire power". Sometimes a shooter would hit the other marble with such force that the marble would splinter and break.

Now and then, they'd use "steelies" as shooters. These were hollow metal marbles that ranked in desirability between the commies and the glassies.

Marbles were also a measure of a boy's wealth and success. If he had a bagful or pocketful of glassies with a few aggies thrown in, he not only commanded attention but prestige as well. Marbles were also stock-in-trade for bartering. Like 10 glassies would go quite a ways toward a good homemade slingshot, if the slingshot owner were the trading kind.

Steelies, as I remember it, were used most often in playing "chase". This is the game the boys played on the way to school and coming home. One of the boys would throw out a marble and his companion was supposed to hit it with his marble. If he missed, then it was the other lad's turn to shoot. When one or the other hit his opponent's marble, he won it.

The marble season didn't last very long. By the time the grass started to grow each spring, the enthusiasm for marbles was transferred to kittenball and the marbles were put away in a dresser drawer or some other safe place where they remained until the snow started to melt the following spring.

Celos Hettinger, who operated Hettinger's Hardware, was glad for the change of seasons, too. By that time, the marble business had dwindled to a few that were bought for replacement of those lost or broken. When this happened, marbles came off the shelves, and in their place went the garden seed display. Not far from the front door Celos would stand the nail keg full of Louisville Slugger bats inscribed with names of such stars as Babe Ruth, Lou Gehrig and Paul Waner. On the shelf beside the bats were Reach baseball gloves, Spalding kittenballs with outside seams, and baseballs ranging in price from ten cents for the kind used for playing catch only, to $1.50 for the better balls that were labeled "guaranteed for nine innings".

These were true harbingers of spring. When you hefted a bat, rolled a ball around in your fingers or tried on one of the gloves and pounded its palm with your fist, it was a safe bet your mother would let you take off the long legged underwear in a couple of weeks.

Springtime was marble time

The game that was most popular was the one where a big circle was made and the object was to shoot your opponent's marbles out of the circle.

It was downhill all the way

Boys would never admit they liked girls but they always found it was rather fun going down the hill, one seated behind the other.

A Short Run, A Belly-Flop And It Was Downhill All The Way

I had another birthday this week.

I found it hard to believe that a whole year had passed since the last one. How does it happen that birthdays seem to recur with so much greater frequency once a fellow reaches 21?

I was thinking about this as I tried to recall some of my most memorable birthdays.

Funny thing is that I remember only a few with any clarity and those that I do remember vividly, the memory relates to the gift I received, more than the event itself.

The first birthday I can remember is the day I was five. That's the day my Mother and Dad gave me my first sled. I'm sure there couldn't have been a happier boy in Rock County that day.

Every boy at some time or other wants a sled, even to this day, although kids whose folks have snowmobiles may not enjoy them the way kids did back then.

My first and only sled was a 30-incher, a "Flying Arrow". The words were printed on the middle board of the sled's surface — the slatted top on which you flopped when you went sliding down a hill. The letters of the words were in script, painted in blue, over a red arrow. The boards were varnished. The runners were bright red. It was beautiful.

It seems that we always had snow by this time each year and sliding provided recreation for us all winter long.

We had several good hills in the pasture on the farm. One was about a quarter of a mile from the District 44 school. Elmer Alink, Harold and Martin Freim, Floyd and Albert Johnson, Clarence and Johnny Top and maybe a couple of others and I would eat our noon lunch in about five minutes and head for the hill in the pasture for our noon hour play period.

As I look at the hill today, I wonder how we ever got enough momentum to even get to the bottom, because it really wasn't very high. But after a few tries and the snow became packed, it seemed we literally whizzed to the bottom.

At the bottom of the hill was a gate which led from the pasture and into the hay meadow. By opening the gate, we had a slope that was a little longer, and at the same time, it meant that the sled operator had to steer it so that it went through the gate and didn't hit the fence.

The "Flying Arrow" had an excellent steering mechanism. A lot better than the "Champion" brand that they sold at Hettinger's Hardware in Beaver Creek and which some of the boys had. But not as good as the "Flexible Flyer" which was the Cadillac of the sled line.

We'd have races. We'd see whose sled could go the greatest distance. We'd have collisions, some accidental and some purposely.

We'd pick up the sled, back up as far as we could to the fence, then run a few feet and flop down. The sled runners would ring as they hit the frozen ground and then came the swishing sound as the shiny bottomed runners would cut through the snow where it wasn't already packed solid.

Once in a while, one of the bigger boys would straddle the slide and we'd steer through his legs. The idea was that he'd sit down on our backs as we went through. It took some intricate timing to know just when to sit. Generally, the boy would sit too late and ended up on the ground.

Other times, a boy would be waiting part way down the hill and would flop down on top of the one riding the sled. Then the two would ride the sled down together, laughing and enjoying every minute of it.

Sometimes the girls would join us, if it happened to be a sunny day.

Boys would never admit they liked girls, but somehow, they always found that it was rather fun going down the hill seated on the sled the girl in front of the boy, with the boy holding the rope and steering with his feet. Only thing wrong was that you couldn't get the distance or the speed you could when you used the belly-flop method of coasting.

I don't know what happened the day I had my accident. But I was coming down the hill — the snow was packed and the slope was fast. I think, perhaps, we were having a contest to see how close we could come to the corner post beside the gate into the meadow — without hitting it.

I hit it.

The steering bar broke. One of the runners was bent out of shape. I sailed through the air, luckily missing the post with my head but the seat of my overalls caught on a piece of protruding barbed wire, ripping through them and a second pair of pants I was wearing. Fortunately the back flap of my union suit was thick enough to save my skin.

I wasn't too concerned about the overalls and what I knew my Dad would say when he learned that I'd been foolish enough to run into a post. What I was worried about was the sled.

Lucky for me, everything turned out for the best. The reprimand was stern — both for the damaged overalls and for being so stupid as to hit the fence post.

But Dad took the sled to Harry Davis, the Beaver Creek

blacksmith, who could fix anything, and the sled came back better than new. He redesigned the steering and it turned sharper than ever before.

The year I was six, I received my first pair of skates — the kind that clamped on with one push of a lever.

I believe I was nine the year Dad gave me a Daisy pump action air rifle. One of the first Daisy pump guns ever made.

The year I was 16, I received a gift I cherished as much as anything I ever owned — a Parker fountain pen.

It was a gift of several high school friends whom Mother had invited out to have supper with us. All had chipped in from their meager allowances to buy the pen.

A Parker pen was something I'd always wanted but could never afford in those days. It was the only pen that didn't have a lever on the side to use for filling it with ink. It was the "revolutionary" pen of its day that filled by screwing off a black cap at one end and using a little pumping device hidden out of sight by the black cap when the pen was in use.

The pen took me through the remainder of my senior year at high school and all through college. What happened to it after that, I'm not sure. I know I don't have it anymore, but I wish I did.

I've had a lot of memorable birthdays since. I suppose as we grow older, every anniversary we are privileged to reach is a significant one.

As I look back now I suppose the reason the four birthdays I mentioned stand out above all the rest is because I associate with them some especially fond memories. Also, the gifts meant so much to a boy then because it was the era of the great depression when most kids my age could count their personal possessions, jack knives and Ingersoll watches included, on the fingers of one hand.

Those birthdays were happy ones, though, and I think that having experienced them, the birthdays of later years have been equally happy because I had learned to be content with what I had.

Hmmm — I wonder if I could still flop on a sled and come within two inches of the gate post without hitting it.

We Played Hockey In An Unsophisticated Sort of Way

Winter doesn't delight me as it once did. And that's kind of too bad. As long as we live in this part of the country, we should be happy with the seasons and what those seasons bring. Maybe the reason I don't like winter is that I don't make an effort to enjoy it, so it's really my own fault.

I thought about that the other day as I drove past the gravel pit ponds south of town. What a place to go ice skating! The ice was smooth as glass. The largest area was several blocks long and nearly as wide. There wasn't a snow drift on it anywhere.

Skating was one of the most enjoyable of winter pastimes when I was a boy and still is for a lot of youngsters. But now, unless there is a rink that is given regular maintenance and a comfortable warming house nearby, nobody skates. The river or pond isn't good enough.

Of course, it's not as easy to go skating now.

First of all, you need a pair of shoe skates. If you're a growing kid, that means the folks have to shell out for a new pair of skates every year because last year's shoes are too small. Besides, it takes longer to put skates on and take them off. And if your shoes aren't left in the warming house, they're mighty cold to put on when you're ready to go home.

Not so with my first pair of skates. About the only thing I needed was a pair of shoes that had leather heels and soles.

Those "Club" clamp skates were really slick. All I had to do was turn the little screw device attached to the clamps to adjust for tightness and I was in business. Just pull a little lever and the clamps would open. Push it back and the clamps would dig into the sole and heel of the shoe and the skate was firmly fastened. Taking them off was just as easy.

When I did outgrow the first pair, I'd saved enough money from my trap line to buy a pair of key skates. They worked the same way — clamps on the soles and heels, but a key was used to tighten or loosen the clamps. A skate key was as important in a boy's overalls pocket as a bone handled knife.

I learned to skate on the rocker bottom skates and then graduated to the key style hockey skates.

They were something else.

The bottoms were flat, not made like a rocker. The back end curved to fit up under the heel as the front curved to fit up under the toe.

The boys of the neighborhood usually would show up on our pasture pond on Saturday and Sunday afternoons during the winter months. If the ice was covered with snow, we'd use scoop shovels to clear the area so we could play hockey. If there was no snow, we'd lay out a rink and play.

A couple of chunks or ice, cut from the water hole where the cattle came to drink each day, were used for the goals at either end of the rink.

We cut our hockey sticks from the trees in the grove, or out of old buggy tops if we could find them. The buggy tops had curved pieces of oak for supports. We'd take the tops apart, cut off one of the curved ends, and we had perfect hockey sticks.

Tin cans made ideal hockey pucks, but after one game, they'd be flattened and banged up so they'd have to be replaced.

We didn't have many rules so the game wasn't as complicated as those we watch on TV today. The game could be played with as few as two players and as many as 20 if the rinks were big enough.

There was only one designated position on each team. That was the center. The others were just plain players — no goalies, no wingmen, no defensemen.

Teams would line up on either side of the center line. The tin can was placed in the center, between the two goals. The two centers would line up facing each other. They'd count one, tap the stick on the ice beside the can, and then lift the stick and tap their opponent's stick about a foot above the can. Then they'd say "two" simulantaneously and go through the same routine. On the count of "three", they'd swing at the can.

If one of the players had a weak branch for a hockey stick, it very often broke at this point, as the opposing player whacked it out of his hands.

When the can was hit, it would skim across the ice with a metallic sound. There was little passing done between players. Anyone who had the can would skate toward the goal, as the members of the opposite team would try to hit the can in the other direction. If the can went between the two blocks of ice, it meant a point had been scored.

We didn't need a warming house. With our heavy jackets and 50 percent wool union suits, we'd perspire playing hockey even if the temperatures were below zero. And we didn't have to worry about cold feet, because we didn't have to change shoes. We just took off our skates and put on our overshoes.

I did get a pair of shoe skates finally, but not the ones I really wanted. The Alfred Johnson skates were the "name" skates then. Mine were Nestor Johnson's.

I enjoyed my shoe skates — at least they didn't pull off my heels like the clamp skates did, or pull the soles of my shoes apart.

But the skates I'll always remember are the gleaming key

hockey skates with both ends curved. I guess the reason is that by that time, I'd become fairly adept on skates, and for some reason, had the opportunity to use them more than any of the others.

I still think a game of hockey with a tin can on the gravel pit pond would be fun for a 12-year-old.

Every Farm Boy Had A Pocket Knife —
And Used It

I never see a display of pocket knives in a store that I don't stop
and take a look at. I think it must be a habit that I acquired when
I was a boy, because I not only stop, I also have an intense desire
to hold the knife in my hand, to open the blades, to feel their
sharpness with my thumb. There's something about the sight of a
new knife that makes me want to own one again.

Every boy owned a knife when I was a youngster. In fact, every
boy and every man that I knew owned one — and used it.

Knives came then, as they do now, in various sizes and styles.
There were the single bladed ones and there were knives with
several blades.

They came with bone handles, wood handles, pearl handles and
metal handles.

The proudest boy in District 44, I remember, was the boy with
the newest knife. No gift a boy could receive, it seemed, would
produce the thrill that came when someone gave him a new knife.

In those days boys did a lot of whittling. I guess they learned
about whittling from their dads who, when sitting around during
the noon hours while the work horses were resting, would pick up
a stick and just whittle.

During the spring of the year, the boys would keep their knives
busy whittling whistles and sling shots. Branches from willow
trees made the best whistles. We'd pick out a limb about a half to
three quarters of an inch thick and with a couple of slices with a
sharp knife, we'd sever it from the tree. The next thing was to
select the piece that had the fewest rough spots. Then the whistle
was cut to length, usually three to four inches long and a notch
was cut on one side. Removing the bark from the stick was tricky.
We'd lay the stick on something solid and rap it lightly with the
knife handle, holding the knife by the blade and using it as a hammer. It was important to keep turning the stick around and
around until the bark was loose. If it wasn't completely loosened,
the bark would crack as we twisted it to remove it.

Once removed, we did the whittling, cutting away part of the
pure white stick that tasted sweet when put in the mouth,
because a little sap still remained in it. The length and depth of
the cut away portion determined the whistle's tonal quality. A little chip removed from the end so you could blow into it, after the
bark was returned to the stick, finished the whistle.

The smaller box elder branches produced another kind of whistle for the boy whittlers. The bark was removed the same way,
but it was thinner, and less susceptible to breakage because the

limbs were smoother than the willows. We'd thin the edges at one end and flatten them. The result was a whistle that resembled an oboe reed. Actually, the sound that the box elder whistle made was not a whistling sound at all, but more of a squawk or a squeak, depending on the diameter and length of the bark tube.

Whistles weren't the only things a boy whittled.

There were sling shots, made from a tree fork, to which were attached long rubber bands cut from a blown out Model T Ford innertube. A piece of leather, cut from the side of a worn out shoe, was attached to the two ends of the rubber bands not fastened to the stick. This leather pocket held the stones that were fired over the top of the barn, at pigeons, at windmill fans and through chicken house windows.

A flat piece of wood, about a quarter of an inch thick, an inch and a half wide and five or six inches long could be shaped into a fan blade in short order with a sharp knife. After a hole was drilled in the middle, it was nailed to another stick, and presto, you had a windmill. Or, if the fan were small, it was used as a propellor for a homemade airplane.

Sides of peach crates and apple boxes made ideal whittling material. I remember I often made jumping jacks from these thin, easy to shape boards. I made the holes in the boards to attach the movable legs and arms by heating a wire red hot in the kitchen cook stove and burning through the wood.

We made pistols and toy guns with our pocket knives. The pistols had a notch at the hammer-end of the barrel and we'd slip rubber bands over the barrel around the notch. A finishing nail was driven into the bottom side to simulate the trigger. Then, we'd play cowboys and Indians, firing the rubber band ammunition by flicking it from the notch with the right thumbnail.

The different blades served different purposes. I remember I always wanted a knife with a long "toad-stabber" skinning blade so I could better handle the animal pelts from my trapline. And it was always nice to have a leather punch blade. This could be used to punch holes in most anything and it was ideal for reaming the pith from the center of a corn cob when making a corn cob pipe. The "little" blade of a two-bladed knife was especially good for sharpening school pencils.

Those who had "Boy Scout" knives were always the envy of their playmates. These knives had the Boy Scout emblem on each side and there was usually a screw driver blade, a combination bottle and can opener blade and once in a while a corkscrew, besides two or three regular blades.

Another blade, not too common, was the pruning blade. This had an end that was hook-shaped for cutting unwanted branches from fruit trees. No farmer ever bought a knife that didn't have a "cuttin' " blade, which was curved upward at the end and kept super-sharp for various types of veterinary surgery that he had to perform from time to time.

Another purpose served by the pocket knife was for carving initials . . . on the walls of the "BOYS" out in back of the school house . . . on barn doors . . . and axe handles. I can still see the FWF and OB skillfully cut by Francis Fagan and my uncle Olaf in the school privy and the RWB, carved by the late Bob Blakely on the wall of the granary at home when Bob was our hired man.

A pocket knife also served as a gaming device. We'd open the small blade the full length of the knife, then open the big blade halfway so it was at right angles to the small blade. Then we'd get on our knees and play mumblety-peg. We also threw knives at targets on wood walls and some of the boys became quite accurate marksmen.

I remember by the time our overalls had worn to the point where the first knee patches were sewn on, there'd be a faded spot, the size of a pocket knife, which showed on the outside of the pocket in which the knife was carried.

Some of the farmers often carried their red or blue handkerchiefs in their knife pocket, to keep from losing it. Crawling around under a binder or other piece of farm equipment that needed mechanical attention was a sure way to have one's knife drop out and get lost unless there was something there to prevent it from doing so.

Yes, pocket knives in those days were as essential to a farm boy as a pair of overalls or a straw hat in summer.

Games People Played Like Pom-Pom-Pullaway

Since school started, I've driven past the elementary playground and watching the youngsters, I've wondered, "What games are they playing anyway?" I'm sure that most of them are games that I never heard of when I was their age.

By the same token, I suppose, they've never heard of the games my generation of "grade school kids" played, either.

The game we played most often at recess time, as I remember, was "Pom, Pom, Pullaway."

First of all, someone had to be "It". He took his place in the center of the playing space, with goals drawn in the dust at either end, and side boundaries marked. We would "choose up sides" so there was an even number on each side, then each team would line up behind the goal lines.

"It" would yell out, "Pom, Pom, Pullaway" and each side would run toward the opposite goal. Any player tagged by "It" would become his assistant. Any player running out of bounds would also be counted as caught. When everyone had been tagged, the game started over with a new "It," usually the last one caught.

Then there was "Blindman's Bluff." All the youngsters with the exception of "It" would join hands to form a circle. "It" was blindfolded and place in the center of the circle. Assuming "It" was a boy, he would start the game by signaling the others to move either right or left. He would then command "halt" at which time everyone in the circle stood still and "It" would point to one of the players in the outer circle who would then step into the ring. With his blindfold still on, he'd chase the person he pointed at around the circle until he caught him. Then he would try to guess his name. If he guessed correctly, the person caught would be "It" and the game would continue. If he failed to guess the person's name, he'd have to try again.

We also played a game called "Last Couple Out." One player was selected to be "It" and the other children were arranged by couples one behind the other. "It" would stand behind a line about 10 feet ahead of the couples, with his back toward them. He or she would then start the game by calling "Last Couple Out."

The last couple then would come stealthily forward, one on each side. Upon reaching the line behind which "It" stood, they'd break and run, trying to join hands before "It" could tag them. If "It" succeeded in catching one of the partners before they succeeded in joining hands, that person would be the new "It", and the first "It" would join the other partner and go to the head of the line.

Another game we played occasionally was called "Rachel and

Jacob". One boy acted as Jacob and a girl was picked to be Rachel. The remaining players formed a circle by clasping hands with boys and girls alternating. Rachel and Jacob would take thier places within the circle. Jacob was blindfolded.

Jacob would then start the game by asking, "Rachel, where art thou?" Upon hearing her voice, he'd run around the circle trying to catch her, continuing to ask her where she was, and she replying. After he would catch her, he'd be permitted to take off his blindfold and take his place in the ring. Rachel would then wear the blindfold and would have to catch a new Jacob.

Our favorite winter recess game was "Fox and Geese." The kids would line up one behind the other and tramp a big ring in the snow. Then they'd walk in a line criss-crossing the ring to make it look like a huge wheel with the criss-crosses as spokes.

One player was picked to be the "Fox". The "fox" would take its place in the center of the hub of the circle. The "geese" would then scatter and the rest of the game was a simple game of tag, the fox chasing one of the geese until he or she was tagged. The only restriction was that the players had to travel only down the trodden paths of the snow wheel. The center of the wheel was a free space for the "geese" after the "fox" started the game so the fox couldn't tag them when they were in the free space.

When the weather was such that we couldn't play outside, we had a variety of indoor games. I remember several we played on the blackboard with chalk, among them "cat and rat" which was merely writing zeroes or x-es in squares and the first one to have three in a row was the winner.

Another blackboard game was "Hangman". First we'd draw several dashes or blanks on the blackboard, each dash representing a letter of a word which the guesser would try to figure out.

If he guessed the right letter, the letter would go above the appropriate blank. If he failed, a part of the man was drawn below the hangman's rope. First it would be one side of his face. Then the other. Then eyes, ears, nose, mouth, body, arms, and legs. If the player guessed the letters right before the drawing of the man was completed, he was the winner. If he didn't, and the hung man was completed first, he lost the game.

Another recess pastime was playing "Hide the Thimble". In this game, "It" would leave the room. In our one room school house, the best "It" could do was turn around, while one or the other players hid some object, usually a piece of chalk, an eraser, or even a thimble if one were to be had.

After the object was hidden, "It" had to find it. If he came close, the other players would say he was "warm" or "hot". If he were quite a distance away, he would be told that he was "cold". When he would find it, he'd get to pick the next person to be "It".

There were a lot of other games we played, most of them
without much supervision by the teacher. I guess that's what
made it fun. Today, I fear, a lot of the games played aren't played
for fun, but more for instructional purposes . . . as they say in the
teaching profession, to develop motor skills and coordination.

I don't argue that this isn't good, but I still think the games we
played for fun, and the games we made up ourselves not only
freed us from a lot of regimentation, but made each of us a little
more independent. And if any of us wanted to snare gophers,
whittle, or play mumblety-peg while the others were playing
pom, pom, pullaway, there was no one telling us "you gotta" play
with the other kids.

There Was More In It Than Money For The Boy With A Trapline

"Do farm boys do any trapping any more?" I asked Ralph Watts, the local fur buyer, the other morning.

"You bet they do," he replied. "And not only farm boys. There are a lot of town boys, and college kids, too, that trap for the sport and for the money it brings in."

I thought that trapping might have been something that had lost its appeal in the years that have passed since I was in grade school, but it seems I was wrong.

What prompted me to raise the question was a visit from Elmer Alink who came in with a handful of fur price lists and other memorabilia relating to trapping dating back to 1922.

How those printed sheets brought back memories!

Every fall about this time the farm magazines would carry ads from fur buying firms, mostly in St. Louis. Each ad had a coupon one could fill out with his name and address. "Mail in the coupon," said the ad, "and we'll send you our newest trapping catalog and fur price lists."

I'd maybe send in a half dozen — to Hills Bros., Abraham Fur Co., F.C. Taylor Fur Co., Funsten Bros. and Co., and Fouke Fur Co., all in St. Louis, and M. Lyon and Co., in Kansas City.

In a week or two, I could go out to the mail box and there addressed to me personally were the big brown envelopes, filled with catalogs, order blanks, self addressed envelopes and shipping tags.

The catalogs were the big thing as far as I was concerned. They were jam packed with pictures of guns and traps and lures which, if one could raise a few dollars to send in an order, he became the .envy of all the neighborhood boys around him.

More than that, they carried a number of "how to" articles of interest to the boy trapper. There were drawings of the various furbearing animals and their tracks. The articles explained where to look for their secret hiding places, and what to look for to ascertain if there were any of the wily creatures there. They explained how to set the traps and how to handle the pelts.

I never sent away for anything because whatever I needed, I could buy at Hettingers Hardware in Beaver Creek. But that didn't mean I couldn't fill out an order blank just for the fun of it, and then not mail it.

My folks would never let me have a rifle. I could have sent for a Hamilton .22 single shot out of the Abraham catalog for only $2.25, or if I'd have wanted to go "first class," I could have ordered a Stevens Marksman with a tip-up lever action for only

$6.75. Postage was 30 cents extra. For $18.25 I could have ordered a Remington .22 Repeater, like the one Hank Christiansen had, which held 14 short rifle cartridges (which we always called shells).

I also wanted, but never could afford, some Newhouse traps. Newhouse was the Cadillac of the trap line. No. 1 size cost 54 cents, Elmer's 1923 price list shows. Dad said I could get along with a No. 1 Victor that sold for 20 cents or a Kompact "jump" trap was a better deal yet for only 13 cents. Some of the kids talked their dads into buying them the No. 91 double jaw Victor, but my dad said, "No, you'll catch just as many with what you've got," and I guess he was right.

I always wanted an Abraham smoker, and I never got that either. I would envision the wholesale skunk trapping I could do if I had one of those outfits that I could attach a hose to and pump smoke, from a special smoke bomb made for that purpose, into a skunk den. F.C. Taylor had a different style. It had a holder for the smoke bomb on the end of the cable and you'd push that all the way to the end of the den.

Another item pictured in that catalog always appealed to me, but I knew Dad would never go along with any of that kind of foolishness. It was a cap, on the front of which was a carbide lamp with a reflector. This was especially designed for night hunting or trapping. With the cap came a tank of what they called carbide, which was also used for lights on cars before the advent of electric lights. You'd light the little jet on the reflector, according to the catalog description, and you could shine the light up into the tree tops where the raccoons were hiding.

About the time school started in the fall, I'd begin checking the likely haunts of the furbearers.

I'd walk along the creeks to see if there were signs of mink. I knew what their tracks looked like from the drawings in the fur catalog. I looked for the tell tale mud mounds along the creek banks. Beneath these little mounds were the underground muskrat dens.

I looked around the pile of pink and white fieldstones in the pasture. Skunks and their smaller cousins, the civets, often set up housekeeping there.

The gravel pit in the pasture invariably had a burrow which a badger had dug in early spring or summer in his quest for striped gophers. Frequently, this was taken over by a family of skunks, and when this happened, it was easy to detect by just kneeling down and sniffing at the den entrance. Another almost sure spot for a den of this kind was in the gully through the field between home and the school house. And in the weed patch at the north end of the meadow.

I never went far beyond the boundaries of our farm, because the boys living on neighboring farms were doing the same kind of scouting that I did.

Skunks and civets were the easiest to catch, minks the hardest. Mothers and teachers would have preferred to have had it the other way around, because a young trapper's encounter with a skunk or a civet made him an outcast. His mother wouldn't let him in the house and the teacher wouldn't let him into the school.

I don't believe I was ever sent home from school, but I perhaps should have been. I didn't recall it, but Elmer Alink said he remembered being sent home one day, and that I was the only kid in school who didn't shy away from him. In fact, I went up and put my arm around his shoulder in sympathy.

During trapping season we'd be up before dawn to walk our traplines before breakfast and before school. The morning air was invigorating. It was quiet and serene. Now and then a pheasant would jet out of a weed patch. Or a blue heron could be seen stretching his neck in search of the source of the unfamiliar sound he had heard. Then, with a spring of his long legs and a flap of his mighty wings he'd head either upstream or downstream, and resume eating his breakfast of minnows and crayfish.

Now and then a family of teal would wing its way from the steam covered stillness of the creek's surface to the nearby cornfield. And occasionally, a flock of geese which had spent the night resting, would hear our steps and decide it was time to get up and start heading south again anyway.

During the trapping season, which generally ended for me about Christmas time, I'd get monthly reports from the fur companies on the prevailing prices.

Prices would be listed for extra large, large, medium and small and umprime for skunks; No. 1 extra large, No. 1 large, No. 1 medium, No. 1 small, No. 2, No. 3, No. 4 and kits for other animals. I'd always figure on getting the extra large price. Generally, the price I'd get was the medium or small, much to my disappointment.

I always dreamed about the day that I'd accidentally find a marten or a fisher or a silver fox in my trap. A No. 1 extra large silver fox would bring up to $600 (the price list showed); a marten would bring $50, a dark fisher $130. This compared to $1.90 for a choice medium sized muskrat; 50 cents for a top quality civet; $8.50 for a medium choice mink and $1.50 for an average medium sized broad stripe skunk. Skunks, incidentally, were classified as black, short stripe, narrow stripe, and broad stripe. The ones that ended up in my traps were generally the broad stripe variety, which brought the least money.

I'm somewhat surprise that some of the more avid do-gooders of today haven't thrown their weight around to have trapping of fur bearing animals banned.

When I was trapping, there were several good reasons why the sport was not only condoned, but encouraged. For one thing, any skunk or mink or weasel that was caught was one less to rob a chicken coop. And every farm in those days had a chicken coop. Secondly, it brought in spending money for farm boys that they would never have had otherwise. Another good reason for permitting trapping was that it kept a lot of boys out of mischief. The exercise and fresh air made them both strong and healthy, while at the same time they learned about nature in the greatest laboratory of all, God's out-of-doors.

Today, trapping is still a good sport. And it still brings in money. Furs are a natural resource and harvesting helps keep nature in balance. And any farm boy who takes it seriously — who makes it a point to study game habits, can pick up a tidy bit of change while he's out enjoying the great outdoors which most folks don't see because when summer is over, they come inside and stay there until spring.

Whatever Happened To High
School Skip Day?

I never hear of schools having high school skip days anymore. My guess is that most seniors today would be far too sophisticated to take a day off to go sightseeing with a chaperone on hand to make sure they didn't get out of line.

Cornball as it may have been, skip day as it was experienced by the Class of 1931, Beaver Creek High School, just happens to be one of the highlights of my high school years.

No one skipped school in those days. Prof. Norman Duckstad, the superintendent, wouldn't have permitted any of us to come on stage for our diplomas if we had deliberately taken a day off for anything except work. But, because we were seniors, we were given the customary day to do something considered worthwhile, but also enjoyable, and which might have some educational benefits.

Our class of 14 decided that what we wanted to do most was visit a real honest-to-goodness radio station, like WNAX at Yankton, South Dakota. It was one of the few strong stations that came in over the three-dial Atwater Kent and Crosley radios, and we had become acquainted with the voices of the personalities who were program regulars every day.

We had little or no money among us, so each of us brought a sack lunch and off we went over the gravel roads that led to Yankton.

We arrived without even having a flat tire.

WNAX was then located on the second floor of the Gurney Seed and Nursery Company warehouse. We inquired how to get to the studio, and someone directed us to a freight elevator which took us to our destination.

When announcers mentioned studios over the radio, we had envisioned something quite classy. They really weren't. Little had been done to the warehouse interior except to hang some burlap around the room for acoustical purposes.

Maybe we had planned it, I'm not sure, but when we entered the studio, we were asked to make a "guest appearance". We had a class song, a parody to "Memories". We sang it with classmate Jessie Spies Allen accompanying us on a piano. The class elected me to be their spokesman, and I had to tell about Beaver Creek and its venturesome class of 1931. After our song, some of the others were asked to say something into the microphone. Several were bothered with stage fright, even more than I was, and disappeared.

Chan Gurney, who later became U.S. Senator, was the announcer for our visit. We were thrilled at the attention that was given us, but much more exciting was seeing and hearing in person George B. German, the cowboy ballad singer, and Eddie and Jimmie Dean, a couple of other vocalists.

Because of the limited time we had, we missed some of the programming with which we were most familiar.

We did, however, get to watch and hear one of the most popular stars with the WNAX listening audience, the rotund Irish fiddler, Happy Jack O'Malley. Happy Jack had an orchestra he called the Old Timers and they'd be on the air as early as 7:30 a.m. with old time square dances, Virginia reels and waltz music, even though they might have come in from a dance engagement someplace in South Dakota only two or three hours earlier.

"Happy" would kid the announcers and the members of the orchestra and there was just a lot of good natured bantering going on all the time. This appealed to a lot of listeners and in many homes, the Happy Jack troupe became a part of the family every time they were on the air which sometimes was several times a day.

Another entertainer we heard regularly was a fellow who called himself the Shepherd of the Hills. He sang a lot of old time songs in a plaintive voice that caused us to picture him as a poor old cowboy who had an erring sweetheart, and who, when he was gunned down, pleaded with bad men to "Bury me out on the lone prairie, where the coyotes howl and the wind blows free. . ." When he wasn't singing alone, he joined the Sod Busters from the Bar O Ranch.

There were a couple of hotshot banjo players called the Banjo Twins. Actually, they were part of the Sod Busters gang, too. Between songs, a fellow by the name of Earl Williams was urging the "listeners out there in radio land" to buy their gasoline at WNAX Fair Price Stations, because alcohol, made from the cheap corn farmers couldn't get rid of during the depression years, was mixed with the gasoline to make the gas better, and at the same time, helped the farmer get a better price for his corn.

There were three other Sod Busters, Rufus, Ezra and Zeb, who talked a lot about the happenings on the "Bar Nothin' Ranch".

Entertainers had to be versatile in those days, believe me. Harvey Nelson, who was the program director, played sax for the Sunshine Four, another musical group that I suppose we'd call a "combo" today. One of the Sod Busters filled in on the banjo.

The House of Gurney, Inc. opened the radio station for the sole purpose of promoting merchandise they had for sale. They had a clothing department then and the announcer would make a pitch for their various clothing specials. George Gurney, whose picture appeared for many years on the Gurney Seed Catalog, came on the air once a day with nursery tips, which helped sell Gurney's apple trees and garden seeds.

A fellow who was called Slim Jim sang songs and read poetry.

Chan Gurney gave the news, weather and markets at noon each day and had a big listening audience. He became well enough known to win a senate seat in Washington some years later.

There were two other Gurneys, "D.B." and "Uncle Phil", who also did quite a bit of the talking and selling.

Another entertainer who was popular was a gal by the name of Esther. I'm not sure if her last name was Williams or Seils. She sang and accompanied herself on the cello.

There was a Bohemian Band that was popular with a lot of folks of Bohemian origin and others who liked their "oom-pah" style of music. It's hard to believe, now, that the whole band would come in to play just a 15-minute program at say two o'clock in the afternoon, only to be replaced on the air by the Sod Busters, Happy Jack, Slim Jim or Beanstalk Jack, who also had 15 minute shows.

There was no tape recording done then. Tape recorders as we know them today hadn't even been invented. Everything was live, and the House of Gurney, Inc. picked up most, if not all, of the tab for the entertainers. I'm sure the entertainers were paid minimal wages. But they were able to make up for some of it by moonlighting — going out to the little towns in the South Dakota, Nebraska, Minnesota and Iowa listening area for dance and stage engagements. They drew good crowds at these events because everybody who had a radio wanted to see their favorites in person.

At night, WNAX live shows were interspersed with network programs. Thus we here in the hinterlands became acquainted with folks like Fibber McGee and Mollie, Jack Benny and Rochester, Phil Spitalny and his All-Girl orchestra, Jack Armstrong, the All American Boy, newscasters like Boake Carter and sportscasters like Ted Husing.

Skip day also broadened our horizons geographically. That day, we drove over the Missouri River bridge into Nebraska. For most of us, it was the first time we'd ever seen the "Big Muddy" as the river was known then and it was also the first time many of us had ever been in a state other than Minnesota, Iowa or South Dakota.

We limited our sightseeing to the radio station and the river because we wanted to get an early start for home. I don't know how we managed it, but we were back in Beaver Creek before dark, tired but happy, and proud to say that we had visited the entertainment capital of our part of the world.

Working On The Farm

You Worked Hard, But Livin' Was Good At Threshing Time

If I could relive any of the "good old days", I'd probably want to go back to the grain threshing days of my youth.

The combines I see in the fields today would have been greatly appreciated then, I'm sure, but they'd have deprived me of some of the most enjoyable days I ever had on the farm.

I thought about this the other day as I saw a teen-age boy operating one of the monster-mouthed machines as it devoured a windrow of newly swathed oats. That kid, I thought, will never know what he missed by being born 40 years too late.

Working with a threshing crew meant you had to be a strong kid. With calloused hands. And a free spirit. Able to laugh at jokes, even though they were at your expense.

One of the best threshing experiences I ever had was the fall I worked for Ben Phillips. I must have been out of high school then, and the offer of $2.00 a day for pitching bundles meant that I had reached the stage of hired-man maturity. It also meant being up at the crack of dawn and milking three or four cows before hitching up the black team and heading down the dusty road, the horses trotting, and the bundle rack clattering. First man "up to the machine" in the morning, was the first to finish at night. It meant something to be early.

I guess the reason I liked to work for Ben was that he not only paid well, but he paid every Saturday night. A lot of the farmers wouldn't pay until you asked them for an advance, and then hardly enough to finance any kind of a Saturday night fling. The meals at the Phillips house, prepared by Ben's sister, Hilda, also made working there a delight for a growing boy. His brother, Reuben, provided live entertainment on his banjo.

Anyway, the main thing at threshing time was to get that rack loaded fast, so you could get up to the threshing machine in time to rest while the wagon ahead of you was still being unloaded.

I can still see Adolph Wallenberg on the old yellow Avery separator, red bandana around his neck, his shirt and overalls wet with sweat and caked with grease, chaff and dust, as he turned the crank on the blower to direct the straw to just the right spot to make the stack solid and properly shaped.

When Adolph wasn't looking, the young punks would try to "plug the machine" by pitching the bundles in so that the butts overlapped. This would throw the drive belt off the pulley and it meant a chance to sit down while the work of unplugging was being done and the belt was replaced.

Adolph never appreciated that kind of monkey business. His

choice of words as he verbally chastised the offender conveyed his disapproval so there was no misunderstanding, believe me.

The Wallenberg threshing rig was a brother-operated deal. Charley was the engineer of the big Case steamer. His brother, Fred, was the water monkey. What clowns they were!

Charley usually fired up the engine about 4 a.m. About the first thing he did after he'd built up a head of steam, was blow the whistle. When you'd hear the signal that sounded like "toot-toot-toot-toot-t--o--o--t, toot-toot-toot," you knew it was time to get going if any work was going to get done that day.

Fred spent his time telling stories and making the crew laugh when he wasn't away from the rig, getting a load of water. When the rig was in our neighborhood, he'd fill the big tank wagon from the creek that ran through our pasture. He'd put the big hose into the water, then get up on the wood platform at the rear of the tank and man the handpump that drew the water from the stream. Filling one of the big tanks — my guess is that it held 600-700 gallons — wasn't easy work, but then, you didn't haul too many loads in a day either.

You could usually count on Fred to have a half pint of moonshine hidden someplace. I don't think anyone ever located the hiding place, but the empty evidence would show up occasionally when it came time to clean up around the straw stack when the threshing season was over, or in the corner of a manger in the barn.

Threshing dinners were out of this world. Every farm wife was at her best when cooking for threshers. Usually, there'd be roast beef, or pork, chicken, or ham, cabbage slaw, mashed potatoes, corn on the cob or fresh string beans from the garden, fresh home baked bread, several kinds of jam and pickles, and fresh baked pie. At supper time, there was leftover meat served cold with American fried potatoes, homemade sauce, cake and cookies. Morning and afternoon lunch meant king size sandwiches, cookies, cake, coffee and lemonade for the "boys". Always, there was the urging from the cook or cooks as the food was passed, "Now, make out your dinner," "there are a lot more sandwiches here" or "it's a long time between now and breakfast."

The ride home was pleasant. The sun would be setting, it would get cooler, and the evening breezes were perfumed with those delightful harvest time fragrances — newly cut grain, growing corn, red clover in blossom. You could sit on the side of bundle rack if you had one of the open-sided kind, and you didn't have to trot the horses the whole way home the way you had to when you started out in the morning.

By the time you got home, had the horses unhitched, watered at the stock tank, unharnessed and fed, it was bed time. And believe me, you were ready to "hit the hay". With crickets chirping their even-song beneath your open window, you were asleep in minutes.

A Steam Threshing Rig

The work may have been hard, but the comraderie that the workers enjoyed made threshing a lot easier.

Grain stacks were a form of rural art

Novelist Frederick Manfred and I had many of the same boyhood experiences, including grain stacking. Frederick Manfred, his grandfather, father, uncle and brother are shown in this grain stacking scene.

Grain Stacks — An Art From That's Vanished From Rural America

Fred Manfred, Sr. and I shared many similar boyhood experiences.

Often, when we're together, we recall those days and reflect on the changes that have come about in the few (?) years that have elapsed, changes that have eliminated so much that was commonplace then to virtual oblivion.

Some time ago, Fred was going through some old snapshots and came upon one of a grain stacking scene, taken in 1919 when he was a youngster on his Dad's farm near Doon.

One day, when we happened to be chatting, he fished the envelope with some reprints out of his pocket, and asked "Did you ever help stack grain?"

"Did I ever!" I echoed. "Just about every fall for a while."

Grain stacking is now a lost art. Maybe there are a few still around who can "set" a stack, but there never were a great many who had the ability. Those who could were sort of specialists — the neuro-surgeons of the grain harvest season.

My Dad learned the tricks of the trade from my grandfather when he was growing up. He did our stacking, and helped some of the neighbors with whom we exchanged work.

Fred's father and grandfather, too, were grain stackers.

Like me, Fred never served an apprenticeship in the trade, because smaller tractors and threshing machines became commonplace, eliminating the need for stacking. There were more farmers buying small rigs, and it didn't take too long to get a fall shock threshing run out of the way.

Fred recalled his father raised an early variety and a late variety of oats.

"That gave us more time to get the harvesting and the stacking done," he explained. "We'd cut the early oats first, and we'd start stacking them right after we got the late oats cut.

"Dad always liked to get a little rain on the shocks before we started stacking.

"He always wanted the grain to be golden ripe when it was cut. But even then, the straw didn't like to let go of the grain."

Something happened to the grain panicles or heads during the period the bundles were in the stack prior to threshing. The grain attained a greater degree of ripeness and it threshed more readily.

I remember Dad walking around the stacks a few days after they were up, reaching his hand a full arm's length into the side of the stack to check if the bundles had begun to sweat. Once the sweating period was over, threshing could begin any time.

That was one of the advantages of stack threshing. After the stacks were in place, the threshing could be done whenever a rig was available. This might even be in mid-winter if corn picking came on real fast in the fall.

A grain stacker had to be skillful. He had to be light on his feet, strong in his arms and shoulders; he had to have perceptive eyes and a feel for symmetry.

"Kind of like a dancer," is the way Fred described him.

He had to make just the right steps with his feet, and the right movements with his hands and arms as he deftly placed the bundles in rows one atop the other to make the circular stack.

If he made a mis-step, the side of the stack was apt to slide out, and it was necessary to take the whole thing apart and start over.

"The middle always had to be kept high," Fred recalled. "The bundles on the outer edge were kept just a little lower than those in the center of the stack."

When I was big enough to haul bundles, Dad made it clear that there were two ways to pitch them from the load to the stacker — the right way and the wrong way.

The right way was to keep your eye on the stacker and pitch them so the butts were pointed to the outer edge of the stack, no matter where the stacker happened to be.

Dad also liked to have them fall binder-knot side up some times, and other times binder-knot side down. That meant less handling for him on the stack. Once a person learned how to do it, it was just as easy for the bundle pitcher to do it right as to do it wrong.

The stack was started by first building a big shock. This meant setting the bundles head up fanning them out as far as possible without permitting any of the grain heads to lie on the ground. The first row of bundles was then laid atop the outer edge, then the second row, etc. always keeping the center higher than the edge.

As each row went up, the stack became just a bit wider until it was about four feet high. Then the stacker would start "drawing" it in, making each circular row a little smaller than the one beneath it.

The stacker took each bundle as it came, laying it down so that it overlapped the one beneath it by just the proper distance. As he stepped on it to pack it into its proper place, he reached out with his fork for the next bundle. He developed a rhythm — reach for the bundle, lay it in place, step it down, reach for the bundle, lay it in place, step it down.

Finally, there was room for only one last bundle, and the stack was finished. By that time, however, the stacker had to be very

careful to lay each bundle perfectly. At the very end, he slid his
fork down the side of the stack, and got down on his hands and
knees to lay the final dozen or so.

The final touch was either sticking a spiked tree-limb or a heavy
lath through the top bundle down into the stack to hold it down,
or tying a bundle to a long piece of binder twine, tossing it over
the top of the stack so it would hang down the other side. A second bundle was tied to the other end.

Four such bundles, with the twine criss-crossed over the top
would keep the top of the stack from blowing off should a high
wind come through before threshing time.

The finished stack had the same rain-shedding qualities as a
thatched roof. No matter how many rain showers a stack would
go through in the fall, the oats came out as bright and golden as
the day they were cut, unless of course, they'd become discolored
while they were in the shock.

There were exceptions, however, particularly if the stack had
been built by someone without know-how, or someone had been
careless in not packing the bundles solidly. When that happened,
rain would soak through and find its way to the bottom. There,
the bundles would become wet and mushy, fit only for a ride back
to the field in a manure spreader.

Each day was a long one during stacking time. It meant getting
up to get the milking, separating and calf feeding done, the
horses fed, curried and harnessed, and breakfast out of the way so
that the bundle wagon could be rattling its way to the field before
7 a.m.

There were three welcome breaks during the day — morning
lunch, noon dinner, and afternoon lunch. Noon dinner was at
least an hour break — to give both man and horses time to eat,
and a few minutes to rest, and perhaps even a quick nap.

After the last bundle went on the stack during the late afternoon, there was supper and the evening chores which quite often
weren't finished until 9 o'clock. There was only one place the
stacker and bundle pitcher wanted to go at that time — to bed.

Fred reminded me of the competition which usually existed
among the bundle pitchers.

Each would start out filling the bottom portion of the rack by
trying to lift up an entire shock of grain at one time, and as rapidly as possible. As the rack began to fill, it was necessary to start
laying the bundles carefully with butts out so the load would not
spill going in from the field to the stack or the threshing rig.

The horses soon learned how to follow the shock rows, starting
and stopping on signal.

The reins (we always called them lines) were tied to the cross
piece atop the ladder at the front end of the rack. When it was

necessary to steer the team along the row, the bundle pitcher would do so by reaching one line or the other with the tined end of his fork, and pulling it taut while telling the team to "giddap".

Bundle hauling, whether for a stacker or a threshing rig, was hot, exhausting work. But it was challenging, and it usually paid 25 to 50 cents more a day than regular farm labor, a lot of money in those days.

Another plus was the food that was served during the stacking and threshing season.

No one had to count calories. Even with the extra food consumed, a threshing crewman could easily lose 10 pounds before the season ended.

If the crop was heavy, and the season lasted longer than usual, a rainy day was always welcome. Fred described it more aptly. He said it was a "blessing". It meant taking it a little easier, maybe a nap in the hayloft, or a trip to town for a game of pool with the boys.

Fred and I agreed that the stack settings as they were called added a distinctive touch to the rural scene in autumn.

Like the leaves turning color, the incessant chorus of crickets as night descended, and the "shypokes" returning to the creek bank, the stacks reminded us that the long days of summer were at an end, and that the long nights of winter would follow in short order.

There Was Something Satisfying About Making Hay

I saw a self propelled hay swather in operation in a hay field the other day and the thought came to me, "Things have really changed in this haying business since I was a boy on the farm."

A lot of the hard work has been taken out of it, that's for sure.

But I wonder if some of the pleasures — or at least what my memory now recalls as pleasure — haven't disappeared because of the machinery and the methods now used.

Dad always made sure we had plenty of hay.

We had wild hay in the meadow of necessity. The creek wound its way through the meadow, and cultivation was impractical because the ground was always wet at planting time. There was always the possibility of a summer flood which would have washed out everything if the ground had been tilled.

Then we had alfalfa. Dad used the alfalfa in his crop rotation plan to give the land a rest and a shot of natural nitrogen, at the same time. The end result was a supply of succulent green hay for the milk cows in winter.

I never could see the sense of Dad's alfalfa haying method, except, perhaps, it provided the best quality hay under all weather conditions.

I always thought that we put a lot of work into it before it went into the barn.

Before the start of haying, Dad would always put the mower sickles in shape. He'd add new sickle sections where they were broken or badly worn. Then he'd go out to the grindstone, under the old maple tree in the back yard, and there he'd pump the pedals to keep the stone rotating counter-clockwise. Now and then, he'd stop to pour water from a Calumet baking powder can onto the spinning stone wheel. It seemed to do a better job of sharpening when it was wet.

Ever so often, he'd have to replace a sickle guard, or one of the ledger plates. The ledger plates were similar to the sickle sections except they were smaller and were serrated on two sides. The sickle would fit snugly against the guards, once it was inserted in the sickle bar, and if both the sickle sections and the ledger plates were sharp, the mower couldn't help but do a clean job of cutting.

Dad was particular about the way the mowing was done.

"You've got to make sure that you drive all the way to the end before you turn the corner," he'd say. "We want square edges, and we don't want to leave any grass or alfalfa uncut."

We never had a side delivery rake, just a dump rake. So when the hay had been cut and had laid long enough to be nearly dry, we'd hitch the team to the rake and form windrows. Making a straight windrow with a dump rake was quite an art, too. I kind of liked raking. I'd hit the dumping lever with my foot, and once I got the rhythm, I could let the horses go at a pretty good clip and keep the dumping mechanism working smoothly so the hay rows would be straight.

Then, Dad would make sure that the hay was bunched. This was done by going the length of the windrow with the rake, piling the hay in bunches. There was some sense to that. It meant less work with the fork when we pitched it onto the rack wagon.

But I never could see the need for going out and making haycocks by hand, once the hay was bunched. But Dad liked the idea, evidently. For one thing, a field of bright green haycocks was beautiful to look at. And if it rained before we could get it in the barn, the haycocks did a pretty good job of shedding water which meant the hay quality would be better, and you could get back to haying sooner, once the rains stopped. It was a little easier to pitch from the cock into the rack, too. But making the haycocks took a lot of hand work with a pitchfork.

Some of our neighbors had hayloaders but Dad didn't like them. "They shake off too many leaves, and the leaves have the most food value," he always said. So, we'd pitch the hay onto the rack wagon, making sure the hayslings were properly laid on the rack, and that the trip rope latch was closed.

The trip rope latch was tricky. It had to be tightly hooked for one thing. Then we had to be sure that the rope attached to the latch to open it was laid flat under the wood slats of the slings.

When the load was a third full, I'd have to get on the rack and move the hay around so it was level. Then, I'd put on the second pair of slings, as carefully as I had the first. Generally, we'd have three slings on a load.

When the load reached a height that we could no longer get a forkful to lay in place, it was time to haul it to the barn.

Holding the pitchfork handle loosely with the thumb and forefinger of the left hand, we'd cradle the butt end of the handle in the right hand. Then, with a quick, forceful movement of the right hand, we'd send the fork sailing upward. Once a person acquired the technique, the fork would sail skyward, tines in the air, then it would arc and the tines would sink into the middle of the hayload. If the handle pointed straight up at a perfect 90 degree angle to the hay. which would be tramped down to make the top of the load flat before we headed home, one could be sure he had acquired the technique.

Riding home on a load of hay, I remember, was great sport before I was old enough to work in the hayfield. I'd climb up the front of the rack, in back of the horses, and sit down beside Dad and to the barn yard we'd go. Sometimes I'd even get to drive Daisy and Bess. But the real enjoyment was sitting in the soft, sweet smelling hay, and being 10 feet off the ground.

At the barn, we'd drive up beneath the big hayloft door, unhitch the team from the wagon and hitch them to the double tree attached to the big draw rope which lay coiled inside the alley-way door.

Dad would remain on the hay load, reach up and grab the pulley hook that led to the carrier track. This he would attach to the slings, which had metal rings, at either end of the rack. I should explain for the uninitated that this was a double hook affair that pulled apart, so one hook went to the rear end of the sling and the other to the front end.

That done, we were ready to put the hay in the barn.

Dad would stand atop the load, directing me, or whoever was driving the horses hitched to the big draw rope, when to start the team in the direction of the house. As the rope went through the pulleys, the ends of the slings came together and the hay started upward toward the carrier at the end of the single rail leading into the hayloft. As the hay started up, Dad would step back and get below the swinging sling load. As it continued upward, he'd grab the latch rope and snap the long trip rope, which he had carried with him to the top of the load, onto the latch rope.

I drove the horses as the rope and pulley system hoisted the hay to the very peak of the barn. There, the hook portion of the carrier device slammed into place on the carrier. This tripped the carrier lock, and sling load of hay disappeared through the big door. Dad could tell by how much of the trip rope he still held in his hand how far the carrier had traveled. When it had gone just the right distance, he'd pull the trip rope, the slings would snap apart, and the hay fell right where he wanted it to drop.

Inside, he made sure that the hay was properly leveled. By moving it around with a pitchfork, it lay just right so when it came time to start feeding it, it was easy to move forkful by forkful without tearing it all apart. It also meant fewer broken fork handles.

After a couple of loads had been hauled in during the afternoon, Mother would bring lunch to us. Lemonade never tasted better, and the sandwiches, fresh cake and cookies made up for the pay I didn't get. Dad sipped his coffee and chatted with Mom for a few minutes, then it was back to the field until chore time or the haying was done, whichever came first.

Today, haying is done a lot differently. The five-foot horse mower, the ten foot dump rack, the pitch fork, the slat slings, the trip rope and the double trees have all but disappeared from the rural scene.

Now there are hay elevators. Or, on some farms, tractor drawn field choppers follow the windrows, grinding the stems of hay into bits and blowing them into self-unloading wagons. This hay doesn't go into the barn, rather, it goes into the silo.

There isn't the manual labor involved in haying — except the bale handling, perhaps — that there once was, and that's good. But tired as we would be at the end of a day, there was a great feeling of satisfaction when Dad would say, "Well, you'd better hang the draw rope back up in the alley and close the big doors. We won't be putting up hay again now for another month or so."

You Did It Differently When You Made Hay With A Stacker

"You didn't say anything about hay stacking," I was reminded after I had written about my boyhood experiences on hay making.

Perhaps readers have already had their fill of hay, but for those who remember hay stacking, recall that it was a different phase of farming entirely. Particularly when you were stacking "wild" hay.

"Wild" hay was the native prairie hay that grew in the meadow, or on the uplands. In fact, Dad always left a strip of hayland about 10 or 12 feet wide at the end of each cultivated field for easy turn around with horse-drawn machinery. This we'd cut and haul to the barn to feed the horses and calves because there wasn't too much and there was room to store a little of it. But the meadow hay was stacked out in the field, to be hauled in as needed for the horses and the calves in the winter.

Mowing the meadow was tedious in one respect, but pleasant, nonetheless. There was a mixture of grasses there — and wild flowers in abundance when the first crop was cut shortly before the Fourth of July. The fragrance was delightful to the nostrils — coming mainly from the white clover and the alsike clover blossoms. The tall stems of timothy and red top stood sentinel-like above the shorter heads of blue grass and the thick white clover beneath it.

The narrow creek snaked its way through the center of the meadow. When the silt settled after a spring rain, the water trickled clear, and minnows darted around the little pools. Along its soft mud banks, the crayfish (we called them crabs) lived in holes which they had dug, piling the mud in a cone shape about them. They'd poke their heads out, but when they saw a person coming toward them, they'd disappear back into their burrows.

The red-wing blackbirds nested in the tall growth on the creek's edge. Bob-o-links wove their nests in the tall grasses where the foliage was dense. In the trees along the creek's edge, the crows raised their families, and now and then, we'd come across a brown thrush who preferred country living. Kingbirds sat on the fence wires, and yellow-breasted meadow larks warbled from their fence post perches.

In one corner was a patch of wild strawberries. We'd never find many, but in late June, we could generally pick a small handful of tiny berries with sweetness and flavor that has never been match-ed in the tame variaties. There were also patches of sorrel to be found, except we called it sourgrass. The stems and leaves had a sour flavor and it was always fun to reach down, pick a few and chew on them.

Violets and bluebells grew near the creek. And there were yellow buttercups and lilies of the valley. Wild roses thrived along the fence line. Before my time, wild tiger lilies grew there, Mother told me.

There was animal life there, too. Once in a while, the mower would pass over a nest of young cottontails. Now and then a plump field mouse would scurry beneath the fallen grass. We'd occasionally see a mother pheasant leading her chicks out of danger. Once in a while we'd catch a glimpse of a garter snake as it slithered out of our way and out of sight. Striped gophers and grey squirrels found the meadow a good place to live, because they could keep out of sight of the boys with snares, traps, and pails of drowning water.

Along the creek, we'd see evidences of wild mink and muskrat, but seldom did we see the animals themselves. The creek was also the home of dozens of frogs who found the grassy area nearby a delicatessen supreme with its gourmet menu of bugs and hoppers. As one walked along the creek bank, the frogs would jump in, kerplunk, and swim under water to the other side to resume their croaking chores. But back to haying.

Once the hay was raked and dry, we'd hitch a team to a buck rake which we always called a "bucker". This wasn't the easiest piece of equipment to operate, because the horses were not hitched together in the usual manner, but were the width of the bucker apart, each hitched to a pole protruding from either side. The bucker had long wooden prongs or tines that resembled those on front end loaders used on today's tractors. We'd drive down a windrow, get a load of hay on the tines, then head for the stacker.

The stacker was an impressive looking device — with pulleys and high beams. Once the hay was pushed onto the stacker tines, the driver of the team hitched to the stacker rope (usually me) said, "Giddap" and up went the bucker load of hay.

Dad usually was the man who built the stack. He'd direct the person on the ground where he wanted the hay dumped and whoever was the ground man would turn the stacker after the hay was well off the ground, with a long protruding handle which gave him the necessary leverage. When Dad would yell, "Dump!" he'd release a metal lever, and the hay would slide off the stacker fork onto the stack. The fork was then turned back to its position parallel with the stack, and it was lowered by operating another lever.

Lowering it was fun, because a lot of wheels and pulleys were turning. It would be moving pretty fast as it neared the ground. If one let it go, it hit the earth with a resounding thud. It was possible to brake the fall, however, and the last few feet were slow and easy like.

One of the neighbors who helped make hay stacking an unforgettable experience was Irvin Aaker. He had the knack it took to load a bucker just right, and to get it onto the stacker so not a wisp of hay fell off. Irvin fought in France in World War I and had learned all the bawdy barracks ballads. As he'd go to and from the stacker with his team and bucker, he'd raise his voice in song, much to the enjoyment of boys like myself, who were the part time "hired men" at haying time.

Dad was an expert hay stacker. When the job was done, the stack was round at the top so it looked like a huge green loaf of bread. It shed water like a shingled roof, and somehow, Dad made his stacks so they never had to be weighted down. They'd withstand the strongest winds once they "settled".

There were more neighbors around to help at stacking time than at alfalfa time, and Mother always made sure that the noon dinners were adequate for the working crew. There was home canned roast beef, new peas from the garden, fresh homemade bread and pie. No one could make hay and not have pie for dinner. The afternoon lunches meant hefty sandwiches, cake, cookies, coffee for the "men folks" and lemonade or "nectar" for the boys.

On the way home, we boys usually stopped for a swim in the pond in the pasture. Then, when we put our clothes back on again, we'd pick out the "foxtail" stickers that were lodged in our socks.

Once in a while, we'd have a special treat when we got home, a glass of Irvin Aaker's home brew. Those were prohibition years, and if anyone wanted beer, he had to make it himself. Irvin would make a batch now and then so it would be ready at haying time.

We had no refrigeration, so the brew was kept in a tub of cold water at the well. Someone would pump fresh water into the tub from time to time during the afternoon so it was refreshingly cool at supper time. By today's legal age standards for drinking beer, I would have been violating the law. But at that time, if we were considered old enough to do a man's job in the hayfield, we were considered old enough to enjoy a man's refreshment at the end of a hot day.

They make hay differently these days, and I don't know but what I'm all for it.

But anyone who has made hay with a bucker and a Jayhawk stacker will probably be like me. He has forgotten the hard work that went with it, and he remembers the good times.

And I guess that's the way it should be.

The bucker, a different haying machine

This wasn't the easiest piece of equipment to operate. We'd drive down a windrow, get a load of hay on the tines, then head for the stacker.

The barn Grandpa built

Grandpa combined American and Norwegian architectural styles when he built this barn in the late '90s. When it was finished, he hired several fiddlers and held a barn dance to celebrate the occasion.

Grandpa Combined Norwegian And American Architecture When He Built His Barn

I hadn't been inside Grandpa's barn for over 40 years — until a few days ago.

I wondered if it had changed much since those days when we played hide and seek by the hour in the tunnels that my uncles and aunts made in the hay piles in the big loft.

Basically, it was as I remembered it. The cattle barn interior was somewhat different. Stanchions had been installed to replace the partitioned cow stalls with their wooden mangers and feed boxes.

Someone in more recent years had raised hogs there, as evidenced by the farrowing crates scattered over the floor.

There was baled straw in the cavernous hayloft instead of hay. There was also straw in the room on the horse-barn side where Grandpa kept his surrey when it wasn't in use.

Grandpa Bjerk built the barn some 75 or 80 years ago. I remember reading a news story about it in an issue of the Rock County Herald some years back. It must have been quite the building in its day.

My mother, who lived on a neighboring farm, remembers when it was built. A fellow by the name of Charley Black, was the builder. And a good job he did, because even today, the framework is very straight, even though the structure has weathered some mighty powerful windstorms in its day.

Grandpa combined American and Norwegian architecture when he had the barn built. He had it constructed into the side of a hill, as so many barns in Norway were built. The bottom part was built of stone and mortar. The top part was built of lumber.

In its day, it was one of the warmest barns in the country. The cow barn, particularly, was warm, because it had no north or northwest doors. All the doors were on the east side; the west, north, and south sides had rock and mortar walls, almost two feet thick.

I couldn't help but wonder where the rock came from that was used in the wall. From its color and appearance, I'd guess perhaps it was quarried at the Blue Mounds, or the Palisades area around Garretson, then hauled by team and wagon to the farm northwest of Beaver Creek.

The horse barn, the carriage room, a grain storage bin and the hayloft were on the same level, above the cow barn. Hay for the cattle had to be shoved vertically down a chute into the mangers. Hay for the horses was pitched horizontally into the mangers because the floor of the stalls and the floor of the loft were on the same level.

The hayloft floor was built of one-inch boards, eight or ten inches wide. Everything considered, the floor is still in pretty good shape.

It was on that floor that one of the big social events of the season was held the year the barn was built. Grandpa lined up some fiddlers, and invited all the neighbors to celebrate the occasion at a big barn dance.

Mother was too young to go to the dance, but she remembers watching the many teams and buggies that went past their home and headed down the lane to Grandpa's yard to initiate the new barn properly.

Grandpa was a great believer in lightning rods when they first came out, and I remember as a boy, the barn had several lightning rods on it, all of them grounded by a cable leading from the peak of the roof to a stake in the ground.

A long wooden ladder, leading from the lower edge of the roof to the peak, still is affixed to the roof which has never had to be reshingled, as far as I know, since the barn was built.

The barn had wooden cupolas when I was a youngster, but they're gone now. It was in those cupolas that the barn pigeons raised their two-chick broods, every summer.

When the loft was full of hay, so that it was possible to reach up and grab the lower part of the slat hayslings, my uncle, Olaf, and I would climb the ropes and hoist ourselves into the cupolas to look at the eggs and baby pigeons, and more times than not, to catch a live pigeon or two.

Today, there's a single metal cupola. In the darkness of the early evening, I could see the form of a pigeon's head and neck craning over the edge of the opening, ready to take off had I come any closer. Boards and shingles now cover where the other cupola had been.

In the horse barn, long metal rods protruded from the wall in back of the stalls. It was there that the harnesses and collars were hung, after a long day in the fields, or after returning from a trip to Beaver Creek or Booge with a load of grain. On the stall dividers were nailed worn horseshoes. These made convenient hooks for hanging tools, harness parts, straps and the like.

Swallows, which have swooped in and out of open doors and windows for three quarters of a century, still build their sculptured nests in the barn.

Each year, before raising their young, the swallows go out in pairs, spending many days bringing in beakfuls of soft mud from around the water tank or the creek, some using bluegrass stems for reinforcing material, and fashioning it into a semi-round bowl against a rafter or ceiling joist. Once the mud hardened, the swallows lined it with grass and feathers, and there laid their eggs.

Within three weeks, a half dozen hungry mouths would appear over the edge of the nest. To satisfy their famished youngsters, the parents busied themselves from dawn until dusk, performing aerial acrobatics while capturing flying insects, the vitamin-protein packed energy food that makes tiny birds grow big and strong in a hurry.

From the barn I went to the granary, the first building on the place. According to the Sept. 18, 1885 Herald, it was built that summer.

The granary served as the family home before the house was built.

The stairs from the ground floor to the second floor are worn deeply, an indication of the hundreds of times they had been used. Grandpa's mother — my great grandmother — once had a loom in the loft on which she wove rugs and maybe even cloth at one time, using skills she had learned in her native Norway.

Both the barn and the granary reflect the passing of time, and the stress of the elements. While both buildings are still used, they are in a state of disrepair, and with changes that have taken place in farming over the years, are obsolete.

When I told Carmen Suurmeyer about re-visiting the old homestead, she handed me a poem, by Carlee Swann saying, "Then you'd enjoy this."

I did enjoy it, and here it is:

INSIDE THE BARN AT NIGHT
With supper done, we'd warmly dress
And wade through snow with eagerness,
To watch our Daddy milk Old Bess
Inside the barn at night.

The lantern hanging on the wall,
Lit up the horses in the stall,
And though we still were very small,
We liked the barn at night.

We perched upon the manger rail,
And watched the milk shoot in the pail,
While Bessy slowly swung her tail
Inside the barn at night.

The barn had such a friendly air
Of warm contentment, now so rare;
Somehow it seemed so peaceful there,
Especially at night.

In dreams I clasp your ready hand
Across the space that years have spanned,
And for a moment we two stand
Inside the barn at night.

Shocking Corn Was A Test Of Patience And Strength

One thing today's farm boys can thank their lucky stars for is that they don't have to shock corn.

If it hadn't been for the modern field choppers and the several methods now used for storing chopped corn stalks and silage, this would have been one of those years when a lot of corn would have been cut and bundled with a corn binder.

Dad always called it "fodder corn". Sometimes he'd plant corn for fodder purposes only, using the tip and butt kernels of the seed corn for the fodder which was drill-planted, and the flat kernels for the regular corn crop which was check-planted.

Fodder corn stalks were usually still a little green when they were cut with a horse-drawn single row corn binder. The bundles, containing about 20 stalks, and measuring about 10 inches in diameter, were not only heavy, but they were hard to handle.

This meant that two men had to work together while shocking, with one holding the first bundles in place, while the other laid more bundles around them until they would stand alone. When the shock was about three feet in diameter, a strand of binder twine would be wound around it and tied to keep the bundles in place until they were totally dry and ready to be hauled to the feed yard.

You could get hired men for most any farm job, particularly in the fall, but not many of them were available if they knew you wanted them to shock corn. There's no question about it, it was a disagreeable job.

Hauling them in to the yard later in the fall also was a miserable job. Invariably it was cold — and windy. Sometimes, the job didn't get done until after the first snow, and if a rain preceded the snow, you could bet that some butts of the bundles were frozen to the ground. Sometimes the bundles were full of snow. Lifting one to the top of the loaded hayrack would mean a whoosh of snow and ice in the face.

If the bundles weren't loaded just right, you could almost bet there'd be a "slide-out" on the way home as the rack wagon would tilt ever so slightly on a side hill.

If the shocks had stood for a time, it wasn't unusual that they were "occupied".

Lift a few bundles and out might hop a cottontail. Or a skunk would pop his sleepy head out from an opening between two bundles. When that happened, it meant moving to another shock immediately to avoid a confrontation. Invariably when the last bundle was raised above the ground, a roly-poly field mouse would scurry down the row in search of another home.

It always seemed to me the cattle wasted more of the fodder than they ate because when it came time to clean up the yard at manure hauling time in the spring, it meant breaking the back all over again, trying to pull the stuff loose with a 4-tine fork.

A lot of artists have drawn and painted corn shocks as a picturesque part of the autumn scene. Chances are they never had to shock or haul corn bundles.

Double-Thumb Mitts And A Good Hook Were Basic Tools Of The Pro Corn Picker

Every time I drive down the road in the fall and see a picker-sheller operating in a cornfield, I find myself wanting to say "Wow!"

Four rows at a time, at a speed faster than a man can walk. And no shoveling!

I'm sure there are many who share my amazement at the marvels of mechanized corn picking. It wasn't ever thus, let me assure you. When I was a "boy ON the farm" every single ear had to be picked one at a time, by hand. Today it hardly seems possible that this was the accepted method of harvesting corn.

Generally corn was picked by hired hands — young fellows who liked to compete with others and themselves in a sport that had some monetary dividends.

It was kind of like golf. Each day a man went out, he'd try to pick more bushels than he had picked the day before, just as the golfer tries to shoot a better game each time he plays at the country club.

Instead of a scoreboard, the corn picker would carry a little pocket notebook, which he probably had picked up at the hardware store or elevator in town. On the cover of the notebook was an advertisement for Plymouth binder twine or some such agricultural necessity. On the inside, he'd write the number of bushels he picked forenoon and afternoon. Usually he had a brother or a neighbor working in the same field with him. Each would see how much they could pick in a day, and also who could cover two half-mile rows in the least possible time.

Each corn picker had to have certain basic tools of the trade. No. 1 was a good corn picking hook, or peg. I always used a hook, a metal device that was attached to a leather harness affair that slipped over the hand. The hook was attached to a piece of steel shaped to fit the palm of the hand, and it was held in place with a wide band that buckled around the wrist. There was another style of hook shaped to fit in the center of the palm of the hand. The peg, which preceded the corn husking hook in time, was a pointed metal prong which was held in more-or-less closed fist fashion.

In addition to a good hook, he needed good double-thumb husking gloves or mittens. A good corn picker would buy a dozen pairs of new brown Yankee gloves or mittens every Saturday night when he went to town. If he bought the cheaper white ones — with the blue wrist band sold under the Boss label — he'd wear out more than a dozen pairs on both sides in a week.

He also wore "sleeves". Sleeves were usually homemade of

denim recycled from the unworn parts of discarded overalls or jackets. They were usually pinned with a safety pin to the shirt sleeve above the elbow. At the other end, a round hole had been cut for the thumb to go through. The gloves or mittens, then, were worn over the sleeves. The main purpose for the sleeves was to save wear and tear on shirtsleeves, and to keep the wrists from being exposed to the cutting edges of dry corn leaves. They served their purpose well.

There was also optional equipment for the corn picker. Sometimes, he wore a leather thumb guard with a rough steel facing. This helped to make husk removal easier, although it may have been a little cumbersome. And then there was the leather wrist band. This was strapped around the left wrist (the hook was worn on the right hand if you were right handed) to give it added strength, or for protection if it had been sprained.

Not everyone had one, but another popular option was an Ingersoll or a Westclox Pocket Ben watch, which was worn in the breast pocket of the bib overall, and was attached to the overall by means of a braided leather watch chain or a narrow "whang" leather strap in which slits had been made in each end with a pocket knife.

Not every farmer had a grain elevator those days, so it meant that the corn picker had to unload with a scoop shovel, after he'd spent a half day picking it. Wagons for this purpose were equipped with "scoop boards" at the rear, which, when opened, provided a platform on which the man could stand when he started to unload. And unloading didn't mean just throwing the corn over the edge of the wagon.

It often meant hoisting it above the top rim of a wire or slat corn crib, that stood 10 or 12 feet high. Usually, though, he was paid an extra cent per bushel for unloading the load by hand. If he had a full triple-box load with a heap on it, that meant he had about 40 bushels. So, he collected an extra 40 cents for unloading his corn.

There were some, however, who could pick a hundred bushels of corn per day or more. At eight cents a bushel, plus room and board, the good corn picker could make his winter spending money and then some.

It takes some doing, however, to pick 100 bushels per day or more. First of all, it takes a big wagon. As I remember it, a regular triple box lumber wagon held 36 bushels. To make it hold more, the corn picker would add extra side and end boards. Sometimes, to keep the corn from rolling off on the way into the farm yard from the field, he'd take the top board off the bang board, and put it on the other side of the wagon.

If you were a right hand picker, then the bangboard was always on the right hand side of the wagon. These were boards stacked one above the other against which you'd throw the ears. The ears would hit the board, then drop down into the wagon.

In the early morning, sometimes even before sunrise, you could hear the sounds in the cornfields of the neighborhood . . . bang, pause, bang, pause, bang as the solid ears hit the bang board. This went on for about half the morning. By that time, the corn had piled high enough in the middle of the wagon that it began peeking over the top of the wagon box. Soon thereafter, corn would hit corn instead of the board, and the sound could be heard only by the fellow doing the picking.

The picking itself took on an art form, sort of a clodhopper ballet. The picker usually husked two rows at a time, picking first from the row nearest the wagon then leaning over the picking the one beside it.

The 100 bushel or better men made every move count. The right hand would husk the husk off on one side of the ear. The left hand would pull the remaining husk from the ear as the right hand jerked the ear from the stalk and tossed it into the wagon with the same arm motion. While the ear was sailing through the air, he was reaching for another, and taking the necessary step to the next stalk.

I admit I was never much of a corn picker myself. I had a city cousin who always was able to do better than I did. My dad wasn't fast either, but for a good reason.

If there was anything Dad appreciated, it was a good ear of corn. He liked to pick ears for showing at fairs and corn shows, and he also picked them for seed to sell to his neighbors. (This was in the days of Early Murdock, Golden Jewel and Minnesota No. 13 varieties, before the advent of DeKalb, Pioneer, Funks and other hybrids.)

He always had a wooden box wired to the side of the wagon. He could tell by "hefting" the ear whether it would be a seed ear or not without even looking at it. He'd toss a hundred or so into the wagon between each seed ear that he'd toss into the little box.

By day's end, he usually had a half bushel of seed corn that he'd hang up in the granary loft on some wire seed corn dryers. There they'd stay until spring unless he decided to pick out the 10 or 25 best ones to show at the Garretson fair or at special corn shows in Luverne, St. Paul or Chicago.

When I first started to pick, before I had my own team and wagon, I'd help Dad after school and on Saturdays. Then, we'd take three rows. I'd pick the one nearest the wagon, while Dad picked the other two.

A lot of times, Mother would help him. She would walk out to the field with his afternoon coffee and lunch about 3 p.m. After the coffee break, she'd help him to the end rows, and sometimes would go another pair of rows with him. It wasn't that she didn't have anything to do at home, or that she liked to pick corn. But she and Dad always enjoyed being together, and this provided them an opportunity to work and visit at the same time. It made a better day for both of them.

Hired man with load of corn

It took a bit of doing to pick a hundred bushels a
day. This load of about forty bushels represents a
half day's work. Author, at age 15, is standing
beside the wagon.

Yesterday's water
jug . . . see it?

As vital a piece of
farm equipment as
a pitch fork or a
nose basket.

Yesterday's Water Jug Has Become Today's Valuable Antique

I am not an antique buff, even though I am interested in personal history.

I can go into an antique shop or store, and what I generally see I would classify as junk.

An "antiquer", on the other hand, would be fascinated with almost everything there, recognizing each item for its value as a collector's item.

An ordinary crockery gallon jug with no marking as to its origin might sell for $5 or $6 at an auction sale, so I'm told. The price goes up from there, depending on the historical value of the jug, and also if it is being "retailed" by an antique dealer. Some get up into the $50-$60 bracket.

They weren't always worth that much money.

In fact, they usually were "thrown in" on the deal when you bought molasses or vinegar at the grocery store.

Back before prohibition, I'm told, they were used as containers for corn whiskey. These are the ones, if so labeled, that bring the premium prices now.

It wasn't until the gallon Thermos jug ("Keeps food or liquids hot or cold") was introduced, that the crockery jug started to disappear from the farm scene.

Before that time, it was as vital a piece of summer farm equipment as a pitch fork, nose basket or spiral roll of sticky fly paper.

About the time the first hay crop was ready to "put up", Dad would locate the old jug in a corner of the wash house, then head out to the granary to find a worn gunny sack.

He'd carefully wrap the jug in the sack, so only the neck and handle were exposed. Next, he found a ball of binder twine which he wound around the burlap covered jug, criss-crossing the strands of twine in all directions, until there was no way that the covering would come loose.

The cob pile was the next stop. There he'd pick out a bright, pink corn cob which fit perfectly as a stopper in place of the original, but long-lost, cork. A hame strap from an old set of harness would complete the renovation. This was run through the jug's handle and buckled.

Now, instead of a plain old buff colored jug with a glazed brown top, it was a water container capable of keeping fresh water, pumped from the nearby well, cool and refreshing for the greater part of a hot morning or afternoon.

The secret, of course, was in wetting the burlap sack that surrounded the jug by dipping the jug in the water tank, after it had been filled at the pump. The evaporating process provided the refrigeration and if kept in the shade during the day, one could return to it time and again, and enjoy the treat of a cool refreshing drink.

The hame strap was fitted into the handle of the jug for carrying purposes. If you were heading out to the field with the horses to hitch up to to the cultivator or binder, you'd slide the strap over one of the hames (the curved metal device that fitted around the heavy horse collar) and old Bess would carry the jug without a bit of fuss, even though surplus water from the wet sack dripped on her and ran down her foreleg.

Or, you might slide the strap over a lever of a machine or through the ring end of an endgate rod of a lumber wagon.

If you were hauling hay or bundles, you could strap it around one of the boards on the hay racks.

At haying time, the jug was tucked under a haycock, or was set on the shady side of the ever growing haystack. At cultivating time, it was placed in the shade of a clump of weeds, or the wild plum tree along the fence line.

During the harvest season, the hired men doing the shocking would tuck the jug under a shock. When they became thirsty, they'd head for the shock, lift up the jug, pull out the corn cob, then lift it to their lips to let its cool contents bubble out.

Most everyone would hold the jug in both hands while drinking from it.

But not Roy McCurdy, one of our neighbors . . . Roy would pick up the jug with his forefinger through the handle, then with a flick of his wrist, he tipped the jug so it was cradled in the crook of his elbow. With his left arm at his side, he maneuvered the jug to his mouth with his right hand, letting its cool contents quench the thirst brought on by the big smoked ham steak that he'd eaten for dinner, and the heat of the summer sun.

As kids would say now, the way Roy handled that jug was "really neat".

When I was finally big enough to handle the jug in that fashion, Dad came home from Hettinger's Hardware in Beaver Creek with one of the new-fangled Thermos jugs with the round aluminum top that doubled for a drinking cup.

It seemed to me that the water from the Thermos jug was never as cool or as refreshing as from the burlap-covered jug. Missing too, was the clucking sound that the old jug made when it was being emptied.

While on the subject of water cooling devices, I should also mention our summer refrigeration that required no energy, other than that needed to hoist or drop a rope.

The cistern beside our house served as our cooler for cream, butter and other foods that "wouldn't keep" if stored at room temperature.

Placed in a bucket and lowered into the cool water of the dark, rain-water storage well, butter would remain firm and the cream would stay sweet until it was hoisted up and carried back into the kitchen.

When you wanted to open the "refrigerator" door, you grabbed hold of the cistern pump which was bolted into the concrete cover and turned the pump. This would slide the cover sufficiently to provide an opening through which the milk or cream or butter could be lowered or lifted.

When you wanted to close the refrigerator door, you merely turned the cover back again.

We, of course, never had ice cubes for our lemonade or cold drinks. Mother always made those drinks fresh as they were needed. To get the coldest water possible from the well, she would send me out to pump about 20-25 gallons into the stock tank first, then I filled the kitchen water bucket.

The water then did come out icy cold and condensation would form on the outside of the bucket. When the pail was sweating, it was a sign the water was cold.

The wild cherry or grape pop they sold for a nickel a bottle at Strand and Tveidt's Booge store couldn't compare with the drink Mother made with cherry or grape nectar she bought in big bottles from the Rawleigh or Watkins man.

A couple of times I made Hire's root beer, mixing the root beer extract, sugar and yeast in the prescribed quantities and then bottling it in catsup bottles that had been saved or collected for that purpose.

To cool the bottled root beer, or watermelons, we'd put them in a wash tub and pump cold water on them, letting the water do the refrigerating, changing it as often as necessary.

After a couple or three hours, the root beer or melon would be as cool as the water around it — and a delicious beverage it was, too, if you could wait long enough after it was bottled to permit the yeast to settle to the bottom of the bottle.

Some of our neighbors who had windmills also had cooling tanks.

Steady pumping meant a steady supply of cold water in the cooling tank, which made it an ideal place to keep the partially filled cream cans, the watermelons and bottles of home brew which a few of them managed to have on hand to sit down with after a hot day in the field.

Mangers, Milk Stools, Hungry Cats
And The Cream Man

We didn't have a dairy herd on our farm.

We simply had milk cows.

We didn't call what we did dairying. We called it milking.

There just wasn't anything sophisticated about it. No Surge milkers, no milking parlors, no electrically refrigerated coolers, no automatic manure handling, no automated feeding systems.

Like every farm boy, the first man's work I ever did was milk a cow.

Because it was a morning and night affair, seven days a week, in the heat and dust of summer and the cold and dampness of winter, it was neither exciting nor rewarding work.

I should add, however, that it could have been worse.

Dad didn't go much for the dairy type cows — the Holsteins, Jerseys, Brown Swiss, etc., so we didn't have a lot of cows to milk, even by those days' standards.

The cows he kept for milking were generally the beef type that at most gave a bucketful of milk per milking when they were fresh, but produced some pretty good calves for the market.

We generally milked eight or ten, enough to produce the milk supply we needed for the house, enough to get the calves started, with enough skim milk left over after separating to feed the pigs. And the cats.

Because he wasn't so keen about milking himself, Dad never felt it was worth the while to have stanchions in the cow barn. Mangers were good enough, each with its feed box, and a tie-chain that I soon learned to toss over a cow's neck and fasten it below in a couple of easy motions to keep her confined to the stall, once she was in the barn.

Summertime usually found the milk cows at the far end of the pasture, both morning or night. So, every morning at a little after daybreak, it meant a walk of a half mile or so to round up the cows and bring them to the barn yard, and the same in the late afternoon. There wasn't much for them to come home for, really.

In the fall, winter and early spring, we'd feed them inside, and then they usually came home to eat. But in the spring and summer when there was plenty of grass, they preferred to stay in the pasture.

We sometimes could get them to come home by calling to them. "Come Boss, Come Boss" was the signal that it was milking time. If they didn't come when summoned, they at least were alerted that someone soon would be coming over the hill to get them headed down the narrow path they had themselves created by walking to and from the barn.

When we did feed them, it wasn't a specially formulated mixture of protein, mineral and roughage pouring out from a push button feed distributing system.

It was alfalfa hay, pitched down from the hayloft and gently laid in the manger with a pitch fork. And some oats or ground corn, distributed in what once had been a gallon corn syrup pail to the feed box in front of each cow.

Dad never went for the one legged milk stool, he wanted something more sturdy, more substantial — something that he didn't have to grab quickly when he stood up. So he made four-legged stools. He liked his a certain height. Mine was a little higher.

I finally got so I could handle the one-legged kind pretty well, however, when I'd "hire out" and work for the neighbors during harvest and haying.

When I first learned to milk, we didn't have a radio in the house, say nothing to having one in the barn where today a radio is standard equipment. But that didn't mean we didn't have music.

We made our own, singing songs that we knew, and providing rhythm accompaniment by squirting the milk into the bucket to the tempo of the song. When the pail was empty, it sounded kind of like the beat of a kettle drum. But as the pail filled with milk; the sound became more muted, like that of brushes on a snare drum.

Milking was less pleasant during the summer months, when the flies started to bite. We'd buy a gallon of "fly dope", as Dad called it, from the Rawleigh man or at Hettinger's Hardware, and each cow would be sprayed to keep the flies away at least while she was being milked. This didn't mean, however, that a fly wouldn't sting her some place, and that would set her tail in motion. Many a time, my straw hat saved me from a sound slap in the face with a cow's tail.

Cats that spent the day hunting gophers or mice, headed for the barn each morning and night for their liquid diet of whole milk. We always had a cat dish and it would be filled with fresh warm whole milk each time one of us finished milking a cow.

A lot of times, we'd aim a squirt of milk at a cat to make him run. But some of them caught on that the milk squirted at them was the same as they were lapping up from the pan. They'd turn around, and as we aimed the stream toward them, they'd open their mouths and drink as though it were water from a fountain. From that stage, they progressed to the point where they would sit on their hind legs and "meow" for attention — and for a stream of milk.

It was fun, but Dad didn't cotton much to those kinds of shenanigans because he wanted to get the milking done as soon as possible.

Today's dairy farmers skip one of the steps we had in producing butterfat for market.

Today, they sell whole milk. We always separated it, and this meant carrying the milk in buckets and cans to the milk shed, which was near the house, to run it through the old DeLaval separator — the hand cranked machine with a bell on it that quit dinging when the number of crank revolutions reached 60 per minute. A narrow stream of cream came out of the one spout, a larger stream of skim milk from the other.

Generally, a good share of the skim milk went back to the barn to be fed to the calves. The cream went to the house and into a 10-gallon cream can in the cellar. That was our milk cooler, and not a very effective one, either, but sufficient for the demands of that era, and the kind that was common at most every farm in the neighborhood.

We always saved enough cream from each milking for coffee, Cream of Wheat, homemade puddings, and all the "creamed" foods Mother prepared.

Some would be permitted to become sour, for use in cooking, on fresh strawberries, and Dad always liked it on Sunday mornings when his favorite breakfast was a slice of bread, covered with sour cream, sprinkled with sugar.

Sometimes Mother let the milk "clabber". She made "Dutch cheese" with the curds, and used the whey for baking homemade bread.

Grandma sometimes would cook the milk in a certain way to make a cheese recipe she brought with her from Norway. (No, it wasn't "gammel-ost" but a kind of primost, as I remember it.)

Twice a week a truck would drive on the yard filled with cream cans, some full, some empty. On the sides of the truck were the words, "Hills Co-op Cry." in big letters.

Chris Sjolseth was the first cream hauler I remember. He'd pick up the full can, leave an empty one, and any butter that Mother may have ordered. She would generally send a two or three-pound stone jar with Chris to the Hills Creamery to have it filled with their "92 score or better" butter. It was a little cheaper to buy it that way than in the pound prints.

We always looked forward to his coming. Generally, he'd bring some words of wisdom or news that he had picked up at other farms along the way, and he no doubt left with some of the same from our place.

His arrival was most eagerly awaited on the day the cream checks were issued. The check we got was never very big, but it usually paid the grocery bill, and that was the reason we milked cows.

Other things we could get along without until the hogs or the cattle or the chickens were sold. But groceries we needed regularly, and the size of the cream check usually determined what our menu would include other than the potatoes, meat and vegetables that we'd grown and canned ourselves.

Usually, there was enough left over, so Dad could give us children a nickel or a dime spending money on band concert nights in Beaver Creek.

Spring - The Queen of Seasons

March 1 Was Moving Day — Exciting For Some, Traumatic For Others

The balmy, spring-like weather we had last week made me wonder how many farm families will be moving the next few days from one place to another.

For as long as I can remember, March 1 has been the official moving day in this section of the country. When a farm is sold, or a farm lease is signed, the effective date is usually March 1. I imagine that was done originally to get away winter's blasts as much as possible, and still give the person who is moving a chance to get settled before spring's work begins.

For those who have experienced moving day personally, it is an unforgettable event.

It always was kind of exciting. But there was a trauma connected with moving, too.

The farmer himself and the bigger boys took it in stride, more or less. Usually they had been on the new place the previous fall, plowing the stubble. And, from time to time, they hauled machinery there when the weather permitted.

Everyone else, however, was keyed to a new and different pitch at the thought of settling in a different home. For the children of school age, it meant saying goodbye to their friends, and of being eyed with wonderment by the students in their new school. There was the worry of whether they would like the teacher and the kids. There was usually the school bully to contend with, and it took a little time to find out who were the leaders and who were the followers.

The lady of the house disliked moving more than the rest of the family, it seemed.

She'd have to learn whose "ring" was whose on the party line, and she'd have to learn to recognize the voices when she "listened in". She had to give up her activity in her ladies aid, and start working in a new one.

The house often didn't please her, and if it did, she had to become accustomed to it. She usually worried about whether the kitchen range would "draw" when it was installed so she could get the menfolks a good hot supper that night. She was appalled by the curtainless windows as she drove down the slippery driveway into the farmyard for the first time.

She found that the house smelled different from the one she just left. She generally could see a number of things she wanted changed right soon, meaning perhaps new paint on the kitchen woodwork, new paper on the living room walls, or new linoleum on the dining room floor.

Although the family had been talking about moving for some time, it came as news for the livestock, and not until they had been in the barns for several hours longer than usual on the morning of moving day, did they sense that something had changed or was about to.

Cows and horses both stared at their owner in amazement as he walked through the alley of the barn and made no attempt to turn them out. When the truck backed up to the barn door, and the loading of the cattle began, a chorus of anxious "moos" from the cows, and "maas" from the calves arose. These would continue until a day or two after all were settled in their new surroundings.

The family dog knew "something was afoot" too, for he followed closely behind the boy of the family to make sure that he was not going to be left behind.

Modern trucks and tractors made moving easier. When horses were more commonplace than tractors on the farm, moving day was considerably more work for both man and beast. You could tell Old Dobbin, who perhaps hadn't been harnessed since corn picking, didn't like the feel of the collar, the backpad and the crouper. And if the person doing the harnessing didn't watch out, the horse was apt to lay his ears back and turn his head around to nip him.

Hitched to a heavy load on a rack wagon, the horses would sometimes balk at the first tug on the doubletrees. But after a few neighbors came with their teams and racks to haul the smaller machinery items and the household goods, it didn't take long for all the horses to get the idea, and the trek began.

An early start was necessary, for no sooner would the sun come out than the frozen surfaces of the dirt roads would melt, and the footing underneath would be almost too slippery for a team to really "get down and dig". Unaccustomed as they were to doing any heavy pulling after a couple of months of inactivity, the team would soon be sweating and steam would rise from their backs as they trotted along in the chill of the morning.

By nightfall, the job had been accomplished, and everyone was tired, the fatigue being the result not only of physical exertion, but of the excitement of the day as well.

Sleep as a rule didn't come as quickly as one might expect as the events of the day and prospects for the future tumbled about in the mind. Lying in bed in the dark in a strange room, one couldn't help but wonder. Will we like it here? Will our neighbors be as friendly and as helpful as the ones we just left? What if the children don't get along in school? And, the one question that seemed to rise again and again, what if we don't get a crop?

On the morning of March 2nd, however, everyone was up early, a little dull perhaps from the previous day's toil, but ready to get things in their proper place. First order of business was putting up the mailbox. The next day, or the day following, for sure, the daily paper would start coming, a few letters or postcards from the old neighbors and relatives would arrive, and then the spring sale catalog from the mail order company.

With that, the family was settled once again and the empty house, with its strange smells and sounds of a few days ago, was a family home once more.

It's Spring — Time For Mayflowers, Pocket Gophers And Pie Plant

Spring has come to Rock County.

Gone are the snows of winter. The creeks are running. The birds are back. Nature has come alive.

Spring on the farm was always a time to look forward to — and when it arrived, it seemed that you wanted it to last forever.

As I remember it, the first sign of spring we looked forward to was the return of the meadow lark. The yellow breasted birds defied the last days of winter by perching on a fence post or barbed wire and warbling their welcome song in the early morning as we headed out to do the morning chores. And do you know what I imagined the words of the song were? "MR. CHARLEY CRAGOE!"

Charley is a real person. He now lives at Magnolia, but he was a kid then, living on a farm near Beaver Creek, so I was familiar with the name. Next time you see a meadow lark, stop and listen. You'll hear it, too. Mr. Charley Cragoe!

About the same time as the larks came, we'd see and hear the wild geese. Large V's and long lines, high in the sky, and sometimes low. Grey honkers and snowy whites, heading straight north without the benefit of compass, road map, radar or directional guidance systems.

Now and then, they'd come in low, and settle on the pond in the pasture, or in one of the corn fields. How fun it was to crawl to the edge of the little hill to look down at them sitting motionless or slowly gliding across the water. A rest stop before continuing their long journey into the Canadian wilds.

It didn't take long for the warm rays of the spring day sun to entice the crocuses out of their hiding places on the hill in the pasture. We always called them mayflowers, but invariably, they made their appearance in April. The lavender blossoms were fragrant as we picked them and held them to our sensitive nostrils. As youngsters, we'd race across the hills to see who could come up with the biggest bouquet of long stemmed flowers. Once in a vase, they would last only for a brief time, but long enough so that Mother had a chance to enjoy them, too.

A few weeks later, the violets and buttercups would make their appearance in the meadow beside the winding creek. Then came the lilies of the valley which grew beside the row of willows near the road.

I always awaited the first pocket gopher mounds with anticipation. Dad always was willing to give a nickel for every one of the pests I could trap. I had several No. 0 (that's pronounced number

ought) Victor traps, just the right size for a pocket gopher burrow. First, it was opening the burrow, and finding the cross-hole.
That's where the trap had to go, and one had to make sure that
most of the loose dirt was removed. If this wasn't done, you could
expect the trap to be snapped and the hole plugged solidly the
next morning.

And what farm boy hasn't had the experience of snaring striped
gophers? A length of binder twine with a loop on the end was
placed into the gopher hole. Then, we'd sit down and wait. Usually, it didn't take very long before the inquisitive ground squirrel
would inch his way out of the burrow and look around. That was
the signal to jerk the string. If you did it right, you had a gopher
on a leash, racing around trying to get away.

In a neighbor's field, a quarter of a mile away or so, was a patch
of horseradish. As soon as the leaves started to show, we'd head
for it with a spade and dig a few of the gnarled roots. Returning
home, we then peeled them and put them through a hand-cranked
meat grinder. Before we were finished, tears would be streaming
from our eyes, but it was worth it. Mother mixed the ground roots
with vinegar, salt and sugar. What a delicacy with fresh pork
chops or home canned roast beef and gravy.

The next culinary delight, as I recall, was the first picking of
pieplant. For the more sophisticated, pieplant is rhubarb, but
when I was a boy, nobody called it anything but pieplant. I could
never wait until Mother cooked the first batch as a sauce, or made
it into pie or shortcake. I'd have to have the first stalk raw. Sour it
was, but delicious.

Another sour taste treat was what we called sourgrass, which
we usually found along the creek in the meadow where the violets
were. In fact, the flower on sourgrass looked something like a
violet, except it was pink. Finding a clump of sourgrass, while
out snaring gophers or on the way home from school was a sure
sign that spring had finally come.

Spring was also a time for streaking, although we never knew it
as streaking then. The minute that the water in the creek was
warm enough so you could stick your foot below the surface of the
water and not have your toes become numb by the time you
counted ten, it was warm enough for the first swim of the season.

You bet your life, we didn't wear swimming suits. We didn't
have to. The neighbors who could see us lived too far away to yell
at us. The girls wouldn't be caught dead any place near the swimming hole, so we had it all to ourselves. Besides, the first dip of
the season didn't take more than a minute. The ritual consisted of
racing down the little hill, holding our noses while we jumped into the water, taking a couple of dog paddle strokes, then hastily

climbing up on the bank and scrambling, goose-pimpled, back into our clothes.

The next day those of us who did it — usually it was just my uncle Buster and myself — could go to school and brag to the other youngsters about how brave we had been the night before. (You can bet, though, we weren't brave enough to tell our mothers.)

Spring was wonderful then. It still is now. I haven't done any skinny-dipping for a long time, but I'm still thrilled at the song of a lark, the sight of a mayflower, seeing the thin black and white line across a bright blue sky as a flock of geese heads northward, tasting a spoonful of fresh horseradish and seeing a fresh pocket gopher mound.

It just goes to prove once again "you can take the boy off the farm, but you can't take the farm off the boy."

Butchering — A Springtime Ritual That Came Between Wood Cutting And Oats Fanning

The balmy weather we had last week made me think of hog butchering time on the farm. It seemed to me that the season for "putting" up the summer meat supply was here.

I wonder if anyone butchers hogs on the farm anymore. Since the locker plants came into being, and home freezers a standard household appliance, most of the butchering is done in the locker plants. There the meat is also cut up and packaged without the farmer or his family having to do a thing except bring it home and pack it in the freezer.

Butchering was a spring ritual on every farm, coming some time between wood cutting and oats fanning; usually on a day when the snow was thawing and it was slushy out of doors.

Like so many farm tasks which required an extra hand or two, neighbors would help each other and the work was accomplished in short order.

An early start was always necessary. Buckets full of water had to be carried from the well into the "wash house", a little building near the house where we had a cook stove, a washing machine, and a number of other things we didn't have room for in our home. There, the water was poured into a couple of copper boilers, and the cook stove was fired up with cobs and firewood until sometimes the top of the old range was red hot.

While the water was heating, Dad and my Grandpa Aaker would pick out the best barrow in the hog shed and snare him with a rope.

Out of the building he'd come, squealing to high heaven. A blow from an eight-pound sledge stunned the animal. Then a sharp knife cut the jugular vein. The blood was collected and quickly cooled for future use in what the Norwegians called "blodpolse" or "klub". Our American neighbors called it blood sausage because it resembled a large summer sausage. Our German neighbors used the blood, too, but made a couple of different dishes, one called "schwartsur" (I'm not sure of the spelling) and another called "blotwurst".

By the time this was done, the old wooden barrel standing under the maple tree between the house and the wood pile had been filled with the boiling water from the wash house stove. Some wood ashes had been added to it, and the scalding process was about to begin.

First of all, however, the tendons of the back legs were exposed so that they could be hooked to the end hooks of a single tree. A block and tackle was attached to a branch in the tree; the block and tackle hook was placed in the center ring of the single tree, and the carcass was hoisted up above the barrel. Then it was dipped into the scalding water, hoisted up again, scraped to remove the hair, dipped again after the outside became cool, and scraped some more until all the bristles had been removed.

This done, the "dressing out" began, and the carcass was permitted to cool for several hours.

When it was cooled sufficiently, the sides were carried into the wash house where a makeshift table had been made from planks or old doors, and the cutting process was started.

Pork chops and ribs were sawed with a hand-type meat saw. Fat was removed from the meat and the smaller portions of lean meat put into a box or container to be ground into sausage. The fat was cut into small pieces to be rendered into lard. The hams were trimmed for curing in brine and later smoking in the smoke house. The spare ribs were cut into small squares or pieces, so they could be fried and placed in half-gallon fruit jars. The same with the chops and sausage balls or patties.

Some of the meat was salted and preserved that way. Other parts of the forequarter were roasted and canned for future use, the same as the pork chops. Sometimes, rather than canning the chops or the sausage, these delicacies were placed in a five or ten gallon stone crock and covered with lard. They would keep in the cellar that way for months. When some meat was needed, all that was necessary was to go to the cellar and remove them from the jar, heat them on the range, and dinner was ready.

One of the "new fangled" ideas that came out which pleased Grandpa no end was the hand-cranked meat grinder. For years, Grandpa made sausage the way he learned to do it in the old country, with a small hatchet and a heavy wooden box. He'd put the small cuts of meat into the box, and then chop it to the consistency of hamburger and sausage with the hatchet. It was a long process that way, but the end result was a fine quality ground pork.

Not a great deal was wasted at butchering time, although we didn't save everything as some other families did. The fresh liver was always considered a delicacy. The head was quartered, cooked, and the meat trimmed from the bones. This meat was seasoned with some special spices and other ingredients, then placed into a cloth bag, and pressed under a heavy weight. This was known as "head cheese" and seasoned the way mother did it, it was a delicious cold cut that was later sliced and served with lunches and on sandwiches.

There's not a great deal of meat on pig's feet, but when they were pickled, they, too, were a delicacy. Both head cheese and pickled pig's feet are available still at some delicatessen counters.

The side pork was either salted or made into bacon. Some people preferred to salt the bacon slabs only, without smoking them. The salt would cure the meat so that it would keep without refrigeration. It would be sliced and fried crisp as one fries bacon. I never did care much for salt pork, but the home-cured, home-smoked bacon was delicious.

Once in a while, when we butchered a beef, as well as a hog, we'd make country-style sausages. We never had a sausage stuffer of our own, but the Will McCurdy's had one that we often borrowed to make ring bolognas from a combination of pork sausage and ground beef. The day the sausages came out of the smoke house was the day we all waited for, as all of us liked their spicy smoked flavor.

I frankly admit that I, for one, didn't enjoy butchering day, and I'd guess that there were a lot of others who shared the same feeling. But the end result was worth it even though the work was strenuous.

There was a lot of satisfaction in slicing thick strips of lean, meaty home-smoked bacon, or opening a big Mason jar of pork chops and heating them for supper on the old cook stove.

But those of us who had these experiences generally agree, I believe, that loading a pig into the back of a pickup and hauling it to the locker plant is a much easier and more satisfying way to obtain a meat supply than the home butchering way that was a springtime ritual on every farm when I was a kid in grade school.

Fanning grain

Oats was placed in the hopper of the mill. By turning the crank, the chaff, the smaller weed seeds and other foreign material were separated from the grain, thus providing "clean" seed for planting.

Fattening the roosters

Mother fed the young roosters by hand. By the Fourth of July, they were ready for the frying pan.

Incubator Lacked The Personal Touch
Of The Old Mother Hen

Most exciting time of the year for a boy on the farm just has to be spring!

It's the time for new life. Birth, whether it be a calf, a colt, a lamb, a pig, a chick, a duckling or a gosling, is thrilling to witness.

Late March and early April was baby chick time, a time to "set" the incubator and the "settin" hens, a time to wait and see how well the eggs hatched.

The incubator brought about the first big change in poultry production.

Before that, chicks came into being the way the Lord intended.

As a person matures, life has fewer mysteries, but even today I can't help but marvel at the way Nature has of replenishing its own.

It was always early spring when the hens would start getting "broody". At this stage, they would tend to stick to their nests, particularly if they had eggs beneath them.

When we had to go out and gather eggs in the hen house, we'd avoid the nests with hens on them, because they (the hens) were very possessive. Reach under a hen and try to retrieve an egg, and she'd peck at your hand indignantly. If you didn't pull back quickly enough, you ended up with a hurting hand.

When a hen became broody, her role in life changed from a "layin' hen" to a "settin' hen". She was ready to sit (we always said set, though) on a batch of eggs until they hatched.

A big Rhode Island Red or Barred Rock could "set" over a dozen or fifteen eggs at a time and keep them covered.

When it was certain she was ready to get down to business, eggs were placed in the nest beneath her, and she went to work. All she did was sit, staring ahead with her glassy eyes, just waiting.

Occasionally, she would change her position. She did this in such a way that the eggs beneath her would roll slightly. Turning the eggs is important during the incubation period, and by changing her position from time to time, the hen did turn them without, perhaps, even knowing it. If they rolled too far, or spread out in such a way that one was out in the open, she'd use her beak to tuck it under her body once more.

Only when she became hungry or thirsty did she leave the nest, and then only for short periods of time. She knew by instinct just how long she could be gone before the eggs would become cool, and lose their hatchability.

Her confinement period lasted but 21 days. Then, when we walked into the hen house, and if everything was quiet, we'd get as close to the nest as we dared and would listen. Sometimes, we could hear the "pick-pick-pick" sound of the baby chick struggling to break the egg shell open from the inside.

By the next day, all the chicks had emerged from the shells and you could hear them peeping beneath their mother, and see their heads peeking out beneath their mother's wings.

When the eggs had hatched, the "settin' hen" had become a "cluck hen". While the hen was quietly waiting for the eggs to hatch, Mother Nature endowed her with a new ability, the ability to make a clucking sound. This was to be her method of communicating with her babies while they were in her care. She'd use a certain tonal inflection to tell them she had found food or water for them. She'd change her tone when she sensed they were in danger, and again, when she merely wanted them to follow her.

When night came, and she wanted to "put them to bed" she'd tuck them beneath her, and then cluck contentedly to herself. By the time the chicks were grown big enough to fend for themselves, she quit clucking and went back to being a "layin' hen".

There always seemed to be some hens who preferred to have their babies in seclusion. They'd seek out a place in a manger in the barn, under the granary, or beside the haystack or a strawstack. There they'd lay their eggs and hatch them, often unobserved, and after a couple of days, they'd make their debut on the farm yard, the mother hen clucking proudly as she displayed her brood.

Once the chicks were big enough to scratch for their own feed and find their way around, the cluck hens would be gathered together in a wire mesh enclosed area near the hen house. There they were psyched out of their maternal instincts, and gradually their egg laying instincts returned to start the cycle over again.

The advent of the incubator completely changed baby chick production and put the cluck hen out of business.

Our incubator was a square, flat, box-like affair, made of red cardboard. It had a door in front, with a glass window so it was possible to look in through it and check the thermometer which lay on the eggs. A copper tube filled with water circled the top of it on the inside. The water in the tube was heated with a kerosene burning lamp, on the outside of the box.

One always knew when eggs were being incubated in a farm home, because of the distinctive odor of burning kerosene.

The tray in our incubator would take a couple of hundred eggs, I suppose. They were laid out carefully on their sides and remained there until hatched.

An evening ritual, however, was taking the tray and turning and testing the eggs. The tester was a conical, cardboard device through which one would look to determine if the eggs were fertile. I don't remember what the tell-tale sign was, but by holding the egg up to the light and looking at it through the tube, it was possible to tell if a baby chick was developing or not. If it wasn't the egg was set aside and later thrown away.

As a small boy, I remember how the three-week incubation period seemed to be such a long time. How exciting it was to hear the chicks breaking the eggs as the hatching began. Sometimes, it sounded almost like corn popping.

Through the window in the door of the incubator, it was possible to watch the chicks struggle to be born. First their tiny beaks would break through the shell. They would keep pecking away until finally their heads emerged entirely. After that, they struggled and squirmed until the opening in the shell was large enough for them to emerge, tired and wet, onto their tray. The warmth inside the incubator would dry them in short order and there they were, fuzzy, cute and cuddly.

Before long, they were hungry and thirsty. Instinctively, they would dip their little beaks into a low dish of water, and once filled, they'd lift their heads and swallow. They quickly learned to eat the ground feed that was placed before them.

When the incubator was about ready to bring forth its brood, Dad would get the brooder house ready. We had a 500 chick size coal fired brooder. Like the parlor heater in our living room, it burned hard coal. How an even temperature was maintained I'll never know.

I do know it took a lot of attention during the first two or three weeks of brooding, at least, because if the temperature became too warm, the chicks would get sick, and if it got too cold, they'd huddle together, pile up and those at the bottom of the pile would smother.

By the time the chicks were half-grown, the weather was warm enough so they could go outside. It was exciting to watch the little rascals as they scratched the ground with their feet, picking up any goodies they uncovered.

Mother also liked to raise a few ducks and geese, so we could have roast duck or roast goose for the holiday dinners.

While the hens laid eggs all year 'round, the geese and ducks laid them only in the spring. If you left a duck or goose to herself, she'd lay just enough eggs to fill a nest and they would start "settin". But, if the eggs were removed from the nest daily, she'd double her production.

In order to take full advantage of all the eggs — because we never ate the duck or goose eggs or used them for cooking or baking — it was sometimes necessary to place them under a settin' hen until they hatched.

We always thought it funny to see a big old red hen surrounded by long necked goslings that would follow her wherever she went. They and the ducklings learned to understand chicken talk; when the old hen would start clucking in a certain way, the little geese or ducks would hustle to her side, knowing that she had found some food for them.

The ducklings or goslings that were hatched by their own mothers, however, didn't understand the chicken talk, but neither did the ducklings or goslings hatched by the hen seem to understand the sounds made by their natural mothers.

It was inevitable, however, that the fluffy baby birds would grow up.

The young roosters were ready for frying by the Fourth of July, when Mother served pan fried spring chicken with new potatoes and fresh peas from the garden.

The potatoes and peas were delicious. The chicken was delicious, too, but I'd rather have had a pork chop or a piece of canned roast beef. Somehow, it didn't seem right that those cuddly balls of fluff that kept poking their heads from beneath an old hen's wings in March should end up on the dinner table in July.

Dad Used A Rag-Doll Tester To Pick
Seed Corn That Would Grow

I think I start looking for the arrival of spring the day after New Year's Day.

I don't know if it is because I dislike winter so much, or if it is because that spring somehow delights all my senses, but I suspect it is the latter. The sights, sounds, smells, feels and tastes of spring have always buoyed my spirits and I hope they always will.

One of the first signs that spring would be eventually arriving, I remember as a boy, was seed corn testing time. I think Dad enjoyed working — or as he said, "puttering" — with seed corn more than anything else. Selecting it, grading it, testing it and then selling it always delighted him.

Dad used the rag-doll method of seed corn testing generally, but other times, he merely planted the kernels in a tin can to see how well they would grow.

The rag-doll method was rather unique, I always thought. First, he'd find a piece of white cloth, and with a crayon would draw 25 or 50 squares on it, maybe there were 100, I'm just not sure anymore. Next, he would pick out as many ears of corn as he had squares and would put them into a wire rack, lining them up in rows to correspond with the squares on the cloth. He'd then take his jackknife and take one kernel from each ear and place the kernels in squares on the cloth.

As each row of squares was filled, that portion of the cloth was folded over, and this was repeated until each kernel was in place. Once filled, the cloth was folded in such a way that the kernels would not fall out during handling, and it was placed in a fruit jar filled with water. This was placed atop the kitchen cupboard, quite close to the kitchen range, so it kept relatively warm.

The top of the fruit jar was capped, so the moisture wouldn't escape, and the kernels of corn were left to germinate. After several days, he began to check the rag doll to see how the seeds were doing.

First a white tip would appear from the kernel. Then another. One was the root, the other the stem. Each day, one could detect some growth had been made. Finally, the growth would start coming through the cloth, indicating the test was complete.

If 99 of the 100 kernels grew, that meant the corn was germinating 99 percent. If only 50 grew, that meant he had a bum batch of seed corn, and he'd have to use the 50 ears that didn't grow for feed.

About this time of the year, the meadowlarks would start showing up on the fence posts around the farm, heralding the forth-coming departure of winter.

When the wild geese began moving through on their return flight to their Canadian wilderness nesting grounds, it was pretty certain that warmer weather was moving in, too. There were days when one could see several flocks of the graceful birds at one time, some grey, some white, winging their way northward in response to an instinct provided by nature that no man has yet been able to comprehend.

Something I've never been able to understand is how the various varieties of the same species have retained their identity over the years. One would think that crossbreeding would occur, and in time, the various breeds as we know them would be eliminated, and one crossbred variety would remain. But this, ap-parently, never happens. Nature has done a good job of keeping her secrets.

Trees also were a fascination to me in the spring time. I remember wondering what God had in mind when he created the pussy willow. It's the only tree I know of that produces the furry ball on its branches before the leaves appear.

And why is the maple tree the only tree that produces sap in any significant quantity? We never had sugar maples, only the soft maples, but I don't believe there was a spring during my boyhood years that I didn't take the brace and bit, bore a hole into one of them, and then hang a Calumet baking powder can below the open-ing to catch the sweet tasting liquid that the tree produced.

When the snow began to melt, the ditches and gullies and ravines would begin filling with water, another sure sign that winter's departure was at hand. I could never resist sloshing through the little rivulets in my red, four-buckle Ball Band rubber overshoes with the white soles, to let the running water wash off the mud that had gathered on them as I walked home from school.

If the winter snowfall had been heavy, and the early spring days especially mild, the water produced by the thaw soon had the creek out of its banks. Sometimes, it stretched the width of the pasture, carrying with it huge rafts of thick ice that had broken out of the main channel. As the water headed towards first, the Beaver Creek, then the Split Rock, on to the Big Sioux, to the Missouri, finally the Mississippi, I wondered to myself, "How long will it take for it to reach the Gulf of Mexico?"

At this stage, the planting season was fast approaching. That meant getting a lot of things done that one didn't do in the cold of winter. Like running the oats through the fanning mill in the granary to get rid of the pigeon grass, rose hips, and other "foul" seeds as they were called.

It meant going through the harnesses and horse collars, replacing the broken straps and missing snaps, then having them oiled at the harness shop so they would be supple and wear longer.

It meant cleaning out the calf pen with a four-tine fork, a back breaking task, particularly under the hay manger if long stemmed slough hay had been fed and some had become mixed with the straw bedding.

It meant getting the hog barn ready for baby pigs, by putting up the board panels that would separate the area into farrowing pens for the sows.

It also meant that the time had come to go back to BVD's after having contended with the long legs, long sleeves and drop seats that were the trademarks of fleece-lined union suits, standard equipment for farm boys from the first snowfall until the first robin.

I awaited the arrival of spring with great anticipation then; and I still do. I never cease to be thrilled at hearing the song of a meadowlark, seeing a flock of geese in flight, feeling the furry surface of a pussy willow, inhaling the fragrance of a clump of just-emerged mayflowers on a windswept pasture hill, and savoring a sip of maple sap from a baking powder can.

Spring indeed is a time when a person can make full use of all his senses and truly enjoy being alive.

Gardening Provides A Closer Look
At Some Of Nature's Mysteries

Right now I'm looking forward to planting my vegetable garden. Just like my dad did every spring.

There was a time when I wasn't too excited about it. I'd much rather have been snaring gophers than helping with the planting and the hoeing and the pea-picking.

Now, I enjoy it and can hardly wait until the ground is ready to work. Hopefully, it won't be too long.

Maybe it was the ground preparation that turned me off when I was a boy on the farm. In those days, you did a lot more to make it grow than pick up a bag of granular fertilizer at the store and spread it with an easy-to-push spreader. And you didn't have power garden tillers, either, to break up the ground to make planting easier.

Dad was a great one for having a well-fertilized garden. And he believed there was nothing better than manure fresh from the horse barn for growing big tomatoes and plump cabbages.

The garden plot wasn't large, but it was fenced in, with a large wooden gate in one corner. There was no way a manure spreader could be used to get the job done in a hurry. Instead, it meant loading a single box wagon and spreading it over the ground with a five-tine fork. It was hard on the back and arm muscles, and the "fragrance" lingered as long as the ground remained unplowed.

Once the plot was covered, and the soil changed from mud to crumbly loam, Dad would plow it with a walking plow. That really beat digging it with a fork or spade, which was the way many gardeners had to do it.

Dad would hitch Daisy and Flossie to the plow, tie a knot in the reins, put one side of the loop over his left shoulder, and the other side beneath his right arm. Pointing the tip of the shiny plow share into the moist earth, he'd grip a plow handle in each hand and say, "Giddap".

As the team walked straight ahead, Dad would maneuver the plow to the right depth. As the glossy, black earth turned over, a clean cut furrow emerged.

I wasn't old enough to do the plowing, but I was big enough to walk down the furrow behind Dad, picking up the plump earth worms as their subterranenan passageways were laid bare. Dad didn't object one bit to this kind of fooling around on the part of his eldest son, because next to gardening, bullhead fishing was his favorite spring recreation, and worms were essential to bullhead fishing. It seemed to please him that I had inherited his enthusiasm for the popular cane-pole sport.

The plowing finished, Dad would hitch the team to the single section harrow and would level the ground leaving a flat, well pulverized surface. Then the plot was ready for planting.

For many years, Dad used a common hoe to make the shallow trenches in which he would plant the seeds. A piece of binder twine tied to two sticks was strung across the width of the garden. This would serve as a guide for making the trench straight.

First the onion sets went in. Then the radishes, and the lettuce. Later the peas, the string beans, the beets and carrots. When frost danger had passed, the tomatoes, the cabbage, the cucumbers, the squash and the melons would be planted. In a matter of weeks there was no space left and vegetables were growing in neat rows from one end of the garden to the other.

By the time the seeds were all planted, we were already enjoying garden delicacies. We had what we called "winter onions". They were a perennial kind of onion, that began coming up about the time the snow started to disappear. What a treat they were! Then, the parsnip shoots became visible, and we'd dig the parsnips, sweet as sugar after having survived the winter in the ground.

Strange, I used to think, that some kinds of onions and parsnips come back year after year, while other plants died once they were nipped by frost.

Once the garden was in, I'd watch it closely to see which of the vegetables were coming up. When the first smooth leaves of the radishes were about a half inch across, I'd pull out one or two of the tiny plants to sample the flavor of better things to come.

As the vegetables progressed, so did the weeds, and it was then that Dad put me to work. With a hoe or on my hands and knees, the weedlings came out but not without effort, and, I might add, without grumbling that I'd rather spend Saturdays playing catch with a kittenball.

Then something revolutionary happened.

Evan Trunnell became the Rock County distributor for a push model garden cultivator. He'd travel around the countryside, demonstrating it, and once anyone saw it and tried it, Grandpa Trunnell made a sale.

It was even kind of fun for me to garden with the tool, and Dad used it for 40 years. It just didn't wear out. I'd almost bet there are still some of them around. I've seen a lot of other cultivators advertised over the years, but never one like that one. It had interchangeable shovels and blades, and it cut down hoeing time by half or even more.

By early June, the garden was a joy to behold, both visually and gastronomically. The first strawberries, the green peas, the fresh carrots, little round onions for creaming. What Dad had said at planting time was true. Every bit of work we'd done was worth it.

As I grew older, I grew to respect gardening more, both for the exercise and for the matchless taste of the fresh vegetables that gardens provide. I've never planted a big garden, but I've always planted something.

I've found, however, that gardening provides more than exercise and goodies. It brings one closer to nature, and gives credence to one's religious beliefs.

A potato with its eyes, a head of cabbage made up of a hundred perfectly formed leaves, a cucumber with its mini-thorns, a pod filled with peas — all different, yet all were formed in the same manner. A seed was buried beneath the surface of the earth. Through a mysterious combination of sun, rain and ingredients in the soil, the seed was transformed into a growing plant. And each plant bore its own kind of fruit.

To me, there's no evidence more convincing that there is indeed an Almighty God.

Christmas Memories

It Wouldn't Have Been Christmas Without The School And Church Programs

Christmas is not only a memorable time.

It is also the time of memories . . . when thoughts turn back to Christmases of other years.

Christmas on the farm, at least during my boyhood, wasn't merely Christmas Eve and Christmas Day, but it was a season a month long that kept building up to that climactic moment when the gifts were distributed on Christmas Eve.

First Christmas my memory now recalls is the one when I was five. I'd been permitted to attend the school Christmas program in the weather beaten grey school house in District 44, northwest of Beaver Creek. I sat with my uncle "Buster", my father's youngest brother, who was still in school at the time. When I began to talk out loud during the performance, he tried to "shush" me, and somehow my head fell against a newly sharpened pencil which he held in his hand. A tiny black dot just below my left eyebrow has served to remind me of that Christmas season ever since.

The next year, I was in the Christmas program myself, and became a hero in that being the school's youngest, I was permitted to give the "welcome address" to the audience of parents and smaller brothers and sisters who had packed into the tiny school room for the "show".

"Merry Christmas parents dear,

"We're glad you came to see and hear

"Our songs and plays and recitations,

"And welcome all of our relations!"

Everyone laughed and I felt I'd made a hit, although what I had said didn't sound funny at all to me.

And I wasn't dressed to look funny, either. I had a new "blouse" (boys of six didn't wear shirts in those days), sharply pressed knickers, long stockings that did, I'll admit, show the bulges of the long legged union suit I was wearing, and smartly polished black high shoes with hooks instead of holes for the laces at the top of the shoe. (No button shoes for the first program, I recall. My last pair had been relegated to every day duty a year or two before, and when they became too small, I was the happiest boy in Beaver Creek Township.)

To anyone who has ever attended country school, the program which followed the introductory recitation will have a familiar ring.

The bed sheets strung over a wire were pulled and there we all stood, some shy, some smiling, facing the audience.

"The first number on our program," announced Miss Brindel, our teacher, "will be 'It Came Upon The Midnight Clear' by all."

"A recitation by Martin Freim, 'A Hole in Mama's Stocking'."

"A drill by Edna McCurdy, Lucille Fenstermaker and Lois Egge."

" 'Mrs. Santa Makes A Trip', a play by Zona McCurdy, Florence Egge, Ethel Alink, Floyd Johnson, Clarence Top and Orville Ohlen."

"A song, 'Jolly Old St. Nicholas,' by all." This song was done with motion: "Jolly Old St. Nicholas, lean your ear this way" — singers put hand to right ear and lean head to right. "Don't you tell a single soul what I have to say." — singers shake index finger of right hand at the audience. "Christmas Eve is coming soon, now you dear old man" — hands stroke chin as Santa would stroke his beard. "I'll tell you what to bring to me" — hand cupped to mouth as though whispering to Santa, "Bring it if you can."

And so it went, song, recitation, drill, song, inevitably concluding with "Silent Night".

Then came the distribution of the gifts. Mine was a big red pencil box — complete with soap eraser, several pencils, a six inch ruler and a collapsible metal drinking cup with cover. Elmer Alink had drawn my name. What a surprise! What a fabulous gift to get from a friend!

I must have been in the third or fourth grade when I started to take part in the Christmas programs at the church. The "practices" were held Saturday afternoon, and memorable they were, too. Quite often it meant making the two and a half mile trip to the church in the bob sled with Dad at the reins guiding Daisy and Flossie over the drifted roads, as we children huddled beneath horsehide robes or heavy horse blankets while seated on the straw covered floor of the bob sled box.

I always felt sorry for the ladies who had to work with the children in preparing for the church program. Never were children more noisy, more mischievous than those who gathered on Saturday afternoons at the old East Palisade Church. And never has more patience been shown than was shown by Effie and Martha Ormseth, Rena Bly, Mable Larson and the others who produced the program that packed the church to the rafters for the annual event.

The "big night" usually meant early chores, hitching the team to the bob sled and the horsehide robe and horse-blanket routine again.

The usual quiet of the church sanctuary was missing on this night. The "Shhhh" of the gasoline lights suspended from the ceiling blended with the whispers of the three or four rows of squirming, excited children in the front of the church, creating a sound one hardly noticed until everything became suddenly quiet as Eddie Eitreim, perennial master of ceremonies, stepped in front of the candle-lighted Christmas tree and announced in articulate tones, "The first number on the program this evening will be Hymn No. 193 by the audience."

Then we'd all sing "The Happy Christmas Comes Once More" and the program was underway.

For many of the families, this was gift exchange night. I recall the space between the altar rail and the altar of the church was nearly full of gifts, a stack one can't imagine unless he has seen it.

After the program, Mr. Eitreim with some of the younger men as helpers would start distributing the gifts, calling out the names to find out where the recipients were.

"Eddie Steneberg . . . Herman Larson . . . Gladys Ormseth . . . Olga Edmundson . . . Ernest Ormseth . . . Otto Rollag . . . Alma Johnson . . . Lucille Jordahl . . . Edna Samuelsen . . . Harvey Eitreim . . . Arnold Edmundson . . ." on and on it went; some went home with armsful of gifts, others with one or two; a few had none.

But one thing all of them had to take home was the big bag of candy, peanuts, and an apple, the distribution of which concluded the evening. Then it was out in the clear chilly night, and the ride home. A wonderful feeling, Christmas was now really here.

Christmas Eve was always observed at home with the traditional lutefisk supper, and the distribution of gifts in the living room where the hard coal heater produced a glow and warmth that has never been duplicated in this era of modern heating systems.

Our tree was small — it had to be because with the hard coal heater in our living room, there was little room for a tree or anything else when the family sat down to open their "presents". Mother always was able to find the little red, blue and green clips which were used in fastening the candles to the tree branches. Strings of cranberries and popcorn, and little card-like illustrations of angels, shepherds and wise men were suspended from the tree branches by tinsel loops. The Aladdin kerosene lamp on the dining room table threw just enough light into the adjoining "front room" (it never became known as a living room until years later), but not enough so that it destroyed the effect of the little flames of the candles on the tree.

We children, sister Lorraine and I, would "speak our pieces" we'd learned for school and church, and perhaps we'd sing a few Christmas songs, and then we began opening gifts. (It was some years later before brother James joined us in the ritual, because the year he was born, on Dad's birthday, three days before Christmas was the year I was nine and Lorraine was seven.)

I can't say that I really missed him, because one never misses something he has never had . . . but Santa Claus never came to our house. Possibly it was because of Grandpa and Grandma. Both had come from Norway, neither of them learned the English language. And Santa Claus was not a part of the Norwegian tradition. So with them joining us in our Yuletide merriment, we never seemed to miss Santa, who called at the homes of our "American" friends.

Christmas Day meant observance of the holiday at church. And for many years, festival days of the church meant that the service was in the Norwegian language. For the older people, it seemed, use of the English language at a Christmas service would have been as irreverent as having Santa Claus pass the offering plate.

Viewing it now in retrospect, I can see why they were reluctant to make the change. What little I now remember of the Norwegian I learned as a child, there seems to be beauty and richness of the words of the Christmas story and the familiar Norwegian hymns and carols, that are not captured in the English translation. For to me, no song at Christmas has ever been sung more beautifully — except of course, the song of the angels — than "Her Komme Dine Arme Smaa" as sung by my grandmother when I was a child of five or six.

Christmas, as long as my grandparents lived, lasted into January, concluding with "Lille Julekveld", or commonly known as the twelfth night of Christmas. After this, the tree came down, Christmas vacation was over, and the long wait for Christmas to come began all over again.

Grandpa

Ivar Levik Aaker

Nov. 1, 1833
Oct. 11, 1927

Grandma

Marit Toresdatter
(Bjornhjell)

Aug. 2, 1847
Dec. 29, 1941

Grandpa And Grandpa Gave An Added Dimension To Christmas

A December whiteness has settled across the countryside. Long, blue shadows stretch before unadorned fenceposts as the setting sun casts a lonely enchantment on the snow covered ground.

The air is cold — when one walks, it is instinctive to walk briskly, shoulders tensed, gloved hands swinging, or deeply entrenched in coat pockets.

It's Christmas weather — the kind we Rock Countians have come to associate with the most enjoyable of religious holidays. For some reason, Christmas doesn't seem like Christmas when the ground is bare, when one can go out of doors without wearing a heavy coat or jacket.

I guess all of us have a tendency to look back on past Christmases and to revel in the memories of the delightful bygone days of childhood. Particularly if those days were spent on the farm.

One of the good fortunes of my childhood was that Grandpa and Grandma Aaker lived with us. This is an experience that few youngsters have these days. Somehow or other their presence gave the holiday season a serenity that it just doesn't seem to have today. (Or have our values changed?)

Grandma and Grandpa were devout Christians. They had their own room in our little farm house, complete with a little round wood burning heater in one corner. Each day they would go to their room at a certain time and have their devotional period, reading from the Bible and singing songs from the tattered hymnal they had brought with them from Norway.

As Christmas approached, they would sing together, without accompaniment, the familiar carols they had learned in their home country. Then, they would read together the "texts" that paved the way for the greatest of all stories, the Christmas story.

Their actions and their attitude told us something about Christmas. It was more than Santa Claus and presents and tinsel on the tree. It was more than "Jingle Bells" and "Up on the Housetop". They made us realize that Christmas was indeed love. They made it plain by what they said and by what they did.

Grandpa and Grandma had no money to speak of. A few dollars, maybe, that Grandpa got from the litter of pigs he raised from a sow Dad had given him for doing the "hog chores".

So they never had money to buy gifts, but somehow they always had something to give us.

Grandpa had a whittling knife and carved wood into crude toys. Grandma knit mittens from wool she had carded and spun into yarn. And sometimes, she would knit me a pair of woolen stockings (not socks, stockings), which were always a valued gift because I always seemed to get cold feet sooner than anyone else.

As long as she was able, Grandma would help Mother with the Christmas baking. She knew how to make delicately thin Norwegian flatbread and soft, tender lefse. It would never have been Christmas at our house without those two staple foods which originated in the "old country".

It seemed we moved at a slower pace those days. We had more time.

Those were the early days of radio, and between morning and evening chores, we would tune to KFNF, Shenandoah, Iowa, or WNAX, Yankton, and listen to Christmas music. Today we hear Christmas music, but it seems we seldom have time to listen to it.

When Christmas time came, it seemed we were prepared for it, and were expecting it. Today it's rush, rush, rush, and the day is upon us and gone before we are ready to greet it.

At our house, festivities began on Christmas Eve. Grandpa and Grandma had told us about the baby Jesus from the time we children were old enough to sit on their knees. (Of course Mother and Dad told us too, but when Grandpa and Grandma related the story to us in Norwegian, there was no disputing its authenticity.)

The evening chores were finished early on Christmas Eve, so we could have our supper early and then open our gifts.

I'd help Dad feed the horses, cows and calves in the barn by lantern light. The sound of the cows chewing contentedly, the sound of the horses as they snorted to clear their nostrils of the dust from the hay, the plaintive "maaaas" of the little calves as they waited to be fed their evening bucket of skim milk, were comforting sounds.

Was this the way it was that night in Bethlehem, I wondered?

The manger there — was it high and deep like those in the horse stalls? Medium high like those in the cattle stalls? Or low, like in the calf pens?

Was the hay sweet smelling like the mixed grasses that we had harvested in the meadow during the summer, and now were feeding the horses and calves? Or was there straw in the stable, such as that we carried in for bedding that morning from the stack outside?

Did the inn keeper in Bethlehem provide Joseph and Mary with a lantern like the one that flickered from its peg on the barn wall? Or did God provide the light of the Christmas star because the inn keeper didn't even give them a candle?

Our barn had no heat, other than that generated by the animals inside. Were there enough sheep and goats and cattle in

Bethlehem stable to make it as warm as it was in our barn? Or, was Mary's burro the only animal there?

Chores over, we went inside, kicking off our overshoes and placing them on newspapers in back of the kitchen range. Our work clothes hung up, we'd "dress up" because this was Christmas Eve.

One of us would light the little candles on the Christmas tree. Then, we opened the gifts.

There weren't many gifts, nor were those that were there expensive. For certain, they were useful — clothing, books to read, pencil boxes for school, mittens, one toy or doll, perhaps, and that was it. But how thrilled we were to open the gaily wrapped packages.

When Grandpa and Grandma lived, we'd hear the Christmas Eve story read in Norwegian:

"Men det begave sig i de Dage, at en Befaling udgik fra Keiser Augustus, at al verden, skulde indskrives i Mandtal."

"Al verden" . . . "all the world." How sweeping were those words. Young eyes looked far. What was the world like out there on Bethlehem's plain? Like the pasture atop the Blue Mounds? And the City of David? Like Sioux Falls, maybe? And wise men from afar? Like way from Norway? Or Minneapolis?

Afterward, we'd maybe sing some of the carols we had learned at school. The hard candy and nuts would be passed. Then perhaps a cup of cocoa (we didn't call it hot chocolate, then) and a Christmas cookie or fattigman, and it would be off to bed.

Looking out the bare spot on the glass above the frost on the window pane, we could see the "moon on the breast of the new fallen snow," the outline of the barn, and the granary, and the big cottonwood tree in the front yard.

We looked in the sky for Mars or one of the other bright planets, and the big Dipper. The night time sky seemed to take on added splendor because it was Christmas.

And it still does, even to this day. I look at the sky and the stars, and wonder what I'd have done had I been wakened by an angel chorus, as the shepherds were that night so long ago.

Christmases have changed, just like the world has changed over the years. But the spirit of the day and season hasn't changed. Love came down at Christmas, and while we may have doubts at times, love is what Christmas is all about — both then, and now.

Bethlehem Hill-Folk Saw Stable Birth As Fulfillment Of Biblical Prophecy

Bethlehem, Judea, December 25 — Astronomers today were inconclusive as to what caused last night's strange heavenly body that appeared over Bethlehem.

"From the information available to us, at this time, there is nothing that would indicate that a star or a planet of this magnitude should be in the skies over this area," said Amos, who has been observing the heavens for over 40 years.

"We have no explanation for it whatever."

Some of the community's religious leaders, however, saw the phenomenon as a sign that Israel's long promised Messiah had come in the person of a baby boy born to a young Galilean couple from Nazareth.

Zachariah, a temple priest, exclaimed, "I'm firmly convinced this is the fulfillment of Isaiah's prophecy when he said, 'The people that walked in darkness have seen a great light; they that dwell in the land of the shadow of death, upon them has the light shined.' "

The star was first observed by a group of shepherds in the hills outside of Bethlehem.

Esrom, shepherd foreman, interviewed this morning, was still visibly shaken when he related the incident.

"We had all the sheep bedded down for the night," he stated. "It was chilly, and those who weren't sitting around the campfire were in their tents.

"Those of us around the campfire were just talking. Like how glad we were that we didn't have to walk a hundered miles just to come to town to sign up for our taxes. Taxes are bad enough without having to walk that far.

"Anyway, the fire was dying down, and you know how it is when you're watching a fire. You get kind of hypnotized, and you just sit there, staring into it, not saying a word."

It was then, he said, that the shepherds were startled by a voice.

When they looked up to see where it came from, they became aware for the first time of a light they hadn't noticed while they were sitting staring into the fire, Esrom said.

"Then we saw him, this angel. I'm sure it had to be an angel, because I've never seen a human being that was so dazzling — I can't explain what I mean, just bright like, so we had to shade our eyes. You can bet we were plenty scared."

The figure, according to Esrom, held up his hand as though giving the sign of peace, and told them not to be afraid.

"I bring you tidings of great joy — that's what he said — tidings of great joy that shall be to all people," Esrom declared.

"Then he told us about this baby that was born in town. A Savior, he said, and he had a name for him. Christ the Lord, he called him.

"Then he told us where we could find him. At the stable in back of Jacob's Inn, at the edge of town. In a manger."

Esrom said the shepherds maybe would have thought they were dreaming had it not been for what happened just then.

"We just started to crowd around him to ask him what was going on," Esrom said excitedly, "when suddenly in the sky and all around us and around this figure there appeared what seemed like a thousand other figures, all shiny and bright. And there was music. Music like we had never heard before. It was beautiful.

"Then this crowd — for want of a better description, I'll just call them a heavenly host, began chanting in time with the music.

"Glory to God in the highest, they were saying. Glory to God in the highest and on earth peace good will toward men."

Esrom said he and the other shepherds were as dumfounded as they were frightened. They fell to their knees.

"You can't help but feel religious out there in those hills," Esrom explained. "We always have our regular prayer times because with all these sheep to tend, we just don't get away to get to the synagogue on the Sabbath.

"I led the men in prayer. When we stood up, we saw this star.
"Funny thing.

"It seemed like it was beaming down on a certain spot. The sheep were quiet all this time, and something — I just can't explain it — kept our eyes focused on that star beam.

"So I said to the men, let's go to Bethlehem and see this thing which has come to pass."

They wasted no time, he continued, and at the bottom of the hill, just at the edge of Bethlehem, on the road that leads into town from Nazareth, they found the star's light beamed on a stable at the rear of Jacob's Inn.

They opened the closed door, and there as the figure had told them, lay a baby boy in a manger, and beside him were his parents. They told the shepherds they were Joseph and Mary, from Nazareth, but because they were of the lineage of David, they had come to Bethlehem to comply with Caesar Agustus' decree that everyone had to report to be taxed, and each one in his own city.

Esrom told how he and the other shepherds stood in awe at what they saw.

"It's not as if we'd never seen a baby before," he said. "I just can't explain it. That's why I am convinced that the supernatural is involved. This was of Almighty God, of that I'm convinced."

The shepherds left the stable a short time afterward, and every time they met someone along the way, stopped to tell what they had seen.

Some laughed, some scoffed, others were curious enough to head for the stable to see the baby themselves, Esrom said. The shepherds, however, had work to do and by that time it was daybreak.

Arriving at the place on the hills where the sheep had been bedded down, they found the sheep on their feet, grazing peaceably, as though the shepherds had been there all the time.

"When we got back," Esrom said, "we just fell to our knees again. This had to be God's doing so we just expressed our praise as best we could for what we had been privileged to see."

This reporter paid a visit to the stable where he was greeted at the door by a shy young man who said he was a carpenter by trade.

Asked about the happenings that surrounded the birth of their baby, the man spoke hesitantly.

"You'd better ask her," he said pointing to the young mother standing over the manger and smiling at the baby wrapped in narrow bands of white cloth, commonly used by mothers to cover their newborn infants.

"No, I can't say I was really surprised," she said, "after what happened to me last spring.

"Did you say the shepherds told you that an angel appeared to them?"

"Well, an angel appeared to me then, and told me that I was going to become a mother, that the baby would be a boy. He said that I was to name him Jesus, and that he would be called the Son of God."

Adding credence to the shepherd's account and the religious aspect of the incident was a late report from Jerusalem this morning, stating that the chief priests and scribes had advised King Herod that the birth of another king had been foretold by the prophet Micah.

He not only had pinpointed the place of birth as Bethlehem, but had referred to his being one with God by saying, "whose goings forth have been from of old, from everlasting."

Only one other person appeared to be as impressed as the shepherds by what had happened.

Jacob, the innkeeper, who had in desperation suggested to Joseph and Mary they could have a stall in his stable because every one of his rooms was filled, his chin resting in his hand, looked out toward the stable.

"I hated to do it, but what other choice did I have?"

Then thoughtfully, he added, "Wouldn't it be really something if the whole course of the world were to be changed by that little fellow out there?"

A Galilean Carpenter Reflects
Upon Becoming A Father

"I just can't believe everything that has happened," said the carpenter, Joseph, shuffling his feet in the straw on the floor of the stable at the rear of Jacob's Inn in Bethlehem.

Looking first toward his wife, Mary, then at the tiny blanket-wrapped bundle in the hay-filled manger nearby, he turned to face the inquisitive stranger who had walked in through the open stable door.

"You see we were just going to come down to Bethlehem to register for the enrollment which the emperor ordered," the young man from Galilee reflected. "Then we were going to go right back home. But this happened." He pointed to the sleeping baby.

With a finger, he flicked a spider's web from a timber cross piece that formed the cow stall.

"It's just not real," he went on, his strong voice modulated to a whisper, so as not to awaken the infant.

"Here we are, 110 miles from home. We haven't even been married six months and now we have a baby."

With his right hand, he stroked his black-bearded chin slowly.

"Can you believe that there are so many people here from out of town that there's not a vacant room in the hotel? That's what the manager told us, 'No room! But if you want to, you can sleep in the barn,' he said. I don't think he expected us to take him up on it, but what could we do?"

"We didn't really expect the baby quite this soon. The trip probably speeded up things a bit. You know, 110 miles, even if you're riding a donkey, is quite a ways. Then, when we couldn't get in at the hotel, Mary was pretty upset. This is the first time she's been this far from home, and not knowing a soul in this town — well, I just don't blame her for being scared."

The young man then went on to relate some of the unusual events he and his wife had experienced prior to coming to Bethlehem.

"Do you believe in angels?" he asked. "I've heard about angels since I was able to walk. My folks talked about them when I was a kid. Mary's folks did too. But neither one of us ever thought we'd see one. You can believe this or not but we actually did see an angel — not at the same time either — and the angel talked to us. Mary, tell him what happened to you."

Mary, who had been listening to the conversation, then told of how she was at her home in Nazareth one day when she heard a voice at the door. She turned away from what she was doing, and there stood a stranger.

"He looked at me," said Mary, "and greeted me by saying, 'Hail, O favored one, the Lord is with you.' That really scared me. I couldn't figure out what he was talking about. Then he told me not to be afraid, that I had found favor with God, and that I was going to have a baby whom I was supposed to give the name Jesus.

"I told him this was impossible. How could this happen when I didn't even have a husband, I asked.

"By this time, I had this strange feeling that it really was God saying something to me. My nervousness went away, and when he told me that the Holy Spirit was going to come upon me and the power of the highest was going to overshadow me, and that this baby he said I was going to have would be called holy, the Son of God, I was so excited my head was swimming."

When she told Joseph about it, she said, Joseph was "plenty disturbed by the news."

Joseph admitted this was true.

"Our family was always strict about doing things the right way," he explained. "Here she was, pregnant, and I knew I wasn't the father. But somehow or other, I couldn't get angry with her. I loved her, I knew that, and I certainly didn't want to hurt her, but being a Jew, I couldn't marry her either under those conditions."

All day long, every day in the shop, Joseph stated, he could think of nothing else.

When he went home for meals, he wasn't hungry.

When he went to bed at night, he couldn't sleep, worrying about how he was going to tell Mary that while he still loved her with all his heart, he was bound by Jewish law to break the engagement.

Some men would have made a big thing about it, announced it publicly, but this Joseph said he knew he couldn't do.

"Finally," related the carpenter, "I decided to just go and tell her than I couldn't marry her, but that I wouldn't spread it all around town."

That night, Joseph continued, he went to bed, and for the first time in many nights was sound asleep almost as soon as his head hit the pillow.

"Then I had this dream," he stated. "There was this angel standing there, telling me to take Mary to be my wife. He said that she had conceived by the Holy Spirit — whatever that meant — and that the baby she would have was to be called Jesus and that he would save his people from their sins.

"You know how dreams are. Some you just can't remember, and some are so real that when you wake up, it's just like it's been an actual experience.

"That's the way this one was. Then I got to thinking about the prophet Isaiah who had predicted so many things that had happened. He said in the early part of his writings that the Lord was going to give the Jewish people a sign. A virgin would conceive and bear a son whose name was to be called Immanuel.

"The more I though about it, the more I thought about what Mary had told me about her experience with the angel, the more I became convinced that this just wasn't something we were both imagining.

"I got up as soon as it was light, and headed right for Mary's house.

"I rapped on the door, and Mary was up. She opened it and I grabbed her in my arms and said, 'Mary, we're getting married. I don't care what anybody thinks or says. Get ready, let's go. We've waited too long already.' "

Mary's eyes met Joseph's. She smiled, remembering.

"What about the shepherds?" the stranger asked. Reports around Bethlehem were that shepherds in the hills outside of town had also seen and heard angels.

"That's another bewildering thing," responded Joseph. "You know how they keep the sheep out there on the hills and let them graze. You should probably go out and talk to them and get the story straight, but I can tell you what they told me."

According to Joseph, the shepherds had laid out their bedrolls on the ground after the sheep had bedded down for the night. It was chilly and they had a campfire burning. The sky was clear. Stars were everywhere.

Several of the shepherds had fallen asleep. A couple of them were still awake and marveling at the brightness of the sky.

The man who seemed to be the spokesman for the group, said he was just lying there when out of nowhere, a stranger appeared.

"The way he told it," said Joseph, "it frightened him almost out of his wits. There this stranger stood, and dark as it was, a weird kind of light covered the hillside. The other shepherds woke up. They were just as scared. Then this stranger started to talk, and they figured out he must be an angel of the Lord, because he told them not to be afraid and that he had good news for them. He told them that a baby had been born in the city of David — that's Bethlehem, you know — and that this baby was a Savior whom he called Christ the Lord.

"You'll find him," the angel told the shepherds, "wrapped in swaddling cloths and lying in a manger.

" He had no more than said that than there seemed like there were hundreds of others, all around and in the sky above, the way that shepherd told it, and they all started to praise God, by saying

'Glory to God in the highest, and on earth peace good will toward men.'

"Then, the shepherd said, they knew it had been angels who had appeared to them because they disappeared from them into the heavens above.

"When they had gone, the shepherds told us, they decided to find out if what they had heard was true," continued Joseph.

"I don't know who was the most surprised when the shepherds opened that barn door, Mary and me or the shepherds. They came in one by one and looked at the baby. Then they started telling us about what they had seen that night before. I hear they also talked about it around town, too, because there are a lot of people out there who are wondering about what's going on.

"All I know is that those shepherds were pretty excited when they left here, because they kept saying, 'Glory to God' and 'Praise God' as they walked down the street and back to their pastures."

Asked about his future plans, Joseph said that they would remain at the hotel barn for eight days, and then take the baby to have him circumcised according to Jewish law and custom.

"We'll name him Jesus," said Joseph, "because that's what the angel told Mary he was supposed to be called.

"Then we'll go back home to Nazareth and see what happens."

Mary nodded her head in agreement, as she walked over to the manger to arrange the blanket around her baby's face.

She patted the little head with her hand, and whispered softly, "Jesus — what a beautiful name for a beautiful child."

The Ways Of The Model T Ford

Snow-Blocked Road Was Just Another
Challenge For Mailman Pete

We haven't had a heavy snow yet. But when and if we do have a
heavy snow fall, and it falls on frozen ground, it won't stay long.
If it falls on mud, it will stay. It doesn't appear that this will apply
this winter, because there won't be much mud, I fear, until early
spring.

Snow that comes in the old of the moon is apt to last; snow that
comes in the new of the moon is soon past.

When snow falls dry, it means to lie, but flakes light and soft
bring rain oft. (Kind of a corny way to say it, if you ask me.)

It takes three cloudy days to bring a heavy snow. (This is one
I'm going to watch. It makes sense to me.)

If snowflakes increase in size, a thaw will follow. (Something
else to watch.)

Speaking of snow, it seems to me there was always a lot more
snow on the ground when I was on the farm.

I mentioned this to one of the "younger generation" the other
day and was told that reason it was so much deeper then than
now is that I was only half as tall then. And that may be true.

However, I remember there were a lot of times I walked to country school in snow that was deeper than my four buckle overshoes. And every car carried a scoop shovel in case the tracks on
the township roads had drifted full again.

What a struggle it was to go anywhere with a car in those days.
Most of the time, we figured it was more trouble than it was
worth, and didn't even try to get the car out of the garage unless
it was necessary to go to town for a few groceries. Otherwise, we
let it sit, and stayed at home.

Our driveway, which was a couple of blocks long, had a way of
drifting full with two to three foot drifts. When formed by a real
strong northwest wind, those drifts would be so solid that the
snow couldn't be shoveled until the crust had first been cut out in
squares.

When the weather settled a little bit, Dad would get out there
and work his way through to the road. It might take the better
part of a day. The next day, the driveway would drift full again,
and he'd have to start over.

Usually, several of the neighbors would get together to open the
road so the mail could get through. Mail was mighty important,
because it always included the daily paper and the Rock County
Star or the Rock County Herald on Fridays.

"Pete" Gibson was our mail carrier, and he'd tackle most any road and get through, but there were on occasion, some that even he couldn't negotiate.

That was during the days before snow tires. "Pete" would put chains on the 30 by 3½ tires on his Model T and would hit the drifts at full speed in the hope that he'd get all the way through.

Sometimes he did get through, sometimes he didn't. When he didn't, he'd start shoveling. Then someone looking up the road to check on why the mail hadn't come yet, would see him, and go to his rescue. Usually going to his rescue meant harnessing up a team, finding a long rope or chain, and pulling him out. There was no towing charge. The farmer was just happy to help and to get his mail.

Those who recall the Model T remember that the low gear was activated by stepping on the pedal with the left foot, and that reverse was the middle pedal on the floor. Getting unstuck from a snow bank meant going forward in low, then going backward by stepping on the reverse pedal. What the pedals did was tighten some bands in the transmission case. Those bands were like brake bands in the wheels on today's cars. A week of heavy snow generally meant that Pete would have to get a new set of bands put in when he came in from the route on Saturday.

The repairs were done quickly and efficiently in the Vopat and Clemens garage. It didn't take a graduate engineer to take the car apart to get the job done, either. All that had to be done was take out the floorboards, loosen several bolts, and the transmission case was laid bare. Take out the old bands, put in the new ones, and the car was ready for another bout with the plugged roads.

A heavy blizzard would sometimes keep Pete from making his route for a whole week. But he'd start out every day and get as far as he could before dark. His job was to get the mail through, and he took his job seriously. I think he had another reason, too, He just liked to put that Model T to the test, so that when he got back to town, he could tell "Sheik" Bruemmer, "Curly" Hettinger, and "Dutch" Newberg how he could get through roads that no one else would even try.

The townships had no snow removal equipment at that time, and the county had only a limited amount. So, the farmers who lived along the roads would do what they could to make it possible for traffic to go through.

They made makeshift single lane roadways on the grades beside the roads, or inside the fences in the fields. They'd pull a few staples out of the barbed wire fences and lay the wires down so a car, a wagon or a bobsled could go over them. Or, they'd open a couple of gates and the makeshift roadways would wind their way across the fields avoiding the big drifts by curving this way and that to the exit at the other end.

Dad often made a snow plow out of the bobsled by attaching a walking plow to the right rear runner. The bobsled track was narrower than a car track, but with a walking plow attached, it was possible to drive one direction, and come back over the opposite wheel track from the other direction, and the road would be just the right width for a car.

Where the snow was deeper than a foot or two, it meant shoveling the track open with scoop shovels. The neighbors would all pitch in, and many hands made light work for what to us today would be an awesome task.

There were times, however, that a snowstorm would last several days, and we couldn't wait until we could get through with a car to get groceries, coal, or whatever we happened to need.

Then we'd go by team and bobsled, filling the bottom of the sled box with straw to keep our feet from freezing. We'd also take along a couple of horse blankets. As we drove to and from town, we used the blankets as robes to keep our legs warm. In town, we used them to cover the sweaty horses.

Needless to say, the stay in town didn't last long. With days short as they are now, it didn't take long until the afternoon sun disappeared. And there were lots of evening chores to do at home.

It was cold on the hands as we guided the horses where we thought they should go. More often than not, we tied the end of the reins, or the "lines" as we called them, in a knot, and slid the loop over our shoulders. Then we'd guide the horses by body movement, or an occasional pull on the lines with the hands. Otherwise, we kept our hands in our coat pockets, or if we got really cold, we'd swing our arms across our chests and slap our hands against our shoulders. That improved the circulation of both hands and total body.

Believe me, it was mighty good to get home, get the horses watered and in the barn, and get into the house to warm up while sitting on a chair and propping our feet on the oven door of the kitchen range.

I guess maybe that's why I think one of the best devices ever invented for the traveler is the car heater.

I think it is also one of the reasons why I can never sing out with much enthusiasm on such songs as "Jingle Bells" and "Over the River and Through the Woods".

It might be fun to ride in a one-horse open sleigh, but as I remember it, it was doggoned cold.

"They Don't Make 'Em
That Way Anymore"

I made the rounds last weekend to see the new car models in the various show rooms.

The hood of this one new car was up, so naturally, I looked in.

The maze of hoses and electrical wires and metal tubing, round things, square things, plastic things, metal things — all jammed together in a neat compact package that makes today's new car engine something to behold.

"Quite a change from what they used to be," commented an equally puzzled viewer, looking in from the other side.

"Yes," I remarked, " a lot different from the first new Ford sedan my Dad had. I remember . . . "

And then it dawned on me, that was quite a while ago. If that Ford sedan were still in existence it would be over 50 years old, because it was a 1923 Model T FORDOR — that's the way Ford spelled 4-door then — FORDOR. (A two door sedan was a TUDOR.)

Man, what a car that was! Not as big as Will McCurdy's Buick touring car and a little smaller, maybe than John Alink's Chevrolet coach, but it was a four-door, with crank up windows. Turn the crank one way, and down would come the glass in the door. Turn it the other way, and up it would go. It didn't have those cold imitation leather seats, either. Real cloth upholstery, that's what they were made of. Grey striped wool.

It had a lot of other innovations, too, that weren't on the 1918 touring car which had served as the family car for several years.

It had a self starter. Just step straight down with your foot and you'd hit a metal knob. Step down a little harder and it would go, "Oo, Oo, Oo, Oo" about four times, and then, the motor would roar into being, the intensity of the roar depending upon how far down you had pulled the throttle lever, which was on the right side of the steering column, just below the steering wheel.

I'd better mention that before you ever stepped down on the starter button, there was a certain pre-start technique that had to be followed.

First, you had to push the spark lever, on the opposite side of the steering column from the throttle lever, up as far as it would go. This kept the engine from "kicking". The throttle lever was usually pulled down about half way between "shut off" and "wide open". You'd turn the switch key to the left. This would start one of the four coils buzzing, and you knew you had current going through. The choke lever was on the right hand side of the dashboard, and the usual procedure was to sit with one hand on the spark lever, one pulling the choke, and the foot on the starter button. Then, when the engine started, you'd pull the spark lever down with the left hand, let loose of the choke with the right hand, move the right hand over to the switch key and turn it completely to right, from "Bat." to "Mag.". Those two abbreviations meant battery and magneto. You'd start on battery power, operate on magneto power.

A couple of other special features on the 1923 Model T sedan that appealed to me were the dome light and the electric horn. The 1918 touring car had a magneto horn. The horn button was on the top side of the steering column. When the motor wasn't running, the horn wasn't functional — it wouldn't honk. When the engine was running, you'd press it, and it made a sound which we youngsters would imitate vocally by saying something like, "Skuirt, skuirt, skuirt." Actually, we didn't pronounce the "R". So, if you can think of the word "squirt", harden the second letter by using a "k" and drag out the sound of the "irt" without giving a true "r" sound to the "r", you have the sound pretty well in mind.

The 1923 model had an electric horn. The horn button was at the end of a tube, protruding to the left side of the steering column. Even if the motor wasn't running, you could honk the horn. And, it had a different sound. This one we imitated by saying "kronnnk", which rhymes with honk, only you drag out the "onk" portion, and sound the "r".

The dome light was the greatest. I remember the first night we drove the new Fordor to a band concert in Beaver Creek, we kept the dome light on the whole way. In fact, this was the only electric light of any kind that we had. Remember, this was 15 years before the REA brought electricity to the farm, and we depended on lamps and lanterns for all other light. It was really exciting to pull a little button on the door post and watch the light come on overhead.

The "big cars" like Chevrolet, Dodge, Overland, Essex, Briscoe, Mitchell, Maxwell, Willys Knight and Buick had shifting levers — on the floor. But with a Ford, you didn't have to fiddle around with a hand shift. The pedal for low gear was on the slanted front floorboard, right beneath the steering column, on the left. There was a middle pedal, which you stepped on for reverse. The pedal on the right was the brake. You started out advancing the "gas" or throttle lever and stepping on the low pedal. This got the car going forward. When you released the low pedal, you were in "high" and you'd govern your speed by advancing or retarding the gas lever as the occasion demanded.

If you wanted to go in reverse, you'd depress the low pedal — which also served as a clutch — about half way, and then step on the reverse pedal. You'd also depress the low pedal half way when you applied your brakes. If you didn't, you'd kill the engine.

Model T Fords didn't come loaded with extras like new cars do today but you could buy them. One of the popular accessories was the cutout. You'd cut a hole in the exhaust pipe right below the front seat floorboard, and install this gadget which fit around the pipe. The gadget had a butterfly valve which was opened and closed with a small foot pedal. By pushing it open, you closed the exhaust pipe ahead of the muffler, and the exhaust was emitted through the cutout. The roar of a car with a cutout was music to the ears of the "young punks".

Another accessory that was popular was the spotlight. And, the tool kit that mounted on the running board. The Montgomery Ward and Sears catalogs carried oversize steering wheels that were hinged on one of the spokes so they could be flipped up. Fat men, particularly, liked these wheels.

By the time Dad bought the 1923 sedan, demountable rims were standard equipment, and that meant a carrier on the rear, complete with inflated spare tire and rim. Before that, the spare tire was a side mounted affair, and had to be mounted on the rim without removing the wheel whenever there was a flat tire.

If you didn't have the tool box on the running board, chances are you kept the tire tools and jack beside the gas tank, which was located below the front seat. Every time you filled your car with gasoline, it meant that everyone in the front seat got out of the car, and the front seat had to be removed before you could unscrew the gasoline tank cap and fill the tank.

Simple as the Model T was by today's engineering standards, it was still quite a car. And once its traveling days were over, it could usually be converted into a stationary engine for sawing wood, grinding feed, and other farm chores. As I have said many, many times, "They just don't make cars like that anymore."

1922 Ford Model T touring car

If you didn't have the tool box on the running
board, chances are you kept your tools beside the
gas tank, located under the front seat. Note front
cushion resting on back of seat and steering wheel.

The Dodge touring car

The "big cars" like Dodge, Chevrolet, Overland,
Essex, Briscoe, Mitchell, Maxwell, Willy's Knight
and Buick had shifting levers — on the floor.

It Took Ingenuity To Start
A Model T In Winter

I seldom get into my car on a 20-below zero morning that I don't think of the anguish we used to go through trying to start a Model T Ford in winter.

How much simpler it is to cope with winter starting problems these days when we have jumper cables and headbolt heaters!

Model T Fords weren't easy to start at best. There was a knack to it that some had and some didn't have.

I didn't.

Particularly in the dead of winter.

I will say that there were very few times that it was impossible to start a Model T. But, boy, did you have to baby it to get that four-cylinder engine to start chugging when the mercury was around the zero mark or below.

My dad's first Model T was a touring car without a self-starter. The next one, and the one I remember as a boy was a 1923 Fordor sedan. It did have an electric starter.

But on extremely cold days, the starter didn't count for much. The six-volt battery might turn the engine a couple or three times, but if it didn't "fire" then, you'd about had it. The starter would make one last groan and that would be it.

Necessity is the mother of invention, and Model T owners, by necessity, came up with a number of ways to cope with their problems.

The first possibility, of course, was spinning the crank.

Every Ford came with a crank in front as standard equipment. Normally, the crank dangled below the radiator, readily available when needed. Optional equipment, I remember, was a strap that was attached somewhere along the bottom of the radiator that would hold the crank in a horizontal position. I can't remember the reason for it, unless it was to keep it from dangling down into the mud when the car had to go through deep ruts on muddy roads after the spring thaw or a heavy rain.

The fellow doing the cranking made sure that the spark lever along the left side of the steering column was pushed up. When it was pulled down, the engine sometimes backfired, or as we called it, "kicked". When that happened, it was easy to end up with a broken wrist if you had a full grip on the crank.

The ignition key on dash was turned to the left, or on "Bat.". It would never in the world start if it were turned to the right, on "Mag.". You could always tell when it was on "Bat." because one of the four coils beneath the dashboard would buzz. That is, if the battery wasn't dead. When the battery was dead, you'd wire up the "hot shot" battery, a four-pack of six volt dry-cells normally used for the gasoline engine that powered the water pump or the washing machine.

Then, you began cranking. If you hadn't switched to winter grade motor oil, it was easy to understand why the self-starter didn't turn the crankshaft. Sometimes the oil was so heavy and stiff from cold, you'd have to stand on the crank to even budge it.

Usually, when it was cold, we'd push the car out of the garage and build a bon fire beneath the crank case, by igniting a few kerosene-soaked corn cobs. By the time the fire was burned out, the oil in the crank case had thawed enough to make turning the crank possible.

Someone would sit in the car and pull the choke button while the other person would crank. After a while, if the car hadn't started, they'd change places.

Another way of making cranking a little easier was to jack up one of the hind wheels. Blocks were placed against the other wheels to keep the car from moving forward, and then one of the rear wheels was raised so it would turn. The transmission was engaged, putting it in high gear. This made cranking a little easier, and if there was a chug of the engine, the momentum of the rear wheel in motion kept the car running.

Another remedy we quite often used when the car wouldn't start was the pouring of boiling water on the intake manifold. This supposedly would heat the gas mixture in the manifold to make it ignite better. A little hot water on the carburetor sometimes helped too.

Putting a little gasoline in the cylinders, might also do the trick. This meant taking out the spark plugs, and pouring a few drops of gasoline through the spark plug openings. If there was any kind of spark at all, it would ignite the gasoline and maybe get the engine going. What a relief it was when this happened, because by this time, we'd be virtually exhausted from turning the crank.

If none of these methods worked, there was one last resort — harness up Queen and Bess, get a whipple tree and log chain, and pull the car around the yard a few times. If there was snow or ice on the ground, it meant putting chains on the rear wheels first, because they'd just slide along and not turn otherwise.

The fellow behind the wheel had to be alert during this operation. The ignition had to be on "Bat.". The choke, way on the right of the dashboard had to be pulled out. The gas lever on the right hand side of the steering column had to be pulled down at least half way.

The emergency brake lever, on the floor board on the left side of the driver, had to be pushed forward. This lever also put the transmission into high gear. As the horses started out, the driver would depress the clutch pedal about half way. This would make pulling easier because the car was in neutral. Then, after the team was moving along fairly fast, the driver would pull back his left foot, and the car was in gear. A few trips around the yard, pulling the choke at the right time, adjusting the spark lever back and forth quite often was enough to get a pop or two from the engine. Then it roared to life.

If it didn't, about the only recourse we had was to call Roy McCurdy. Roy was our neighbor who could do more with a monkey wrench, a pair of pliers and a piece of baling wire than any man I've ever known. He'd approach the ailing Model T with a gleam in his eye and the determination that there did not exist such a thing as an unfixable Model T engine. Trouble with Roy was that he was hard to find at home. He, more often than not, was out shelling corn, helping repair somebody else's car or gas engine, or lending a helping hand to a neighbor in some other way.

Model T Fords had a few other shortcomings, too. They never had heaters but we'd try to fashion something by covering the exhaust manifold, and letting the radiator fan blow air across it, through a metal tube, and then through an opening below the dash on the right side. Sears Roebuck and Wards had some special heater manifolds with fittings that included a little floor register. Model T owners who had those were considered to have the very best equipped cars in the country.

Model T's had no water pumps, either, unless you bought them as special equipment through the mail order firms. This didn't make for the most efficient cooling system, and many a radiator froze, even if it had alcohol in it.

Alcohol then was the only anti-freeze available, and it was very volatile, evaporating at a much lower temperature than water. If you had your radiator filled with a water-alcohol mixture that would stand 20 below temperatures, it would likely begin to boil and steam when it reached 160-170 degrees. By the time the car had traveled 10 miles — the distance from our farm to Luverne — it wasn't unusual to have lost enough alcohol by evaporation that the radiator would freeze at the zero mark, or even above. This was something we watched of course, and when we arrived in town, we'd throw a big horse blanket or robe over the radiator and hood to keep as much cold out as possible while we were in town. When we got home we'd replace the evaporated alcohol to keep the radiator from freezing until the next time we went out with the car.

Despite what I've written about the Model T, it was still a great car in its day. As a vehicle, it was hard-working, commonplace and heroic; a possession that produced happiness and excitement when conditions were right; irritation, hot temper and high blood pressure when they weren't.

I don't mean that these reminiscences should be an indication of irreverence. But they certainly make me appreciate Die-Hard batteries, permanent anti-freeze, dashboard controlled heaters, and car dealers who have tow trucks.

Those Were The Days

The Day The Bank In Beaver Creek Failed To Open For Business

A couple of weeks ago when I interviewed Les Rolfs for a story on the new Hardwick State Bank, he and I were talking about the problems the banks had in the 1920's. Rock County had 13 banks then, one or more in every town, including Magnolia and Ash Creek.

Then came the "hard times". Banks began to close or they would merge, keeping their doors open by pooling their resources. Too many had outstanding loans without sufficient collateral, and prices went to pot. When the liabilities exceeded the assets, it was good bye bank.

Some of them, which had relatively wealthy directors who stuck in a lot of their own money to keep them solvent, came through the troubled times.

And some of them didn't, among them the First National Bank in Beaver Creek.

My dad was a director of the First National.

I was about 10 years old when it happened. The impact was so great on our family at the time that I remember it to this day.

I recall it was vacation time, because I was home from school. Dad, it seemed, had been going to Beaver Creek to a bank meeting almost every other night. I couldn't figure out why. He'd leave about 7:30, and I know he didn't get home until past midnight.

Dad was a happy-go-lucky chap. Problems, he felt, were something everyone experienced some time or other, and when they came . . . well, it was just a matter of rolling with the punches.

Dad was never an emotional man, but he was pretty choked up that sunny morning he drove home from Beaver Creek, after learning that the bank had not opened its doors that morning.

"The bank is closed," he told Mother, with tears filling his eyes. "We're broke. We don't have anything."

He had some livestock and some grain, as I recall, but the prices weren't good. In order to buy coffee, flour, sugar, syrup and kerosene, life's main necessities, he had to sell some hogs that weren't yet ready for market.

The task Dad would have liked to have avoided that day was telling my Grandpa Aaker what had happened. Grandpa was an old man then. He and Grandma lived with us. After coming to this country from Norway, he never earned any more than enough to care for his family's needs. When Dad bought the farm, they were living there with my uncle, and when my uncle moved, our home continued to be their home. Grandma helped Mother with housework, Grandpa helped with the chores, and for it, they received their board and room.

Dad, however, felt Grandpa should have a little money of his own, so he had given him a brood sow for helping care for the hogs. The sow produced a good litter. They grew big and fat on Dad's corn; Grandpa sold them and banked the money. This happened several times, I suppose, because when the bank closed, Grandpa had $900 in a savings account.

He'd trusted the money to the bank because Dad was a stockholder and director. Now the bank had failed, and Dad had to tell him so.

Grandpa couldn't believe that a bank could fail in America. He had left Norway to come to America because there was no hope of getting ahead in his homeland. Now, he and Grandma were in their declining years, and all they owned was the clothing they were wearing, what they had in their room, and a little change which Grandpa kept in his pocketbook to buy an occasional tin of Union Leader pipe tobacco.

Dad had to tell me, too, that my savings account was lost. I had $30 in the bank. Not much, but it represented a lot of pocket gophers caught and birthday and Christmas presents from parents and relatives.

Times didn't get better for several years. In fact, they became worse until the big crash of 1929, and the depression that followed.

But Dad didn't become disheartened or bitter. Neither did Grandpa and Grandma.

Somehow, we managed to come through it all, although it took Dad until he was almost 80 years old to recover from the financial setback, just because he was a stockholder and director of the bank.

The bank never reopened. Later, the building was sold, and the Beaver Creek State Bank, the other bank in town, moved into it.

Sometimes I wonder if what happened at Beaver Creek and Ash Creek and Magnolia and elsewhere during those financially troubled years could happen again.

Deposits and savings accounts are insured now, of course, but supposing there would be a rash of bank failures such as there were then. Would Federal Deposit Insurance Corporation have enough money to pay every depositor?

A lot of people who lost their life's savings in bank failures would have nothing to do with banks ever again. They kept their money in cash, some place or other, and paid for everything with cash.

Dad never felt that way, however. He opened an account in a bank as soon as he was able to sell something and dealt with bankers all the rest of his life. He taught us children, too, that handling money was easier and safer if we dealt with a bank than if we tried to keep it in cash.

While some of the lessons in economics taught us by the bank failures in the 1920's were tragic, they were valuable lessons as well. I for one have faith that our country will never again experience what it did at the start of the Great Depression.

Whatever Happened To A.S. Johnson Fish Company?

Every time a local store advertises a fish sale, I wonder whatever happened to the A.S. Johnson Fish Company at Duluth.

Maybe it is still in existence, I don't know. There were other fish companies in Duluth too, many years ago, but as stores added frozen food departments, the fish companies just couldn't make it any more.

I remember well A.S. Johnson's advertisements in the farm magazines. The firm's trademark was a picture of a fisherman attired in rain hat and foul weather gear.

You could buy combination boxes with varieties of different fish, or if you preferred, just one kind. The ad explained several of its offers and listed prices. Or you could write for a price list.

Our family liked variety, and as soon as the ad appeared, Dad would figure out how many pounds to buy of each variety, and would send in his order.

In a couple of weeks, we'd get a notice from the freight depot at Beaver Creek that the shipment had arrived. This meant going to town with a team and wagon, or team and bobsled, as the box was too big to load into the back seat of the Model T.

We had a small shed near our house that served as the milk house or cream separator house in the summer. In the winter time, it housed the box of frozen fish. We could shut the door of the building, and there was no way that the cats could get in. There the fish were kept frozen until the supply was gone.

You could buy the fish "dressed" or "round". If they were dressed, they were headless and the innards were removed. If they came round, that meant that they had been frozen as they came out of the ocean or lake, and you did the dressing. You saved a little money by buying them this way because the price per pound was less, but they weighed more, so really, it didn't make an awful lot of difference.

Dad usually bought a few Alaska salmon, some whitefish, and the rest Lake Superior herring. He had a table of some kind in the old milk house that he used to lay the salmon on so he could cut the steaks with a meat saw, a common household tool of that day. How luscious they were the way Mother prepared them! Plump, red steaks, with little or no bone. With mashed potatoes and home-churned butter, a side of home canned peas or corn, and a couple of pieces of thin, homemade Norwegian flatbread, the meal was a gourmet's delight.

The smaller herring were tasty, but had more bone, so they

weren't quite as popular at mealtime. But then, they were cheap. Kind of like having hamburger for a few nights, after you have had one night with a big juicy steak. The whitefish were plump and fat, and when cooked (or I should say, pan broiled in butter) they dripped with their own juices that made them taste a little fishier than the other two varieties. Later, when I was introduced to cod liver oil, I realized that the whitefish for years supplied the same vitamins, because their flavor had a slight trace of cod liver oil flavor.

The supply in the big wooden box dwindled with the passing of the winter days. When the box was empty, it was a sure sign that spring was near at hand. It also served as a reminder that it was spring butchering time; time to replenish the meat supply that had dwindled during the fall corn picking season when there were usually a couple or three hungry corn pickers around for several weeks. There was usually enough left after corn picking so that we didn't have to eat fish with every meal.

The days of the big fish boxes and the spring butchering are gone. Now we pick up our salmon steaks (when they are available) at the frozen food counter, and our pork chops, wrapped and packaged at the self-service meat counter and think nothing of it.

Milk house served a dual purpose

Building at left served as a cream separator house
in summer. In winter, it housed the box of frozen
fish. Grandpa is shown at the water pump.

A source of countryside sound

On a still winter day, we could hear distinctly the
whistle of the steam locomotives as they headed
into Beaver Creek or Booge.

Noiseless Countryside Has Variety Of Sounds For Those Who Listen

Horst Witschonke is the noise control specialist for the United States Environmental Protection Agency Region V.

Recently, I read an article he wrote entitled "Noise in the country" in which he admitted that he was a "city slicker" who spent his childhood in Berlin, Germany, and the rest of his days in Chicago.

Like too many bureaucrats in government jobs today, he wrote the article without doing any research in the field, but rather after "a search of the literature and a lot of imagination."

His conclusion was that "most of the rural areas are necessarily quiet."

The books he read on the subject and the visions he conjured up in his mind, led him to the conclusion that noise in rural areas is caused by highways, grain dryers, aircraft, motor boats, automobiles, trail bikes, chain saws, farm equipment, crickets and snowmobiles.

It's too bad that Mr. Witschonke didn't take the time to come out into the country and do a little listening.

He'd have found that there are a lot of noises that are pleasing to the ear, and that the quiet of the countryside has sounds that must be listened to or listened for to be heard.

Some of the countryside sounds that I recall are no longer heard, but are a pleasant memory to those of us who were privileged to have listened to them when we were kids. And there are others that are still there to be enjoyed by those who take the time to listen.

See if you remember any of these:

The squeaking of snow on a sub-zero morning while walking in broad soled overshoes over hard surfaced drifts.

The explosive cracking sound of ice on a pond on a crisp, cold moonlit night.

The whoosh of bobsled runners and the tinkle of the chain links of the harness traces worn by the team of young bays pulling the sled.

It always seemed to me that sounds carried a greater distance in winter and were more sharply defined than at any other season of the year.

We lived four miles from Beaver Creek and three miles from Booge. On a still winter day, we could hear distinctly the whistle of the steam locomotives as they headed into the two little towns.

The Palisade Church was two and a half miles away. It was not unusual to hear the sound of the "first bell" which was rung by the janitor a half hour or so before church time.

Voices seemed to carry an unbelievable distance at times.

I remember a neighbor by the name of Ralph Gritters who would call his hogs with a lusty, "poo-ooey, poo-ooey!" that we could hear a mile away.

Animal calling was an ability not everybody possessed, but those who practiced it were fairly successful in bringing their livestock in from the pastures and fields with their calls if they rewarded them with some ears of corn or a gallon pail of oats once they reached the barn.

Dad used this method, although he generally supplemented his calling with a walk out to where the animals were.

The cattle came when he called, "come boss, come boss."

The horses responded to his summons of "koo-op, koo-op, kop, kop, kop!"

I never did know the significance of the words, nor their origin, but most farmers who did any livestock calling used the same words.

Animals and birds made a variety of sounds that one learned to distinguish and sometimes understand.

A cow's moo is an example. She'll make a different sound when her newborn calf is in the barn and she is turned out of doors than she will make if she is thirsty and the water tank is empty. Likewise, the calf's response is different when he is first separated from his mother than when he's hungry and it is past feeding time.

The herd bull develops a different sound, once he reaches maturity. When he asserts himself to other males, whether it is one in the herd or to the neighbor's bull across the pasture fence, he'll walk slowly in the direction of his counterpart, pawing dirt and bellowing. He uses a low pitched rumbling sound several times before bawling a louder, higher-pitched vocal rendering that will carry a good half mile on a calm day.

There were other distinctive rural sounds a few years ago that aren't heard very often today:

The chorus of roosters crowing at "first light".

The cackle of a hen to announce that she had laid an egg, and the clucking sound she'd use to summon her baby chicks once they were hatched in her own private nest beneath a feed box in the horse barn.

The peeps of baby chickens in a brooder house. The somewhat similar peeps of baby ducks and goslings.

The hiss of an angry goose when approached at nesting time.

The lively quacking of a flock of white Pekin ducks at feeding time.

Pigs at any age are noise makers. The little ones will squeal if stepped on by their mothers, or shunted aside at feeding time by a bigger brother or sister.

Then there's the mother pig's contented grunting as she lies quietly on her side as her babies nurse hungrily.

Squeals take on a different quality completely when they come from barrows and shoats at feeding time.

I remember that cats, too, provided a variety of sounds.

There were the muted mews that came from the haymow, heralding the arrival of a new batch of kittens.

There were the louder, cacophonous mews that came from the mixed voices of the barn cats at milking time, which was their feeding time.

There were the belligerent, defiant meows of the tomcats when they vied for amorous attentions of one of the females.

And, there were the outraged, screaming meows that cats of either sex used when embroiled in a fight with an unsuspecting, half-grown pup.

Wild birds, too, provided a variety of noises and sounds.

There were the barn pigeons in the hayloft that cooed contentedly.

The brown thrushes used a clucking sound of sorts if you came near a nest, but their vocal solos in the evening from the top of a cottonwood tree were among the most melodious of bird songs.

Speaking of bird songs, I wonder if there are still bobolinks around? We used to see them in the meadows which had creeks. Not only were bobolinks distinctive to look at, but their songs were distinctive as well.

The meadowlark, of course, was the bird whose song was awaited early each spring. When the yellow-breasted bird with the V-neck began his serenade from the roadside fence posts in early March, there was no doubt but that spring was near at hand.

There are, of course, birds that make noises as opposed to sounds.

I think of the crows and their raucus cawing. And the woodpecker, who often disturbed my early morning slumber with a rat-tat-tatting on the roof above my bedroom.

The flickers nested in holes in trees. You could tell when their new home was about finished by the slower peck-peck sound that came from within as the tree was being hollowed out to size. A few weeks later, when the eggs had hatched, a buzzing sound announced that a hungry brood of babies were impatient because the parents weren't bringing in the insects — their favorite baby food — fast enough.

Then there were familiar sounds of machinery, many related to the season of the year.

There was the cluck of the wheels of the high-tired lumber wagon.

And the click-click-click of the corn planter as the long strand of wire with its many joints moved though the mechanism which dropped the corn at set intervals.

The clatter of a mower sickle during the haying season.

The kerchunk of the grain binder as another bundle flopped onto the bundle carrier.

The steady puff-puff-puff of a steam threshing engine.

The clanging and clunking of a grain elevator at corn picking time.

The sneezing and chugging of a one-lung gasoline engine.

The whine of a buzz saw at winter wood cutting time.

The shake-shake-shake of a fanning mill.

There are sounds of nature that are heard in the city as well, but somehow, the sound is more defined in the country.

I think of the sharp claps of thunder, the whoosh of a miniature whirlwind through a field of knee-high corn, the steady patter of a spring rain on a barn roof, the howl of a blinding blizzard, and the quiet bubbling of water from a spring.

I guess I'd maybe agree with Mr. Witschonke that most of the rural areas are quiet. There is a stillness that one doesn't find in the city, that is certain, although there are noises now that I never heard as a boy on the farm.

But as quiet as it may be, one has only to listen to find that while there may be relatively few noises, there are a multitude of sounds that are pleasing to the ear — if one just takes the time to listen.

It's Hobo Time, But There
Are No Longer Hoboes

I never see a freight train in late summer and early fall that I don't look it over as I pass it or it passes me to see if maybe there isn't a hobo aboard. But, I guess the days of that kind of bumming are gone, because I never see one.

When the trains were more numerous, and in the days before the combine replaced the grain binders and threshing machines, it was commonplace to be able to count a dozen or more men as they sat in open boxcar doors, particularly on north bound trains. They'd start in the south — Texas, Oklahoma, then Kansas and Nebraska. As the harvest progressed northward so did they, working as day laborers shocking grain and pitching bundles until winter closed in on them in northern North Dakota or Canada.

I don't know whether these men could be called hoboes or not. I guess maybe they could be more aptly called itinerant harvest hands.

They came in a wide variety. Some rough, some soft spoken. Some young, some old. Some good guys, some real bums. Many made the same stops year after year. Others made the trip only once. Still others chose different routes to see different parts of the country.

They had an opportunity to make pretty good money for the time they were out, and the best ones went home with a pretty healthy bank roll.

For one thing, their travel cost them nothing. It may not have been first class, nor was it speedy, but the train ride got them to where they were going.

When they'd arrive in town, there'd usually be a gathering place, like the old Gimm and Byrne corner in Luverne or the Beaver Creek pool hall, where farmers of the area could come in and pick up a couple of men to shock grain or haul bundles. The trip to the farm didn't cost them anything either.

After they arrived at the farm, they were assured of both room and board. Some slept in good clean beds in the house with the rest of the family. Others had makeshift quarters in haystacks or in the barn.

They'd eat with the family, and the fare was usually excellent. They came when garden produce was at its peak — green peas, sweet corn, string beans, carrots, beets and the like, and green apples for the best of apple pies.

The farm wives usually prepared more sumptuous meals at harvest time, because the work was hard, the days were long, and the men were hungry.

The pay was also the best. Day laborers made 50 cents to a dollar more a day during harvest time than they did during corn cultivating or haying, or if they were hired by the summer rather than by the day.

The men who "rode the rails" had only a few clothes to buy, their tobacco — Copenhagen, Beech-Nut, Prince Albert, Bull Durham, Camels or Luckies — and that was it, unless they stayed around town on Saturday night. So the pay they got, small though it might have been, was all take-home. No social security, no insurance, no withholding. The money was all theirs.

There were some tramps in the bunch, of course. But I can't recall of a single farmer who hired one of these men who was cheated or robbed. He might get one now and then who'd spend his first day's pay on a half-pint of "moon" or "alky" and take the next freight out, and once in a while there was one who didn't know the butt end from the head end of a grain bundle. Generally speaking though, they'd give a day's work for a day's pay.

And in the evening, they'd delight the farm kids with tales of their travels and experiences during the years on the harvest trail.

I suppose it was before and after the harvest season that the real honest-to-goodness hoboes would ride the freight. Mainly, they were men who liked to travel about the country, or did so to keep away from the law or to avoid supporting a big family they'd left behind somewhere.

Some of these would work. Others would just stop at a farm place or in town and ask for a cup of coffee and a slice of bread. Still others would con a business man out of a dime or so, and in that way, end up with a dollar or so in his pocket. With this — if he didn't spend it for booze — he'd maybe pick up a few items of groceries, then head out to the hobo jungle which many of the towns had if they had wooded river areas not too far from the railroad tracks.

There, they'd meet others like themselves and have cookouts over a campfire. After dark, and when the fire died down, they'd lie down on the ground, cover their faces with their battered hats, and sleep until they were awakened by the birds at dawn.

Those were the hard time years for a lot of people. But it's difficult for us to say now whether the hoboes had it bad or good. For many of them, it was doing what they liked to do — to see the country, meet different people, and work as little as possible. For others, bumming was degrading and demeaning, but one way they could earn a meager livelihood to support their families without seeking relief from their county poor fund.

The world has changed a lot in the last 40 to 50 years.

Today, the hobo, the tramp or the bum — whatever you choose

to call the boxcar traveler of four or five decades ago — is about as extinct as the whooping crane. Social reforms have made it easier for him to live — whether he is unable to work, whether he is out of work, or whether he just doesn't want to work.

I suppose there are still some who ride the rails, but I never see them.

How long is it since you've seen a hobo?

Back Then, Ice Came In
Chunks, Not Cubes

One of the great inventions of our time, in my estimation, is the ice cube.

Even on the coldest day in winter, I like an ice cube in a glass of water. I like the taste and the feel of ice in my mouth. And water is never more thirst quenching than when it has been cooled by an ice cube.

As a boy, I always enjoyed breaking off a piece of icicle and letting it melt in my mouth. Or when I went skating, I'd chip some of the creek ice loose with the point of a skate, and suck on it.

There was a time when ice from the Rock River was pure enough so it could be used to cool the "ice cold lemonade" that they sold at the Rock County Fair.

And the fellow who provided it was a man I remember as the ice man when I first moved to Luverne, more years ago than I care to remember. His name was S.S. Toms, but everybody called him "Vet".

Vet had the corner on the ice business and made regular deliveries of cake ice to the homes and business places going into the back door with a chunk of ice held by a pair of ice tongs tossed over one shoulder to fill the compartment in the wooden chest which kept milk and butter and other perishables cool before the days of the electric refrigerator.

The ice he peddled was natural ice. No electricity or other energy source was needed to manufacture it. But it took a certain amount of human energy to make it available to ice box owners in town.

The ice harvest always took place during the dead of winter, usually when the temperatures were the very coldest.

There were a couple of reasons for this. One was that the ice by that time had attained its maximum thickness. This was important, because it meant more weight per block or chunk. It was also at the time of the year when day laborers could be hired by spreading the word at Gimm and Byrne's, and the business on the ice route wasn't anywhere near as rushing as during the summer months.

Luverne's ice came either from the Rock River, Dybedock's Pond, or from the railroad sandpit south of town.

Ice harvesting was something like the grain harvest on the farm. It was a lot of hard work, but the ones who were working at it usually had fun doing it.

It would be a lot simpler task today with power tools. Then, manpower and horsepower combined to get the job done, although I can remember during the last years of the ice business, circle saws, powered with a gasoline engine were used to cut the rectangular chunks to size.

The first task in preparing for ice cutting was to shovel off the snow so that the surface of the ice was clear and smooth. Lots of times, the ice was so clear that it was virtually transparent like glass.

Once the snow was removed, the ice would be marked with a marker that would scratch the surface and make straight lines so that when the ice blocks were sawed, they would be uniform in shape and size. I can't just remember the dimensions of a block of ice, but I'd guess they were perhaps 24 inches wide and maybe 24 to 30 inches long. The thickness would depend on the winter. An exceptionally cold winter would produce thicker chunks than if the winter was mild.

The saw usually didn't cut all the way through, but did go deep enough so that the ice would break with a jab from an ice chisel or crow bar at the line which had been cut by the saw.

As the chunks were cut and loaded, the water area would get wider and wider. Men would then float the blocks downstream or toward the loading platform by using pike poles.

Chunks would be pulled onto a platform. Then the wagons or sleds would pull up, and the owners would load from the platform. Farmers of the community provided the wagons and teams, and were able to make a little spending money that way. They made sure, though, before they started, that their horses were properly shod with shoes that had heavy caulks for walking on slippery surfaces.

Luverne's ice house was located on South Cedar between the railroad track and the fairgrounds. There, Vet stored the big blocks until he delivered them in the summer time.

There was a trick to stacking the ice in the ice house, too. Particularly when it started filling up. They had some kind of a hoist at the door to the building. A horse would be put into use as the heavy blocks were hoisted from the wagon up to the necessary height to get them inside. There, men and boys would wrestle the chunks and pile them in neat stacks, packing each cake in sawdust which was shipped in by box car from a sawmill someplace. The sawdust kept the ice from slipping around, and also served as insulation to keep it from melting once the weather warmed up. In addition the sawdust also helped absorb what water did come from the melting ice.

A lot of times, a man spending a day at the ice pond would come home looking like a walking icicle himself. When a chunk of ice would slip loose from the tongs and fall back into the pond, water would splash up, covering him from head to toe. On a cold day it would freeze before it soaked through the several layers, so it never reached his skin.

During the summer months, Vet would deliver the ice by horsedrawn wagon to the homes and business places. At the rear of the wagon was a platform and a scale for weighing the ice. The cake would be chipped to size and weighed before being lugged inside.

On a hot day, one could usually locate Vet and his wagon by following the black line that formed on the street by the water which trickled from the crack in the bottom of the wagon box as the ice melted.

Neighborhood kids often ran up to the wagon to get ice chips to suck on, as Vet chipped the ice block to the right size and weight. The ice may have come from the river, but it was pure enough so the youngsters didn't become sick.

I've been told that a black Laborador dog always followed Vet's ice wagon. As the dog became older, he romped less and less. But he'd become so well acquainted with the route that he knew where Vet would be heading next and he'd take short cuts to beat him there. While he was waiting, he'd lie down to rest and catch his breath.

Old Vet's been gone a long time and so has his ice wagon. It's hard to imagine that it was ever possible to get along without refrigeration as we know it today, but the people managed somehow.

I suspect Vet and a lot of others in the ice business put up a fuss when they heard that mechanical refrigerators were going to be produced in such quantities that there no longer would be a need for ice men and ice houses.

But just think of how many people are employed in the field of refrigeration today.

Problems seem to have a way of working out, don't they?

The Day Doc Anderson's Car Stalled In The Middle Of The Roaring Beaver Creek

We no longer seem to have the winter snow runoffs and early rains that filled creeks and rivers to overflowing every spring.

Sometimes, the creek through our farm overflowed its banks and spread out to cover our entire pasture. It was an awesome sight, particularly during the ice breakup when huge chunks would be bobbing up and down as they floated downstream.

The Beaver Creek, which drained a larger watershed, became a mile wide lake at times when unusually warm weather caused a heavy winter snow cover to melt rapidly.

I never will forget the time that Dr. A.M. Anderson tried to cross the "roaring Beaver" during one of those floods. Doc was a veterinarian in Rock County who established his practice in 1915 and served the county's farmers for a half century.

He made his daily farm calls in his personal car. On this particular day, he was driving his nearly new Model A Ford coupe. He started across the stream which was perhaps a foot deep for a distance of five or six blocks. But he must have gotten the engine wet because it stopped right in the middle of the stream.

Doc was never one to let rain or sleet or snow or hail, the heat of summer or the cold of winter deter him from answering a farmer's call to treat an ailing cow or horse. And going to a farm in a round about way was nothing but monkey business if there was a straighter line to his destination. Doc must have been heading up to the Frank Kelling, Adolph Wallenberg or Clifford Helle place when his car stalled. Doc wasn't for wading a quarter of mile in either direction, so he just climbed out on the roof of the car, waved his hands and yelled until someone heard him. If I recall correctly, a nearby farmer came with a team and lumber wagon. The car was left standing until the flood waters subsided.

Veterinary medicine in those days was a far cry from what it is now. Doc Anderson and Doc Haggard were the only two "vets" in Luverne at that time, and they took care of the whole county. How they worked! No radio communications, no pickup trucks equipped with refrigeration and hot and cold running water to ride in from farm to farm. Just head out on a call or two, then head back to the office to learn, often times, they had just come past a farm from which someone had called during their absence.

Those were the days when draft horses accounted for a big share of the veterinary work done. In fact, I don't believe I ever heard Doc being called a veterinarian until about the time he retired. He was always "the horse doctor".

The year the veterinarians really got the workout was the year of equine encephalitis epidemic. It was a form of sleeping sickness, very contagious, and hundreds of fine work horses died that year. Since the horses were the main source of power for pulling machinery — cultivators, binders, plows, mowers, wagons — the loss of a horse not only meant digging down into the pocketbook to buy a replacement, but it also meant delays in seasonal farming operations.

Doc worked night and day, getting little or no sleep as he raced over the rough country roads treating the sick animals, and, if I remember correctly, vaccinating those which had not been exposed to the disease.

Hog cholera was another disease which caused heavy losses to farmers. Then, cholera vaccine was discovered, and when pig vaccinating time rolled around, there were more long days and short nights for the veterinarians.

How Doc Anderson and Doc Haggard ever managed to do the work they did and still devote time to community affairs, I'll never know. Doc Anderson also read a lot, and had one of the very fine private libraries in town.

Their main concern, however, was to serve the farmers in the county whose livestock needed medical attention. They dared venture out in all kinds of weather and over all kinds of roads to answer their calls. That's how it happened that Doc Anderson was sitting atop his car, calling for help, when the "roaring Beaver" overflowed that cold spring day in the early thirties.

Peddlers And Gypsies Were
A Part Of Rural America

It used to be that when spring came to Rock County, the season brought not only the birds, the bees and the flowers, but gypsies, horse traders and peddlers as well.

The gypsies, horse traders and peddlers were itinerants — no one knew exactly where they came from, no one knew where they went. But one thing was certain, they'd show up at the first sign of warm weather.

Some of the peddlers had wagons. Some of them walked.

I remember the peddler and his wagon. Every year, for many years, the same man came to our farm. We thought he was Jewish, and mentioned it one time.

"Not a Jew, not a Jew," he said indignantly. "Syrian. I come from Syria."

He lived in Sioux City and had a regular route through the countryside, driving a single horse hitched to a small covered wagon or buggy in which were suitcases jampacked with goodies that appealed particularly to the housewife.

There were pins, needles, thread, and other items used in sewing. Sometimes he'd have a bolt or two of calico or muslin. And cheap jewelry. Cheap perfume. Pots and pans. Shoe laces. Lamp wicks and lamp chimneys. Knick-knacks and everyday needs.

He and other peddlers, unlike the gypsies, were considered honest. They'd be invited in to dinner, lunch or supper if they were on premises at mealtime, and over a period of time, learned to know who the best cooks were, and usually stopped there when it was time to eat.

In addition to getting free meals, they also generally had free lodging. Sometimes, they had to sleep in the barn, but if there was an empty bed in the house, they were often invited in to spend the night.

They never had to pay for the meal and bed, so in return, they'd let the housewife, or more often, the kids go through their satchels and pick out a ring or some other trinket to show their appreciation.

One of the last peddlers to travel through Rock County died the night of the day he visited our house. This was in the fall. It was cold. He drove on the yard, and Mother went out to greet him. He asked if he could come in and get warm. All he had for a jacket was a black suit coat which he always wore.

Mother took him into the kitchen, put some more cobs in the range, and opened the oven door so he could warm his feet. She gave him a cup of coffee and a bite to eat, but she could see he wasn't feeling well and he told her so.

After he had overcome his chill to a degree, he went back to his wagon and headed west for a couple of miles, then south toward what was then the town of Manley.

He stopped at a farm place near there. I don't know who lived there but they gave him shelter for the night. That night he died.

They Watched The World Series Long Before There Was TV

Watching the World Series in color from an easy chair in the family room at home Saturday, I thought to myself, isn't this great?

Seeing the two best teams from the two leagues match their abilities and their wits without having to shell out the price of a ticket, or look for a parking space, has to be one of the marvels of the electronic age, if you are a baseball fan.

I couldn't help but think how it was when I was a kid about seven or eight years old, when we didn't even have a radio to keep up with sports events of the day.

Unless we went to Sioux Falls to watch what was going on by means of an electrically lighted scoreboard at the Daily Argus Leader, the only way we knew how the game came out on a given day was to read about it in the paper when it came in the mailbox the following morning.

A fellow by the name of Bill Whitcomb was the Associated Press telegraph operator at the time. His office was in the Argus Leader building, which was then located on North Main Avenue.

Bill was an avid baseball fan, and felt that World Series reports should be current, not a day late if it was at all possible to provide that information as it was happening.

I'm not sure whether he designed the scoreboard, or if he had some electrician do it. But every fall, at World Series time, a platform would be set up outside the Argus building, and Bill would put the board up and man it for the duration of the series.

There were switches on the back side to light the various bulbs on the front of the board.

Bill would get the reports over the AP wire by Morse code, direct from the ball park where the game was being played.

Names were placed on the board so that spectators knew who was in the lineup.

When the batter went to bat, the light would flick on at home plate. If he singled, the light over first base would flash on. If there was someone on first when the hit was made, and he advanced to third, for instance, the bulb over second base would flash on, then disappear and the one over third base would light up.

There were bulbs to show strikes and balls on the man at bat, and to show if an outfielder caught a fly. Other bulbs showed runs, hits, and errors, the innings, the number of outs, and other statistics.

When game time rolled round, the crowd would start to gather in front of the Argus building.

When the first man got up to bat, there could well be 300 to 400 persons standing around, watching the game. Traffic had to slow down or detour around the block. Most of the local drivers knew about the scoreboard, and made it a point not to travel down that block while the game was in progress.

Sioux Falls still had streetcars then and they, of course, had to follow the track. That meant that the spectators had to get out of the way every 20 minutes or so that a street car would go past.

Needless to say, the street car operators weren't too happy about the situation, but neither were the spectators, who had to step out of the way or move back about the time the count on Babe Ruth was 3 and 2, the bases were loaded and the Yanks had two men out.

Man for man, fans watching the scoreboard were as vocal as the fans in the stadium.

All the ball park enthusiasm was present there on North Main Avenue. Each team had its supporters, and cheers went up each time a hit or an out was made. A home run or a double play that brought the crowd to its feet at the park captured similar enthusiasm from the Sioux Falls scoreboard spectators.

A little money changed hands, too, there on Main Avenue. If the Yankees were playing the Cubs, there were New York fans who'd have a few bucks that said the Yanks would win, and there were Chicago supporters who had cash to lay on the line to say that they wouldn't.

All this time, Bill Whitcomb was busier than a cranberry merchant the day before Thanksgiving, translating the Morse code messages that were coming in over the wire into flashing lights on the big board.

When the game was over, the lights were shut off, the fans would leave, and Whitcomb would go back to his desk to handle the routine news that continued to come in over the wire.

In those days, the World Series was the No. 1 sports event of the country.

The teams would play all summer, and the fans followed the newspaper reports and boxscores, but most of them never got really excited until World Series time. The excitement became contagious, and even those who didn't follow baseball all year long became enthusiastic and followed the series so that when it ended they knew who the stars were, at least, and who were the World Champions.

World Series enthuisiasm also was developed in another way — through pools which those who had a little gambling know-how would sell at series time.

The big ones had numbers on them which sold for $1 or sometimes $5 a number. They had them worked out so that the person who had the game score was the winner, the one who had the number denoting the number hits each team had would also win one of the prizes. The promotor usually ended up with $10 for making up the board and selling the numbers. The big winner ended up with maybe 50 to 70 bucks.

When radios came on the market, World Series broadcasts, the heavyweight boxing matches and some college football were the only sports events that were carried.

Fans who didn't have radios would crowd around the loud speaker of one of the sets in the dealer's store to hear the game. A lot of them, who had resisted the sales pitches given them before series time, were convinced, after hearing a game or two, that radio was here to stay, and that they might as well buy one and enjoy it at home.

Today, professional football, basketball, tennis, hockey and golf have taken over a lot of broadcast time, both television and radio, and baseball maybe doesn't have as big a following as it did when Bill Whitcomb had his unique scoreboard at the Argus Leader building.

Nevertheless, when World Series time is at hand, the stadium seats are filled, and a lot of people who don't pay a great deal of attention to who's who in the American and National Leagues are glued to their TV sets while the series is in progress.

There's still something about the game of baseball that puts the game in a class by itself, at least during those days in October when the championship is being determined.

The players put forth their best efforts, teamwork is superb, and the crowds, the color and the pageantry provide excitement and entertainment that is not duplicated at any other time of the year.

Weather Forecasting May Not Have Been As Scientific, But It Was Almost As Accurate

Weather forecasting wasn't always as sophisticated as it is today. More often than not, it was based on lore, not scientific evidence. This made it a hit and miss situation, with those most interested in weather conditions using a variety of theories as basis for their predictions.

We used to have several weather prognosticators in Luverne who held to theories that had been handed down from father to son for who knows how long. Max Voelz, Bill Engelking, Herman Jochims and Fred Mitchell had certain signs they looked for, and based their long range forecasts on those signs. Today, with radar, computers, and all the other gadgetry providing information for television and radio weathermen to disseminate to the public, many of the old folklore methods have or soon will be forgotten.

When I worked as a cub reporter for Ed Townsend, one assignment I had four times a year was to check with Bill Engelking, Max Voelz, and Herman Jochims after the Ember Day periods. Not many people know about Ember days any more because practically no one consults almanacs any more.

The first Ember days each year are the Wednesday, Friday and Saturday that follow the first Sunday in Lent. They were established, or I perhaps should say, set apart by the Council of Placentia in 1095 A.D. as days of fasting and prayer. The others, always Wednesday, Friday and Saturday, come during the week following Pentecost, the week after September 14 and the week after December 14. How these church designated holidays entered into the weather picture, I don't know, but here's the Ember days theory:

The kind of weather that prevails on the first Ember day sets the pattern for the next following month, the weather on the second determines the pattern for the second month, and that of the third day for the third month. If the weather is sunny, for instance, the weather for that month will be fair. If it is sunny for a half day, and cloudy and rainy the other half, the month will be half fair and half rainy, and so on. Maybe it just works out that way, but more often than not, the theory holds.

Another old timer, Henry Vande Velde, swore by the wet and dry moon theory. He maintained that if the points of the moon on the first night of the new moon (you can find moon information in almanacs, too) are aimed up, then the weather during the upcoming month is going to be dry. But if the point is down, so that it looks like a dish that is tipping and water could run out of it, then the weather will be relatively wet for that month.

It has to be the new moon, though, and the very first day of the new moon if this theory is to be valid.

Some maintain that the Northern Lights have a bearing on the weather. If the lights are bright, according to this theory, a change in the weather can be expected. For instance, if the weather has been warm, colder weather will follow in two or three days, and vice versa.

The title of Fred Manfred's novel, "Morning Red" comes from these rhymes pertaining to the weather:

Evening red and morning grey
Sends the traveler on his way.
Evening grey and morning red
Sends the traveler home to bed.

This says much the same as the old sailor's adage:

Red sky at night
Is a sailor's delight.
Red sky at morning
Sailors take warning.

I've watched the skies many times. When it's red in the morning, the weather most generally changes during the day or before nightfall. When the sun sets in a glow of red at night, the prospects are for beautiful weather the day following.

Another weather rhyme says "snow that comes in the old of the moon is apt to last; snow that comes in the new of the moon soon is past," and one that says, "When snow falls dry, it means to lie, but flakes light and soft bring rain oft."

Somebody has come up with this observation, "It takes three cloudy days to bring a snow."

Another says, "If snowflakes increase in size, a thaw will follow," and there's the saying, "If the first snow falls on frozen ground, it won't stay long; if it falls on mud, it will stay."

I'm not saying that any of these are accurate predictions, but here's one I know to be true: "When you say that snow always was much deeper when you were a kid, remember you were only half as tall then as you are now."

My grandmother used to say that when a dog eats grass, it is a sign that is going to rain.

When there are sundogs, say some, it is sign that it will be cold, or colder.

If there is a ring around the moon, count the stars in the ring, and it will rain within that many days.

If it rains on Easter Sunday, it will rain every Sunday for seven weeks.

Watch the smoke come out of a chimney. If the smoke goes downward, toward the ground, there will be rain soon.

If it begins raining on the day the moon becomes full, it will continue to rain until it quarters, about a week's time.

If the sun shines while it is raining, that means it will rain the same time the following day.

When the wind blows from the north or northeast, and it begins to rain, you can expect rainy weather to continue for three days.

Fred Mitchell always maintained that the first frost would come exactly six months from the date of the first thunder-shower.

I've check this several times, and found that generally, it comes very close to being accurate. Try it some time. On the spring day that you first hear a thunder clap, go to the calendar and write "first frost" on the same date six months hence. Six months later you can easily check on the validity of the theory.

I Wasn't There, But They Say
This Is What Happened

The girl walked into the boss' office and asked for the day off.

"What's wrong?" the boss asked.

"My father broke his leg."

"I'm sorry," the boss said. "How did he break it?"

"You won't believe me if I tell you," she replied.

Her boss insisted and she unfolded his story:

Her mother and father had spent the previous day at a nursery digging shrubbery, binding the roots of the bushes in burlap. They took a pickup load of shrubs home and put them on the front porch.

Father, grimy from the long day's work, went into the house to take a shower.

Mother, still feeling industrious, begin peeling burlap from the shrub roots.

Father, standing in the shower and enjoying the warm flow of water over his body, suddenly heard Mother scream. "Help! Help!!"

Father dashed out of the shower, down the hall and into the living room, not even bothering to grab a towel on the way.

Mother was standing at the front door screaming.

"Snake!" she cried at the top of her voice. "There's a snake in the house."

The snake had been bound with the roots of a shrub. When she released it, it slithered across the porch, through the front door and into the house.

"It's under the couch!" she cried.

Father got down on all fours, peering cautiously under the couch, his whole body tensed in anticipation of meeting a rattler eyeball to eyeball.

Enter Rover, Father's faithful old hound dog. He came creeping in the front door, silently crossed the living room, his pads making no sound on the carpeted floor. Stopping a couple of feet behind Father, Rover also peered under the couch to see what Father was looking at.

Father, focusing every ounce of his attention on the space beneath the couch, didn't see Rover.

As dogs will, especially faithful old hound dogs, Rover walked the last couple of steps, paused at Father's heels, reached forward and cold-nosed the old man.

"You can imagine what raced through Father's mind," the gal told her boss. "Thinking snakes, when he got that cold shock in the rear, he knew immediately he was facing the wrong way. The snake must have been behind him."

"He thought he was snake-bitten, sure enough," the gal continued. "Flop! He keeled over on the floor in a dead faint."

Mother screamed again.

She thought Father had suffered a heart attack.

Swiftly she raced to the telephone and called the rescue squad.

Realizing the nature of the emergency, the rescue squad responded at full speed.

The men swarmed into the house, armed with oxygen and all the necessary paraphernalia and began their efforts to revive the unclothed man lying sprawled on the floor.

Someone broke an ammonia ampoule and stuck it under Father's nose.

It revived him.

The first thing he remembered when he snapped out of the fog was that he'd been snake-bitten.

He went into temporary shock and began fighting, lashing out at anyone who moved.

He was a big man. And very violent.

Several men wrestled him under control and put him on the stretcher.

He continued to struggle and when two men picked up the ends of the stretcher and started for the door, Father took a vicious swing at one of the rescue squad boys.

Unbalanced, he fell off the stretcher.

Broke his leg just above the ankle.

The boss who had been listening in utter amazement, was too stunned to even comment.

"See, I told you, you wouldn't believe it," said the gal.

"Honey," said the boss, "if that story's true, you can take the rest of the week off. Your father needs you more than we do."

Funny thing, the story ended there. No mention was ever made of what happened to the snake.

Embarrassing situations are not limited to having a dog interfere with snake hunting in a living room. This one is reported to have taken place in the laundry room of a home in Philadelphia suburbia where the lady of the house had just carried an armful of soiled clothing.

Depositing the accumulation in the automatic washer, she applied the non-phosphate soap substitute and was about to touch the button and initiate the cycle when a vision of Ben Franklin's Poor Richard's Almanac flashed before her. "Waste not, want not."

Realizing the single garment she wore was soiled, in the spirit of Poor Richard thrift she stripped it from her, added it to the load, and — with a dramatic sweep — touched the button. About that time she realized the precipitating pipes overhead were ruining her coiffure.

In the spirit of Ben Franklin's innovative resourcefulness she reached for the nearest protection which happened to be her son's football helmet.

There she stood, the personification of all that is basic and great about America: clean, thrifty, resourceful, imaginative. She stood there wearing her son's football helmet, a radiant glow — and nothing more. She stood there statuesque, and alone . . . she thought.

Enter the energy man, the power man, the ubiquitous, omnipresent meter reader.

"Aaahhummmmmmpf!" (The seasoned meter reader's triumphant clearing of the throat.)

"Lady, I don't know who you're playing for," he said, "but I sure hope your team wins." The story ended there. I don't know what happened to the immaculate housewife — or the meandering meter reader, and I suppose it really doesn't matter.

It just goes to show that it seldom fails — what may be embarassing to one person turns out to be extremely funny to someone else who sees it or hears about it.

The fellow who told me this story said the fellow who told him vowed that it was gospel truth.

A fellow drove onto a supermarket parking lot. A cat ran in front of his car, and he couldn't stop in time. The car's front wheel ran over the cat, killing it. No one saw it happen except the driver. Rather than leave the cat's body on the parking lot, he picked it up, put it in a brown paper grocery bag he happened to have in his car trunk, and gently stashed the bag in the corner of the trunk while he went into the store, evidently to pick up a box of groceries he had bought earlier. In any event, he left the trunk lid open.

About the time he placed the bag in the trunk, a lady was walking toward the store. After the man was inside, he happened to look out the window, and noticed the lady standing beside his car. She looked one direction, then the other. Certain that no one was watching, she deftly picked the bag out of the trunk and headed for the restaurant across the street.

Curious as to what might happen next, the man loaded his groceries, and he, too, went into the restaurant. There he found the woman just being served a cup of coffee. Her purse was beside her, and so was the bag. As she sat there sipping her coffee with one hand, she reached over with the other hand to open the bag to see what goodies were in it. She looked, gave one loud shriek, dropped her coffee cup and fainted dead away.

Efforts to revive her were unsuccessful, so an ambulance was called. The attendants placed her on the stretcher and were walking out the door when one of the waitresses ran out with a purse in one hand and a brown grocery bag in the other. "Here," she said, "don't forget her purse and groceries."

The attendants took them, placed them on the stretcher with the woman, and headed for the hospital.

The story, as it was told to me ends there.

I can't believe that the nurse in attendance at the hospital wasn't curious enough to take a look into the bag, too.

I'd like to have seen the expression on her face.

Then Came Adulthood

Newspapering — It's Been Fun, Fascinating, Sobering

"How would you like to come to work for me?" asked the genial gentleman who had just walked down the stairs from the office in Nelson's store.

"I've just talked to Ben," he continued, "and he says you're free to go if you want to."

I'd just finished wrapping a pair of Lee overalls for a customer and was still standing at the wrapping counter. I was speechless.

The man addressing me was Edwin S. Townsend, publisher of The Rock County Star. The day was Oct. 5, 1938.

I couldn't believe what I was hearing. A job at The Star? What I'd been wanting so badly for several years! And he was offering it to me!

"You mean me--me?" I stammered in amazement.

I remembered I'd asked him for work a couple of years before, but he said he had no openings. I'd gone from The Star to Nelson's, and Ben Pelstring, then the manager, hired me. I'd wanted to be in the newspaper business — I'd studied for it, but jobs were scarce and I grabbed onto the first thing I could get, and was happy to get it.

Ed told me he was going to be needing a reporter. His daughter, Lucille, then editor of the paper, wanted to leave Luverne.

As soon as I gained my composure, I said, "You bet I'd like to go to work for you, when do I start?"

"Come to the office on Thursday, Oct. 18, after the paper is out," he replied. "We'll go over the things we want you to do, and you can start right in."

I started that day, all right, hardly daring to believe that I'd last out a week. I knew some fundamentals about news writing, but the only typing experience I'd had was what I could find time to do after work from the day he hired me until the day I went to work.

I managed to last out the week, and a few more besides. Tomorrow, Oct. 18, one thousand eight hundred and twenty weeks later, is my 35th anniversary in the newspaper business in Luverne.

Those many weeks have been good to me, and good for me. I've enjoyed them thoroughly. This is not to say that each day has been one of joy, because it hasn't. There is tragedy in news as well as things pleasant, and even after 35 years, it's not one little bit easier for me to write a story that deals with sadness. It's impossible, I've found, to overcome my sentimental nature.

The Star was published by a small staff. Lucille Townsend, the owner's daughter, was the editor then. She wanted to try her skills at a larger newspaper, so I was hired to replace her. Ed was the publisher. He also wrote a column which he called "Chats" and handled advertising sales. Georgia Molitor McIntosh was his gal Friday who could do about anything that had to be done around the newspaper office except run the linotype or feed the press. The foreman was Frank Heiges, and the linotype operator was a fellow by the name of George Northrup. Young Eddie Townsend, Jr. came in to run the press now and then. Later Glenn Leech was the printer's devil.

I hope that I don't sound as though I'm living in the past. But newspaper work is nothing more, nothing less, than recording history on a day-to-day, week-to-week basis, and I have been privileged to have done much of the recording that has been done by this newspaper for the last three and a half decades.

It's been fun, it's been fascinating, it's been sobering.

As I was writing this, your last week's Star-Herald was being printed. When you read this, I will already have written "Boy Off The Farm" for next week.

In this business, you can't spend much time looking back at yesterday, because if you do, today will be past, and you're into tomorrow before you know it.

Maybe that's why October 18, 1938, seems so very close to yesterday . . . time has a way of flying by so rapidly.

Print Shops Lost Some Of Their Fascination With The Demise Of The Linotype

The last remaining vestige of the old Star-Herald printing plant has been unceremoniously hauled to Abie Thone's salvage yard.

The old "Model 5" linotype turned a few heads as it proceeded down the street, suspended from the crane at the rear of Abie's aging but trusty truck.

"What on earth kind of a machine is that?" someone wondered.

The Model 5 was undoubtedly the most ancient piece of printing equipment left in town.

I have no idea how old it was. I'm sure it was older than the Goss Press which was hauled out eight or nine years ago. And that was 48 years old when it was taken apart and removed from The Star-Herald basement.

The press and the Model 5 were moved into The Star-Herald building by Orval Kannenberg and his crew from the old Herald building in 1943. The press had to be brought up from the basement. The linotype was tucked away in the northwest corner of what is now Harvey Ball's barber shop.

Al McIntosh always said that a devil rode in, uninvited and unnoticed, on one or the other of the machines as they were tugged, lifted, pushed, pried and dragged into the building. In the years that followed, he (the devil, not McIntosh) would emerge from hiding and, just for kicks, would gum up the works sometimes on the press, other times on the linotype.

The devil's trickery had a way of affecting the men and the women who operated the machines from time to time. Particularly, the linotype.

I don't know who might have been the first to sit down to its keyboard. Al Haines operated it when I first came to town. Whether someone was there ahead of him, I don't know.

What a change that must have made at the old Rock County Herald when it was installed. Up to that time, every line of type, large and small, had to be set by hand, one letter at a time, and once the paper had been printed, the individual letters had to be put back in the case from which they'd been taken.

Linotype operators were a different breed.

Among them were what the trade referred to as "boozers" and "boomers". The boozers were those who were addicted to the bottle. The boomers were those who couldn't get along with their fellow workers or the boss, and those who just liked to see the country, going from print shop to print shop, earning just enough to make it to the next town.

We had all three varieties — good hard workers, boozers and

boomers. Not that boozers and boomers weren't hard workers. A good share of them were, but you couldn't count on them to be there when you needed them most.

Going back before Al's time, there was George Northrup. Not over 5 foot 5, George was conscious of his stature, and confident of his ability. He disliked women, or so he said, and being a preacher's son, he liked to quote Scripture passages such as the one from Proverbs: "It is better to dwell in the corner of the housetop than in the same house with a contentious woman."

He left when Ed Townsend sold the paper to Al, and the next operator I remember was Al Haines' son, Eugene "Heinie" Haines. "Heinie" wound up in Omaha and became head of the Omaha World Herald's "chapel" (union local). "Heinie" died in Omaha unexpectedly a few years ago, just several days before he was to have attended his high school class reunion in Luverne.

One chap who deserves mention was a fellow by the name of Perry Bullers. He spent as much time "fixing" as he did setting type. In addition to liking to fix things, he also had a liking for "mountain dew" of the hill country variety. What he lacked in competency, he made up for with ego and gift of gab.

Frank Nodland was another "mountain dew" enthusiast. But a most engaging person. Al thought he'd really hit the jackpot after watching Frank for a day or two. He set county board proceedings in 6-point legal type at an unbelievable speed, and made only two mistakes an hour.

Word got back to Al on Saturday night after pay day that Frank had boasted he'd held 140 different jobs in four years. Sure enough, he wasn't there when the doors opened on Monday morning.

But Frank came back a couple of times after that. One time he left, and Al started getting cards from him postmarked Winnipeg. One day, during Christmas week, he showed up and needed a job. Al was again overwhelmed by the amiable fellow and said, "O.K., you've got a job."

But he was broke, he said, and could he have an advance? Al dipped into the cash register drawer and came out with $2.

"Oh, Mac," he moaned, "I've got to have more than that."

I don't remember now if Al gave him more than that or not, but Al went home for lunch, then something hit him.

"I'll bet he's leaving town on the noon train," he told Georgia as he grabbed his coat and headed downtown. He stopped at Frank's favorite watering hole, Eberlein's Tavern, and Don the bartender waved him on, "He's catching the noon train out," he said.

The train was just pulling up at the depot when Al got there, and sure enough, there was Frank, just reaching up for the handrail on the coach when Al grabbed him.

Looking back and seeing it was Al, Frank kept his cool. "Aw Mac," he said, "I hope you didn't think I was skipping town, I just had an errand to run over at Worthington and I was coming back on the four o'clock."

"Nothing doing," responded McIntosh firmly, as he escorted him to his car. "You're going back to the shop to work out that advance I gave you this morning."

Unlike Bullers, Frank was an excellent machinist. And no matter how often he quit or under what conditions, Al always welcomed him back whenever he showed up. In spite of his faults, you just couldn't help but like the guy.

We had two mutes who worked for us. Husky Bob Taylor could be surly, and was not to be crowded. The other was Bill Royce, a curly haired guy who had a great sense of humor and also a great sense of rhythm. The fact that he couldn't hear or speak didn't bother him when he was on the dance floor, and he always had several girl friends with him when he drove down the street in his car.

If there was one thing that irked Bill, it was the teams of mutes that would hit town, selling needles, pencils, or whatever. When they came into the office, I always called Bill. He told them in no uncertain terms — with his hands — to get out and get to work.

Both Bob and Bill were good operators. And they were never bothered by noises, that's for sure.

A fellow we enjoyed having in the shop helping out during summer vacations was Paul Jess. A competent workman with an infectious laugh, he went from here to the Brookings Register as I recall.

Seba Vail came to The Star-Herald from Sioux City. He was dependable and skilled, but one who became antsy when under pressure. He and his wife, Helen, had a son who was a "blue baby", a lad who had to stop to rest several times on his way home from elementary school because of a heart condition. One of the first to undergo successful "blue baby" surgery, he grew up to be a healthy young man.

Most of the operators didn't become too well known in the community, but one of them, a genial Irishman by the name of Russ Mahoney, did. Russ was small and wiry, and always on the "juice". He underwent treatment several times, but not of his own accord. When he came back from Willmar, the first thing he did was head for the liquor store to get a six-pack.

Russ generally set type on the other machine, a Model 14, that had two fonts of a head-letter type called Erbar. I used to make him set a lot of Erbar heads on Wednesday, his busiest day. One day, I'd imposed on his good nature once too often. In no uncertain terms he told me that if he ever had the opportunity to set my obituary, it was going to be set in Erbar type.

The trouble with most linotype operators was that if something went wrong with the machine, they could neither diagnose the problem nor repair it. Al used to have a machinist come out of Sioux Falls on a regular basis for preventive maintenance until he had the chance to hire Vic Blessing.

Vic was the last operator to set type on the Model 5. In fact, he had set some type on it the day before he suffered his fatal heart attack.

Vic fought the Model 5 the very first day he went to work. Mistakes were coming out in every line, and the perspiration was dripping from Vic's forehead. But he stayed with it, and got it back in shape. We wondered afterward if the machine had been purposely thrown out of adjustment by a "boomer" who operated it before Vic came.

There must have been a dozen others, or more, who sat at the keyboard of the Model 5 during those years. I remember Fritz Cramer and Ruth Cooch who were here at the same time. It was evident that Fritz and Ruth had been friends before they came here. Fritz had been a strike breaker. Ruth had the ability to make the air blue with profanity whenever something went wrong.

Bill Christian operated the Model 5 about the same time Russ Mahoney was with us. They made quite a pair. Walking down the street together, they looked like Mutt and Jeff because Bill was over 6 feet, and Russ was about 5-5.

Others I remember are Elmer Fehrman, who came from Lake Benton, Stanley Van Vliet, Allen Frigaard, Loren Page, Elton Grimm, Ruth Bergquist, Larry Eskelson and Jean Boone. For some reason, I can't remember Jack Nichols, Bill Devlin, Morris Olson, Berlin Gilman, Norris Wulf and Donald Blazell, but Al remembered them, and I can readily understand why.

Now, the Model 5 is gone. Were it able to speak, it could tell far more and livelier tales that I've related here.

It served the newspaper and the community well because on its keyboard was set the type for the thousands of news stories, columns and columns of "locals" written by out-of-town correspondents, plus the classified ads, and legal notices published over a half century of time.

But linotypes have been replaced by machines of the electronic age, simpler in design, and with greater capabilities.

I am just thankful that I was able to be around to see that ingenious machine in operation, to have heard the click of the matrices as they fell into place, and the groan from the melting pot as molten metal was pumped out to form the lines of type.

Print shops lost a lot of their fascination with the demise of the linotype.

A "back shop" birthday party

Eugene "Heinie" Haines, who is cutting the birthday cake, was one of the Rock County Star
linotype operators. Others in photo are Frank
Heiges, "Boy Off The Farm", Georgia Molitor
McIntosh and a young printer whose name I no
longer remember.

The Speed Graphic
Camera

Together we
recorded Rock
County history as
it was being made
between 1940 and
1968.

The Speed Graphic Camera —
Together We Recorded History
As It Was Being Made

I bade a fond "welcome home" to an old friend the other day — a working companion of some years back — now a retiree from the pleasures, the excitement, and often the tragedies that are a part of life, but more particuarly a part of the life of a newspaper reporter.

I'm referring to the Speed Graphic camera that was used in taking 99 percent of the photos that appeared in the Rock County Star, and later The Rock County Star-Herald from 1940 until 1968.

Al McIntosh brought it with him when he came to Luverne from Lincoln in July, 1940.

Up to that time, very few weekly newspapers published news photos, and the dailies hadn't been at it too long. But Al became sold on photo-journalism while he was on the staff of the Lincoln Journal, and one of the first things he did upon assuming ownership of The Star was to make sure that the paper had at least one or more locally-taken news photos each week.

The Speed Graphic was the news camera used by all serious news photographers then. There were imitations, but the 4x5 Graphic was the top of the line.

By today's standards, the Graphic was a big camera.

Now, we use 35 MM cameras with roll film of 20 to 36 exposures that produce negatives an inch and a half wide by one inch deep.

The Graphic negative was five inches wide by four inches deep.

We used sheet film, which we loaded into what we called "plate holders" — black wooden frames with two plastic slides, each slide tipped with a strip of metal that was black on one side, silver on the other.

The holders had to be loaded with film in absolute darkness, and after a year or two of struggling to learn how to put the sheets of film in correctly, I was able to load a holder in a matter of seconds.

The film had notches on one end, so it was important those notches were to the edge through which the slides were inserted. The notches also had to be at the bottom side, not top. If the notches were on the top, it meant the film was in backwards.

The metal ends of the slides, in addition to being black on one side and silver on the other, were also made to be sensitive to the touch for handling in darkness. The silver side had a rough edge, the black side was smooth.

In taking a picture, it would be necessary to pull the slide out, snap the picture, then put the slide back in. While the silver or rough side was to the outside, it meant the film was unexposed. When the black or smooth side was to the outside, it meant that the film had been exposed.

Once a picture had been taken, and the slide returned, black side out, the entire plate holder was pulled out of the camera, flipped over, and the opposite side, or the second sheet of film in the holder, was ready for exposure.

Flash attachments had just come into use, too, a few years before Al brought the Graphic to Luverne.

The flash bulbs were the same size as a 50-75 watt light bulb. At first, they contained what looked like a sheet of metal foil in them, which burned brightly to form the light. Later, the same size bulb contained the magnesium wool, or whatever it was called, that is still used in some flash bulbs. It was several years later, that the "peanut bulb" came out, and then came the revolutionary "strobe" or electronic flash, used exclusively now when flash is needed in press photography.

I mention this to point up the fact that every press photographer in those days needed a big carrying case for his equipment, or he had to have a lot of big pockets to hold any film or flash bulbs he was carrying on his person.

It took a little time for me to catch onto the routine of handling the Graphic.

First, of course, was remembering to put a plate holder in the proper place in the back of the camera. Next thing was to make sure the exposure and speed settings were right.

Al wasn't one to fool with light meters and gadgetry, and I learned from him to gauge the light to get the proper exposure.

He made it a firm rule, "Don't change the speed. Leave it at 1-200th, no matter what." It was a good rule because it eliminated one check point at picture taking time.

If it was a normal, sunny day, we'd take two shots of the same scene or person, one at f-16 and one at f-22. If it was a little dark or cloudy, we'd shoot at f-11 and f-16. If it was nearly dark, we might open up to f-4, the largest of the f-stops on the Graphic.

Very seldom did we ever end up without a usable negative.

The standard procedure then was to (1) Determine the proper exposure and set the f-stop, (2) focus on the subject, (3) cock the shutter, (4) pull the slide, (5) snap the picture, (6) put the slide back, black side out, (7) pull out the holder, flip it over, and put it back in the camera so it was ready to take another picture.

When we went out at night, we'd focus on the object we were to take by having someone light a match or a cigarette lighter and hold it over the spot we wanted to be the most sharply in focus in the picture. When the two flames visible in the range finder became one, we knew we were "right on".

Al had shown me how everything was to be done, but I hadn't had any practical experience the day he had to go to Sioux Falls, and Georgia and I were left alone in the office.

The phone rang and it was Jessie Roberts, the sheriff's wife, reporting an accident south of Luverne on Highway 75.

I'd never been to a fatal accident before. I'd never used the camera before, so you can well imagine how nervous I was when I drove onto the scene and saw the crumpled up 1939 model Ford two-door with three men in it.

Doc Wright was the coroner then. He examined them one by one, and declared them dead.

I don't remember how many negatives I shot. I double exposed on some. A couple of times I forgot to pull the slide after I cocked the shutter. On one or more I failed to change the exposure, and I overexposed.

When Al came home he was concerned. Of all the days he had to be out of town, it was on a day when there was a three-fatality auto accident.

He took the films into the dark room and developed them. He came out with a big grin on his face. "They're darn good pictures, Irid. I couldn't have done better myself," he said. I've been paid no greater compliment before or since.

From that time on, Speed Graphic became a close working partner, and remained that way until 1968 when Bob and Jim Vance bought the Star-Herald and we switched to the smaller Rolleis and 35s.

When the paper was sold, Bob Vance took the Graphic to Worthington for some restoration. He kept it in his office until one day, a couple of weeks ago, when he turned it over to Bruce Harrison who brought it back to The Star-Herald.

"Remember this?" Bruce asked, as he handed it to me.

I reached for it gently and held it admiringly as though it were one of my grandsons.

"Do I ever!" was my response.

I cocked the shutter, focused on the parking meter across the street, pulled the slide from the plate holder.

How memories came back to me then, of the times, we had spent together! And the Rock County history we had observed!

I remembered one of my first assignments — a picture of the first draft board — Cliff Reirson, Theodore Goehle and Gerhard Ahrendt. Gerhard resigned a week later. And Doc Bofenkamp, who was the medical consultant for the draft board.

I remember one I took of Carl Bly, who was the corn picking champion about that time.

Of the officers and men of Battery E, when they were called to active duty at Camp Haan, as war clouds gathered over Hitler's Germany.

And of every draft contingent that ever left Rock County during the war years and afterwards.

Of Rock County's oldest twins, Paddy and Mart Connell, who observed their 83rd birthday on St. Patrick's Day in 1941.

It was about the same year that I took one of Rick Welch, the most unusual 4-H boy of that era, because he was enrolled in the cake baking project.

Of Luverne's first police car. Hugh Fay was mayor then. Evan Paulsen was chief of police. Pat Ryan, Arnold Schneekloth, and Mac McKay were on the police force. Only Hugh is living now.

One picture I remember was of Art Schmidt on horseback, belly-deep in flood water in his corn field at the east edge of Luverne, holding a cane pole as if he were fishing catfish in his corn field.

I took a shot of Ernie Hamann's fat cattle in 1942. They brought the highest price paid for cattle in eight years — $15.25 per hundred.

I took one of August Hamann when he had 27 head of mules he was raising for sale to farmers in the south who preferred mule power to horse power.

And there was one I remember taking of E.A. Brown at his farm near Ash Creek. Of Doc Wright, after he'd practiced medicine a half century. Of Celia Stephen when she retired from the meat market which her husband had founded years earlier.

Of Pat Larkin, closing the door to his barber shop, after a half century of hair cutting and shaving in Luverne. And of William Spease, who at the age of 80, could shovel 40 tons of coal onto a wheelbarrow and wheel it from a freight car into a coal shed in a 10-hour day.

There was one of Arlen Steen and his dance band that played a dance every Saturday night some place in the area.

Another — I think in 1949 — showed the Luverne first graders at the depot buying tickets for nine cents each from Art Hoff for their first ride on a train — to Magnolia.

I had the pleasure of staging one photo, which could easily have been a picture of a tragedy. The old grade school building, located where Fledging Field is now, had a cylindrical fire escape through which children would slide during fire drills. There had been problems with kids opening the door at the bottom, so it was kept padlocked when school wasn't in session.

This particular day, the lock had not been removed. A fire drill was called. Kids started sliding down. The door wouldn't open, and they started piling one onto the other, screaming in fear.

A janitor had it open before anyone was hurt. Later, I had a few of the kids who were in the tube pose for me in the open doorway.

I can't begin to enumerate the many fires, the many tragic accidents, where the Graphic and I recorded the event.

Together, we covered two homicides.

Together, we also captured the cherubic facial expressions of probably 2,000 kindergarten students over the years. And high school queens, class play casts, 4-H winners, class reunions.

We met our share of leading state and national figures — Harry Truman, Richard Nixon, John Sparkman, Hubert Humphrey, C. Elmer Anderson, Ed Thye, Luther Youngdahl, Karl Rolvaag, Orville Freeman, Val Bjornson and many, many more.

And Speed Graphic was there to take the first pictures of our two babies, just a few hours after each was born.

Maybe this helps you understand why I was happy to see the camera once more. And why I'm happy it's come back home where it, too, in its inanimate way, saw history being made.

I Cried The Day I Said Goodbye
To Nelson's Store

I can't stand to see a grown man cry.

And yet, there I was myself, with tears in my eyes, as I walked through the "big store" crowded with people who had come to attend Nelson Brothers closing out auction sale. Many of those who came, came to buy. Others were just curious. But there must have been many like myself, I'm sure, who came to pay their last respects to an old and a dear friend.

I know there are many like myself who are saddened at the passing of the venerable old store that has served this community for 99 years. As so often happens when we lose a loved one, we have the tendency to ask, "Why?"

Advancing years have a way of exacting their toll, and while there were other contributing ailments, we can console ourselves, perhaps, in that maybe it would be asking too much to expect Nelson's to go on forever. Life just isn't that way.

Better, then, that we reflect on the good things of the past and let the future take care of itself.

There were people at the auction sale that afternoon who can remember more about Nelson's than I do. However, I have some very poignant memories, and if you will bear with me, I'd like to share them with you.

My first recollection of Nelson's is the day I opened my first charge account. I needed a pair of dress trousers. I had come to Luverne with a neighbor so Dad told me to go to Nelson's, find Jack Ulrich, and give him a note saying that he was to sell me the trousers and charge them. I didn't find Jack Ulrich, but I found Jay Helgeson. He fitted the pants for me, and the charge slip went to the office in a miniature monorail car that whizzed up to the mezzanine office at the pull of a cord in the men's wear department. They extended credit to me, as they had to my grandfather and father before me, and to thousands of others down through the years. I never forgot the trust they placed in me that day.

My next recollection is my going to that same office and asking Ben Pelstring for a job. I didn't get it that day, but a couple of months later, he telephoned me and said there was an opening in the men's department if I wanted it. I snapped it up. Who could lose on a pay check of $12 a week, every single week?

For three years, I worked in the men's department and shoe department under the direction of two of the finest gentlemen I have ever known, Jay Helgeson and Gus Remme.

I thought about them and the others I came to know and respect at Nelson's as I inched my way through the auction crowd to see what there was to see.

I smiled to myself as the auctioneer shouted "Sold for $17!" as he handed a happy buyer a salesman's stool from the shoe department. I'll bet I'd sat on that stool a thousand times. It was probably the same one Gus was sitting on when he was selling a pair of shoes to Albert Christensen. Al was wearing short socks, and Gus just couldn't resist the temptation. He reached above the top of the sock, pulled out a hair from the calf of Al's leg, saying as he did so, "Hair, hair, wotta you got on your head?" Al's immediate and surprised reply was a loud, "Hey!!"

The chairs which the customers sat in when they were buying shoes reminded me of the story about my grandfather that Rodney B. Nelson, son of Senator Sam Nelson, one of the original Nelson Brothers, told me on several occasions.

Grandpa Bjerk, when he was alive, did most of his "trading" at Nelson's. He had a large family — 23 children in all, so when it came time to buy shoes, it meant bringing with him a good sized crowd of kids. When the family would march in, they'd fill all the chairs, and each one would be fitted. They didn't leave, however, when they had picked out the right pair.

When the last pair had been selected, the clerk would figure the cost, and then Grandpa would start to bargain. Meanwhile, there were other customers wanting to buy shoes, but they couldn't get into the chairs to get service. When Grandpa finally got the saving he thought he ought to have (I guess you'd call it quantity discount today), he'd pay the bill, and the whole tribe would get up and walk out. The distraught clerk would wipe the perspiration from his forehead and go back to waiting on more reasonable customers.

But, back to the store. . . the next thing I noticed that brought back memories were the old hat stands — the kind that were used to display women's hats when Elizabeth Voelz managed the millinery department. What a gal she was. Straight as a pin, and straightlaced, too. But friendly, a good saleslady, and a gentle woman.

Then, there was a table heaped high with electric fans waiting for the auctioneers to get to that part of the store. One of them once stood on a shelf above the shoe department to circulate air down to Gus' customers. It's funny how some things stick in one's memory, while others are forgotten immediately. The fans reminded me of one of the Nelson daughters, Thelma Hansen, who'd come into the shoe department with her youngest son, Jerry, who was then about two. Gus would inevitably point to the fan and ask Jerry, "What's that?" He would reply, "That a pwopeller goin' wound and wound and wound."

One thing I looked for but didn't see was the inseam measuring device that we used when selling men's trousers. The customer would be asked to straddle the machine, which consisted of a T-bar which was drawn up to the spot between a man's legs from which the inseam is measured. Some men like their pants to fit up snugly there, others prefer them loose. When the customer decided where he wanted his inseam measured from, the clerk had only to look at a dial on the bottom part of the machine, and that would show in inches what the inseam would be.

One Saturday night, a Norwegian "newcomer" came in and told me that he wanted "et par Boksa" which I understood to mean a pair of pants. He had an ice cream cone in his hand from which he would take a lick now and then while he picked out the pair he wanted. I then measured his waist, and told him to come over and I'd measure his inseam if he would straddle the machine. He stepped over it and I raised the bar. But I hadn't counted on that he was that ticklish. He yelled "Yike", his lanky arms went up with a jerk, and the ice cream cone splashed against the mirror. I don't recall whether the man bought the pants or not. But if I remember correctly, Jay Helgeson, who saw what happened and laughed until he had tears in his eyes, decided we'd better go back to using the tape measure in the future.

As I continued my walk around the store that afternoon I saw the door to the second floor elevator. For years, it was the only passenger elevator in town. It was one of the things that made Nelson's a real "uptown" department store such as very few small towns ever had.

I sauntered up the stairs to the office. The tubes that carried the cash and sales slips from the various departments to the cashier were silent. No one was sitting there. The chairs where three or four cashiers were kept busy every Saturday night were down below, waiting to be sold.

I walked down the stairs again, back to the men's department, and looked toward the auctioneers, standing where the shirt counter used to be. That's where I was standing that June day in 1937 when Patty Koehn Paske introduced me to "my friend, home for summer vacation from Carleton College, Roberta Gilbert." Fifteen months later, Roberta and I were married.

I walked out the front door for the last time.

A tear trickled out of the corner of my eye as I bade farewell to an old friend. And strangely, yet maybe not so strange, these words popped from memory: "Well done, thou good and faithful servant . . ."

Nelson's Store in Luverne

This view of Main Street of Luverne shows Nelson's Store as it looked when I started working there.

Roberta Gilbert Bjerk

Among the many memories I have of Nelson's Store is that of being introduced to Roberta Gilbert by a mutual friend when they were shopping in the store. It was love at first sight for both of us. We were married about a year and a half later, on September 7, 1939.